HIKING UTAH'S
HIGH UINTAS

HELP US KEEP THIS GUIDE UP TO DATE

Every effort has been made by the author and editors to make this guide as accurate and useful as possible. However, many things can change after a guide is published—regulations change, facilities come under new management, and so forth.

We would love to hear from you concerning your experiences with this guide and how you feel it could be improved and kept up to date. While we may not be able to respond to all comments and suggestions, we'll take them to heart, and we'll also make certain to share them with the author. Please send your comments and suggestions to falconeditorial @rowman.com.

Thanks for your input!

After ascending the pass from Erickson Basin, Big Elk Lake comes into view.

HIKING UTAH'S HIGH UINTAS

A GUIDE TO THE REGION'S GREATEST HIKES

THIRD EDITION

Revised and Updated by
Andrew Dash Gillman

FALCONGUIDES

ESSEX, CONNECTICUT

FALCONGUIDES®

An imprint of, the trade division of
the Rowman & Littlefield Publishing Group, Inc.
Ste. 200
20706
www.rowman.com

Falcon and FalconGuides are registered trademarks and Make Adventure Your Story is a trademark of The Rowman & Littlefield Publishing Group, Inc.

Distributed by NATIONAL BOOK NETWORK

Photos by Andrew Dash Gillman unless noted otherwise.

Detailed help on hiking information from USDA Forest Service officials Kathy Jo Pollock, Ryan Buerkle, Bernard Asay, and Loyal Clark

Maps by The Rowman & Littlefield Publishing Group, Inc.

British Library Cataloguing in Publication Information available

Library of Congress Cataloging-in-Publication Data

Names: Dash Gillman, Andrew, author.
Title: Hiking Utah's High Uintas : a guide to the region's greatest hikes / revised and edited by Andrew Dash Gillman.
Description: Third edition. | Essex, Connecticut : Falcon Guides, [2024]
Identifiers: LCCN 2023042723 (print) | LCCN 2023042724 (ebook) | ISBN 9781493075690 (trade paperback) | ISBN 9781493075706 (epub)
Subjects: LCSH: Hiking--Uinta Mountains (Utah and Wyo.)—Guidebooks. | Uinta Mountains (Utah and Wyo.)—Guidebooks. | LCGFT: Guidebooks.
Classification: LCC GV199.42.U82 U564 2024 (print) | LCC GV199.42.U82 (ebook) | DDC 917.9214—dc23/eng/20230929
LC record available at https://lccn.loc.gov/2023042723
LC ebook record available at https://lccn.loc.gov/2023042724

∞™ The paper used in this publication meets the minimum requirements of American National Standard for Information Sciences—Permanence of Paper for Printed Library Materials, ANSI/NISO Z39.48-1992.

Front cover photo: Aerial of the Three Divide Lakes and Clyde Lake, foreground, John Lake, center, and Twin Lakes, at right, below Notch Pass. Near Crystal Lake trailhead.
PHOTO COURTESY UTAH OFFICE OF TOURISM/MORE THAN JUST PARKS

Contents background photo: As the sun sets, shadows rise on the ridgeline below Wall Peak, Big Elk Lake.

CONTENTS

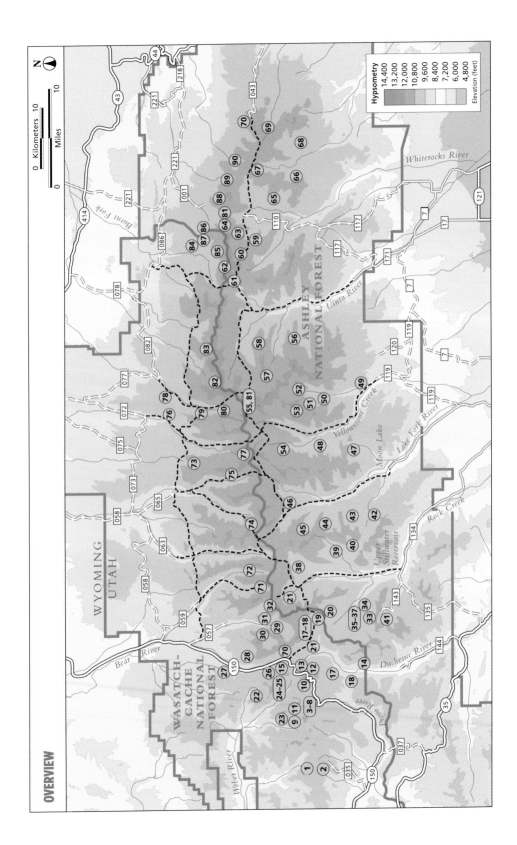

OVERVIEW

N

Hypsometry
14,400
13,200
12,000
10,800
9,600
8,400
7,200
6,000
4,800
Elevation (feet)

0   Kilometers   10

0   Miles   10

WYOMING
UTAH

WASATCH-
CACHE
NATIONAL
FOREST

ASHLEY
NATIONAL
FOREST

Whiterocks River

Burnt Fork

Bear River

Weber River

Provo River

Duchesne River

Uinta River

Yellowstone Creek

Moon Lake

Lake Fork River

Rock Creek

Upper
Stillwater
Reservoir

You may not get as perfect a shot as pro wildlife photographer David Winegar, but hikers frequently spot mountain goats on Bald Mountain and throughout the High Uintas. PHOTO BY DAVID WINEGAR/ PARKCITYPHOTOGRAPHY.NET

INTRODUCTION

I locate my earliest hiking, fishing, and camping memories in Utah's Uinta Mountain Range. It's the place where I first hiked to the top of a mountain. It's where I learned to tie a basic clinch knot to attach the hook to the line and somehow, occasionally, out-fished my dad, the man who taught me that knot. It's certainly where I learned a form of patience and stillness in nature, having cast a baited hook into the deep and sat back to await a bite, straining my eyes to watch for tension on the translucent filament. It's where I first saw a moose.

When I rediscovered the outdoors as an adult, it was in the Uintas, on a car camping trip to one of the same roadside campgrounds frequented by my family. That trip kicked off the long, gradual process of accumulating gear to make the next trip incrementally better in some specific way. (Years later, visiting with my wife and dogs, we're still dialing in our setup.)

And the Uintas are where I finally saw the Milky Way. I had missed out during several consecutive camping trips in pursuit of that goal due to cloud cover or my inability to be awake at the correct hour for the time of year (after astronomical twilight when the night sky settles into its darkest phase).

A primary reason for all these firsts is proximity. The closest campgrounds and trail-heads are less than 90 minutes from parts of the populous Wasatch Front in Northern Utah—the unbroken metropolitan area stretching some 80 miles from Ogden in the north to Provo in the south (with Salt Lake City in the center). There are closer camp-grounds and wilderness spots, but the Uintas have always felt like a destination. They possess a unique identity. Indeed, they used to teach us that the Uintas were the only mountain range in the lower forty-eight states that runs east to west. (That's not exactly correct, but it's an atypical orientation for the range's size.)

The Uintas are the source of several major rivers that make up Utah's watersheds, including the Provo, Weber, Duchesne, and Bear Rivers. There are more than 400 miles of streams in these mountains, along with 1,000 ice-cold lakes, reservoirs, and ponds, half of which are managed fisheries.

The Uintas are Utah's highest mountain range, with nineteen remote peaks over 13,000 feet. No other range in Utah boasts a peak above 13,000 feet and even Utah's famous Wasatch Front peaks don't eclipse 12,000 feet. They are the High Uintas, after all, an identifier drawn from the designated "High Uintas Wilderness," a 60-mile-wide patch of 456,705 acres within two even larger national forest areas that, combined, make up the Uintas.

Population growth in Utah is in no small amount due to the state's access to year-round outdoor recreation. With growth comes pressure on natural resources. The Uintas are a land where previous generations reminisce about favorite places they once had all to themselves. Perhaps this is true of most wild places. Perhaps everyone's parents or

Soft morning light over Bear Lake in Henrys Fork Basin welcomes hikers to a new day.

grandparents (or you) "remember a time." Solitude seekers may have to plan weekday visits or hike a little farther these days, but so long as everyone who visits demonstrates respect for natural places and one another, there is still plenty of space to spread out.

Through ninety chapters, this book shares a variety of hiking experiences in Utah's High Uintas. Some are short, ideal for families with young children or almost anyone looking to get outdoors, even if it's your first time on a proper trail. (And if it is, pay extra attention to the elevation and the importance of staying hydrated and taking it slow!) Other trails are clearly meant for very experienced, very prepared adventurers, whether on foot or on horseback. You'll also read a lot about the lakes of the Uintas and their fishing prospects. It just goes together with the geography. If you're not an angler, that's okay. Simply being outside and appreciating nature and high-mountain scenery are the main attractions.

This book leaves out trails, some deliberately, some from ignorance. It can no more catalog all the trails than it could the 1,000 lakes, and some trailheads are far too difficult for casual visitors to reach. You may notice there are only a few peaks mentioned. That is because, with one or two exceptions, Uinta peaks are notoriously rocky—piles of shifting boulders, talus, and scree (aka loose rocks)—and devoid of designated routes to the top. These attributes don't necessarily make their summits unattainable, but they do require ascending and descending with extreme care.

Whether you reserve a roadside campsite or backpack into the designated wilderness, the High Uintas area has an outdoor adventure waiting for you. You could spend a life-time exploring the high-elevation topography of meadows, basins, mountain passes, and river drainages. And each time you return you're bound to learn or see something new. You'll add to your own list of favorite places you'll want to simultaneously keep secret yet share with others—its beauty is too great to keep all to yourself.

HIGH UINTAS PORTFOLIO

The Uinta Mountains span the entire northeastern corner of Utah below the "notch" of Wyoming on ancestral, traditional, and/or contemporary lands of Shoshone-Bannock, Eastern Shoshone, Timpanogos Nation, and Ute Indian Tribes. The name Uinta (or Uintah in other uses) comes from the Ute word for pine tree or pine forest, *Yoov-we-teuh*. Today, three bands of Utes make up the federally recognized Ute Indian Tribe of the Uinta and Ouray Reservation, which runs along the South Slope of the Uintas.

Two geologically distinct ranges make up the Uinta Mountains—the Western Uintas and the Eastern Uintas. This book focuses on the Western Uintas.

Most of the destinations in this book lie within the official High Uintas Wilderness Area established by Congress in 1984. The High Uintas Wilderness Area is Utah's largest wilderness area. Other destinations lie within the encompassing national forests and the Ashley Karst National Recreation and Geologic Area, a 2019 designation of existing forest area designed to "conserve and protect the watershed, geological, recreational, wildlife, scenic, natural, cultural, and historic resources."

The geography of the Uinta Mountains covered in this book is contained within the Uinta-Wasatch-Cache National Forest and Ashley National Forest, which are managed by the U.S. Forest Service. Ranger districts include Heber-Kamas, Duchesne-Roosevelt, and Flaming Gorge-Vernal in Utah, and Evanston-Mountain View in Wyoming (which includes the Bear River Ranger Station open seasonally on the Mirror Lake Scenic Byway).

Regulations have helped immensely in keeping a pristine environment. Livestock grazing continues in some localized areas, but there is plenty of space where you can avoid running into them or their droppings. Their presence is perhaps the clearest reminder of the fact that the U.S. Forest Service falls within the multi-use management mandate of the U.S. Department of Agriculture. Cattle and sheep are often found around timberline (about 11,000 feet), where they can feed on high grasses then retreat to the shelter of the pines—but do not be surprised to find them at lower elevations.

Utah's tallest mountain is nestled deep in the center of the Wilderness area. Kings Peak (elevation 13,528 feet) stands between the Yellowstone and Uinta River drainages, but is probably best reached from the North Slope via Henrys Fork drainage. Because it is Utah's highest point—and can be conquered without the aid of climbing gear—it is extremely popular among "peak baggers." It's a long hike though, no matter which approach you attempt.

Blue-ribbon backpacking is abundant throughout the High Uintas. Enjoy true wilderness experiences in rugged places with names such as Spread Eagle Peak, Highline Trail, Dead Horse Pass, Toquer, Lightning Lake, Yellowstone Creek, Amethyst Lake, and hundreds more.

Thunderstorms build over the Uinta Mountains almost every afternoon during the summer, and lightning can strike without warning.

The western half of the High Uintas is most popular, due simply to its proximity to Utah's main population centers of Salt Lake City, Provo, and Ogden. A 1.5- to 2-hour drive from any of these cities can put you at any one of a dozen Uinta trailheads. Generally, the farther east you travel by car, the more solitude you will find when traveling by foot or horseback.

The terrain is characterized by large stands of pines that lead into alpine basins and cirques—a mountainside hollow formed by glacial erosion. Small lakes and reservoirs generously dot the backcountry. They can be found almost anywhere: along a stream, at the foot of a talus slope, adjoining a lush meadow, or at the bottom of a towering cliff. Encase all of this within steep, rocky peaks that rise thousands of feet, and you'll have a pretty fair picture of what's in store for you.

Winter lasts a long time in the High Uintas. Much of the backcountry is not accessible until late June, and mountain passes may be snowbound until mid-July. Any time after the middle of September, you risk being caught in a serious snowstorm. As you can quickly figure, the backpacking season lasts only three months, if we're fortunate. The best time to plan a trip into these mountains is during the second half of August. Then the days are warm, the snow is long gone, and those pesky mosquitoes have mostly died off. If you don't mind cooler temperatures, try these mountains after Labor Day.

Those familiar with mountain travel know the weather can change rapidly. Regardless of the forecast, you should always be prepared for searing sun, pouring rain, lightning, and even snow. Wear and pack your clothes in layers and remember longer sleeves double as sun protection. With a T-shirt, long-sleeved collared shirt, sweater, jacket or puffy, poncho, and brimmed hat, you can adjust your attire to match any weather condition.

Pay close attention to how you can protect Wilderness areas and practice Leave No Trace principles when recreating outdoors.

Thunderstorms build over the Uinta Mountains almost every day during the summer. Lightning is generated by thunderheads and can strike without warning, even several miles away from the nearest overhead cloud. The best rule of thumb is to start leaving exposed peaks, ridges, and canyon rims by about noon. Read more in Falcon's "The Art of Hiking" at the end of this book.

The High Uintas vary in elevation from 8,000 to more than 13,000 feet. Most likely you will be camping somewhere between 10,000 and 10,800 feet. Going any higher puts you above timberline, where campsites are scarce and uncomfortable—and where the fragile alpine environment means packing out all human waste and toilet paper. At these elevations it is essential to know the effect elevation has on humans. Altitude sickness is dangerous. It can kill. If someone develops a hacking cough, spits up blood, or seems irrational or confused, then that person may have altitude sickness. The only solution is to go down. If you have suffered from altitude sickness in the past, limit yourself to an altitude gain of 1,000 feet per day. Unfortunately, this includes any elevation gained by your ride to the trailhead.

Bugs are a nuisance in the High Uintas backcountry. Mosquitoes can be terrible around moist meadows and ponds, so remember that when selecting a campsite. Bring your repellent or, as suggested earlier, wait until late in the season when the "skeeters" are gone. Deerflies and blackflies are pesky too. If bugs are bad, try camping in an open area where the wind can blow them down. There's no shame in sporting a mosquito head net.

Giardia, cryptosporidium, and a range of other bacteria and microorganisms are present throughout the lakes, streams, and ponds of the Uintas. Tiny parasites can cause a severe flu-like disorder about one to two weeks after ingestion. In the past, spring water was considered safe to drink without treatment but, according to the Forest Service, there is no safe water source anymore. Spring water sources are identified throughout this book because a good rule of thumb is to start with the cleanest source when treating water, and spring water sources may have fewer pathogens present. (A seasoned forestry tech I ran into recently swore by the quality of a couple favorite springs.) But all water should be boiled, treated with purification tablets, or filtered. When you filter, be sure your filter will remove giardia and crypto. If you choose chemical treatment, follow the instructions closely to ensure that parasites are destroyed. Many hikers carry purification tablets solely as a backup option.

There are rules and regulations to be aware of when recreating in the High Uintas, particularly in the federally designated High Uintas Wilderness. But if we all hike and camp sensibly, we won't burden hardworking U.S. Forest Service staff. Permits are not needed, but a use fee applies for trailhead use on the Mirror Lake Scenic Byway Recreation Corridor and for parking and recreating at China Meadows. It is helpful to carry several small bills, though some concessionaires may accept digital payments. Registers exist at a few trailheads. Please use them. They are one of the few management tools the forest service utilizes here. During dry spells, certain areas may have fire bans imposed. Check with the appropriate ranger district if the summer has been dry. In 2005 the forest service implemented a ban on campfires and wood stoves within 0.25 mile of more than 150 popular lakes both named and unnamed within the High Uintas Wilderness Area. The ban was instigated due to a depletion of dead wood required for fires and a healthy ecosystem. Campers planning on fires will often attempt to unsuccessfully harvest live wood and kill remaining trees in the process. Carry a camp stove to Leave No Trace.

FISHING

Anglers should always review the fishing regulations set by the Utah Division of Wildlife Resources. The trout limit when this book was published was four, but another four could be kept if the additional fish were all brook trout. There are some stream closures when salmon are spawning. A few lakes have restrictions on watercraft with motors.

Fishing is often superb in the High Uintas backcountry, but it is also unpredictable. A lake that provided fast fishing one year might be poor the next. Winterkill can take a toll, as does fishing pressure on popular lakes. If you're serious about catching lots of fish, then opt for an area with several lakes in the vicinity. If one doesn't produce, try another one nearby. Explore remote lakes, especially those that are off the trail or tough to reach. These are the real fishing gems of the High Uintas. You may find a lake where a pan-size cutthroat will hit your fly on every cast, or maybe you'll fool a chunky 2-pound-plus brook trout that has never before beheld an artificial lure.

Catch-and-release is commonly practiced by backcountry fishers and is often considered a good conservation ethic. Biologists now suggest that keeping some trout can help a fishery produce larger, healthier fish and prevent stunting (an overpopulation leads to fish not reaching their growth potential due to a lack of food). Releasing larger fish for other anglers to enjoy catching is a good thing to do, but don't hesitate to keep smaller fish for the frying pan.

Fishing nearly every lake in the Uintas was not something the first European travelers could do—at least not successfully. Colorado and Bonneville cutthroat trout were found in drainages of the Uintas below upstream obstacles like waterfalls when settlers started fishing, but the vast majority of the lakes and streams in the Uinta Mountains likely did not hold fish at that time, according to state fisheries biologists.

Early fisheries management of the Uintas involved introducing new trout and salmonoid species to the numerous lakes in an effort to provide food and opportunity for people visiting the range.

Brook trout made up the majority of the fish introduced into the Uintas. The aggressive trout are native to the eastern United States and Canada, but not the West.

Through the years, the list of nonnative fish grew to include rainbow trout, Yellowstone cutthroat trout, kokanee salmon, brown trout, golden trout, arctic grayling, and two hybrid trout (tiger, a sterile mix between a brook and a brown trout; and splake, a mix between a brook and a lake trout).

Colorado and Bonneville cutthroat felt the squeeze and started to become more and more isolated. In more recent years biologists have also turned their attention back to native species—in fact, anglers interested in supporting Utah's native trout legacy can sign up for the Utah Cutthroat Slam and challenge themselves to catch four cutthroat in their native range. A trip across the Uintas could catch three out of four. Visit utahcutthroatslam.org for more information.

Brook trout will likely always have a place in the Uintas. Rainbows and tiger trout will continue to be stocked in high-pressure put-and-take areas in the most easily accessed areas.

The first trout introduced into previously fish-free lakes of the Uintas arrived in milk cans carried into the backcountry on horseback. The state started using small planes to aerial stock the lakes in the mid-1950s. Horses are still used by biologists doing fish surveys in the backcountry. A plane can stock seven lakes on one trip and a total of forty to sixty lakes in a single day, depending on weather conditions. Aerial stocking is done in the spring. The fish—roughly 2,000 per drop—average 2.5 to 3 inches. Larger fish are less likely to survive the free fall of 50 to 150 feet.

Approximately 150 Uinta Mountain backcountry lakes are stocked by aircraft each year. One key to fishing success, particularly for those hoping to land larger fish, is to check the Division of Wildlife Resources fish stocking plans (wildlife.utah.gov). Fishing lakes that have just been stocked will not be as productive as hitting water that was stocked three or four years previous.

Small flies are the most effective lure in these alpine lakes. That makes sense, since tiny bugs make up more than 80 percent of their diet. Give them what they are used to. Good sizes are #18 and #16. Successful patterns include Renegade, Adams, black gnat, and an olive scud. Small spinners (sizes 0 to 2) are also effective, particularly on brook trout in deeper lakes. Streams are best fished with a flashy, lightweight spinner or a fly.

WILDLIFE

Fish are, of course, not the only wildlife that find a home in the Uintas.

Mule deer and elk are found scattered throughout the entire range and are the dominant big game species found on the Uinta Mountains. Visitors to the Uintas also commonly see mountain goats, including on the popular Bald Mountain trail, and moose everywhere, even along Highway 150. Moose are known to wander through camp-grounds. Give them space and keep dogs on a leash. Bighorn sheep are sometimes spotted on the North Slope of the range. Carry binoculars!

Mountain lion and black bears, Utah's two largest predators, also frequent the Uintas. They are rarely seen, but the presence of bears—and many other creatures that might find human food too tempting to resist—are a good reason to keep a bear-safe camp both in the backcountry and at developed campgrounds. Read more about protecting yourself from bears and other natural hazards at the end of this book.

Numerous small mammals, such as pika, marten, and snowshoe hare, are often sighted during excursions. Raptors, owls, and songbirds are also common in the Uintas. Attesting to the wildness of the Uintas, wolves and wolverines have been documented with sightings and trail camera photos.

Hunting is a popular activity in the Uintas, and hikers can expect to see hunters pursuing game from mid-August into November.

VISITING RESPONSIBLY

LEAVE NO TRACE

Let's talk about minimum-impact outdoor recreation. There are a few rules we all must follow to keep these mountains in their pristine state. This shouldn't sound like scolding or nagging, but rather a quick education in the basics of backcountry manners.

The national nonprofit Leave No Trace (lnt.org) has provided a list of suggestions. Forest Service officials encourage all visitors to forest and Wilderness areas to follow these simple but important tips. Note that motorized equipment and mechanical transport of any kind, which includes mountain bikes and e-bikes, are prohibited in designated Wilderness areas. The Forest Service manages e-bikes as motor vehicles. E-bikes are not permitted on trails designated for non-motorized used, meaning hiker, horse, or mountain bike trails. For tips to manage and reduce your impact from motorized outdoor recreation, see treadlightly.org.

PLAN AHEAD AND PREPARE

- Know the regulations and special concerns for the area you'll visit.
- Prepare for extreme weather, hazards, and emergencies.
- Schedule your trip to avoid times of high use.
- Visit in small groups when possible. Split larger parties into smaller groups.
- Repackage food to minimize waste.
- Use a map and compass to eliminate the use of marking paint, rock cairns, or flagging.

TRAVEL AND CAMP ON DURABLE SURFACES

- Durable surfaces include established trails and campsites, rock gravel, dry grasses, or snow.
- Protect riparian areas by camping at least 200 feet from lakes and streams.
- Good campsites are found, not made. Altering a site is not necessary.
- In popular areas: Concentrate use on existing trails and campsites; walk single file in the middle of the trail, even when wet or muddy; keep campsites small. Focus activity in areas where vegetation is absent.
- In undisturbed areas: Disperse use to prevent the creation of campsites and trails and avoid places where impacts are just beginning.

DISPOSE OF WASTE PROPERLY

- Pack it in, pack it out. Inspect your campsite and rest areas for trash or spilled foods. Pack out all trash, leftover food, and litter.
- Deposit solid human waste in shallow holes dug 6 to 8 inches deep at least 200 feet from water, camp, and trails. Cover and disguise the cathole when finished.
- Pack out toilet paper and hygiene products.
- To wash yourself or your dishes, carry water 200 feet away from streams or lakes and use small amounts of biodegradable soap. Scatter strained dishwater.

LEAVE WHAT YOU FIND

- Preserve the past: Observe, but do not touch, cultural or historic structures and artifacts.
- Leave rocks, plants, and other natural objects as you find them.
- Avoid introducing or transporting nonnative species.
- Do not build structures or furniture. Do not dig trenches.

MINIMIZE CAMPFIRE IMPACTS

- Campfires can cause lasting impacts to the backcountry. Use a lightweight stove for cooking and enjoy a candle lantern for light.
- Where fires are permitted, use established fire rings, fire pans, or mound fires.
- Keep fires small. Use only sticks from the ground that can be broken by hand.
- Burn all wood and coals to ash, put out campfires completely, then scatter cool ashes.

RESPECT WILDLIFE

- Observe wildlife from a distance. Do not follow or approach them.
- Never feed animals. Feeding wildlife damages their health, alters natural behaviors, and exposes them to predators and other dangers.
- Protect wildlife and your food by storing rations and trash securely.
- Control pets at all times, or leave them at home.
- Avoid wildlife during sensitive times: mating, nesting, raising young, or winter.

BE CONSIDERATE OF OTHERS

- Respect others and protect the quality of their experience.
- Be courteous. Yield to other users on the trails.
- Greet riders and ask which side of the trail to move to when encountering pack stock.
- Take breaks and camp away from trails and others.
- Let nature's sounds prevail. Avoid loud voices and noises.

SEARCH AND RESCUE

"Be Prepared" is far more than just a motto for Scouts. It's the *all-caps* plea of land managers and the search and rescue (SAR) teams who are regularly deployed to save poorly prepared, unprepared, and, yes, unlucky individuals or groups from mishaps in the outdoors. Utah sees hundreds of rescue missions per year. These are costly and sometimes dangerous.

Being prepared means carefully planning for your outdoor experience and thoughtfully communicating with everyone in your group about the expectations and demands of the trip. It means checking forecasts, being prepared for changing conditions, staying alert when out recreating, and knowing your limits or the limits of those in your charge. In some instances it may mean carrying—and knowing how to use—first aid and wound closure kits. It may also mean having evacuation plans and communication devices in the event of an emergency.

Since cell phone coverage cannot be guaranteed, well-prepared backcountry adventurers carry two-way satellite communication devices and know how to use them. They also tell people where they are going, when to expect them back, and when to call local sheriffs' offices who coordinate SAR for help.

If you need a rescue, shelter in place. If lost, STOP (Sit, Think, Observe, and Plan). If in a group, stay together. Have the appropriate gear to protect yourself—see the Ten Essentials. SAR efforts in Utah can be supported at rescue.utah.gov.

THE TEN ESSENTIALS

The Ten Essentials is an outdoor adventure survival system to help ensure low-impact, safe recreation. There will be variations to the essentials based on whether you're hiking, camping, backpacking, or mountaineering, but generally speaking these categories in the system include the things you'll need to help ensure a successful trip.

1. Water (extra water is essential in Utah's dry, high-elevation landscapes)

2. Extra clothing, layers, and insulation, including rain and wind protection

3. Extra food—especially nutrient-dense foods

4. Navigation—maps, compass, GPS, backup battery, satellite messenger (and knowledge of their use)

5. Sun protection (sunglasses, sunscreen, lip balm, and sun hat)

6. Waterproof matches or lighter

7. Flashlight or headlamp (make sure they are in working order and have extra batteries)

8. First aid supplies

9. Tools and repair kit (such as a small knife and a little duct tape)

10. Emergency shelter (lightweight emergency bag or space blanket)

HOW TO USE THIS BOOK

The High Uinta Mountains offer a variety of fishing and hiking opportunities, from brief day outings to extended overnight trips. This guidebook provides information on ninety hikes to streams, ponds, and lakes in this expansive forest and wilderness. There is also some beta on a handful of peaks, but be aware most Uinta summits are remote, rugged, and relentlessly rocky. Tackle with extreme care.

There are three sections: Highway 150, U.S. 40 to the South Slope, and I-80 to the North Slope. The road in each section is generally the best initial route to the trailhead, though several hikes on the western side of the North Slope are easily accessed from two directions.

Each hike includes a short introduction to the area as well as the pertinent information you will need for a visit, such as hike distance, trail usage, nearest town, and trail contacts. Many trails begin from the same trailhead. This book groups together trails and information when they share a trailhead to make it easier to understand some of what's available in that area. Be aware that some trails traverse more than one USGS quadrangle and even cross national forest boundaries.

Note: Utah's Uinta Mountains seem permanent, but they are ever-changing. Deadfall from fires, devastation from mountain pine beetles, impacts from water runoff, and other phenomena can cause changes to trails and trail access. Routes and access also periodically change from Forest Service updates or users generating "social trails." A forestry tech I ran into in 2023 mentioned they had just recently reopened part of the Middle Fork Weber River after twenty years and a section of Lofty Lake Loop had to be rerouted below Kamas Lake. Keep your navigation tools handy and stay alert.

Deadfall can block your path. As the signs say, "Look up, look around . . . trees may fall."

Follow this remote dirt road on the North Slope to your next trailhead.

The difficulty rating for the hikes is based on the average hiker's ability and may vary depending on a number of factors, including your physical condition and state of mind, the amount of gear you are carrying, and the weather conditions.

Approximate hiking times are based on the average hiker. You'll often read an average hiker can travel 2 miles per hour or 30 minutes per mile. Many can hike faster, even with a loaded pack, traveling uphill, at elevation. Many hike slower. If you're in a group, consider varying speeds and abilities, including the most careful hikers, and plan for stops. To be safe, most hiking times listed are conservative estimates; you may make a trip in less time. It's best to plan your outing based on how long the hike will take rather than on the distance, including factoring in the importance of taking breaks at high elevations.

Also included are directions to the start of each hike, followed by a description that highlights key points along the route, campsites, and fishing opportunities.

ELEVATION PROFILES

The elevation profiles show the general ups and downs of the route. You can see, at a glance, the general terrain of the route; however, the graphs are compressed (squeezed) to fit onto the page, so the actual slopes you will hike will not be as steep as the lines on the graphs (it may just feel that way). Also, many short dips and climbs are too small to show up on the graphs.

MAPS

The maps in this book use elevation tints, called hypsometry, to portray relief. Each tone represents a range of equal elevation, as shown in the scale key with the map. These maps will give you a good idea of elevation gain and loss. The lighter tones are lower elevations and the darker tones are higher elevations. The darker the tone, the higher the elevation. Narrow bands of different tones spaced closely together indicate steep terrain, whereas wider bands indicate areas of more gradual slope.

MAP LEGEND

Municipal

≡(87)≡ Interstate Highway

≡{40}≡ US Highway

≡(150)≡ State Road

≡[037]≡ Local/Forest Road

= = = = Unpaved Road

= — = — Unimproved Road

═ ══ ═ Featured Unimproved Road

·· — ··· — State Boundary

Trails

- - - - - Featured Trail

- - - - - Trail

············ Featured Faint Trail

·········· Faint Trail

Land Management

National Forest

Symbols

⊃⊂ Bridge

▲ Campground

Overlook

⊃⊂ Pass/Gap

▲ Peak

Ranger Station

⊶ Spring

○ Town

① Trailhead

⊢⊣ Tunnel

Water Features

Body of Water

Marsh

River/Creek

Intermittent Stream

PART 1: HIGHWAY 150, MIRROR LAKE SCENIC BYWAY

When most Utahns talk about heading up to the Uintas, they're referring to the Western Uintas, accessed from the Mirror Lake Scenic Byway. That's because the area is little more than an hour and a half from downtown Salt Lake City to some of the closest trailheads. You'll spend much more time getting the car packed than driving. One translation: Many of these hikes are immensely popular, as evidenced by the U.S. Forest Service's ongoing effort to expand or improve parking access. When this alluring accessibility combines with the high-elevation destination's limited hiking season, it's no wonder campsites and parking spots fill up fast. But there's still room to spread out along the 42-mile highway on these trails or others not covered by this guide. After exploring or fishing some of the roadside lakes or hiking Bald Mountain, the solitude-seeker need only set out on a short hike in almost any direction and backpackers will have countless options for pitching a tent far from the crowds. A recreation fee applies to the Mirror Lake Scenic Byway corridor—look for self-service fee tubes—or have your America the Beautiful pass handy (this federal recreation pass covers standard day-use fees at national forests).

Views from the rough Upper Setting Road reach out across the high-elevation Mirror Lake Scenic Byway and northeast into the High Uintas Wilderness.

1 UPPER SETTING ROAD TO EAST SHINGLE CREEK AND ERICKSON LAKES

Shortly after stopping at a self-serve fee tube to recreate along the Mirror Lake Scenic Byway, drivers can consider the left turn onto Upper Setting Road. Though earlier on Highway 150 than the road and trail to Big Elk Lake (the next hike in this guide), Upper Setting accesses North Slope terrain with drainage into the Weber River, whereas Big Elk is in the Provo River drainage. Upper Setting Road can be rather rough but, if recently graded, it should be passable in most vehicles—which was not the case a few years ago. Just don't travel on threadbare tires and keep your eyes on the road. From the trailhead, some quintessential Uinta Mountain lakes are just a couple of miles away. Speaking of which, there aren't many lakes in the High Uintas with such a short, easy hike that are capable of yielding trout as big as those in North Erickson Lake. Depending on the year, this area of the Uintas may be accessible for hiking in June.

Start: End of Upper Setting Road
Distance: 5.6 miles out and back
Destination elevation: 10,020 feet
Approximate hiking time: 4 hours
Difficulty: Easy—one steep section
Usage: Moderate
Nearest town: Kamas, Utah
Drainage: Weber River
Maps: USGS Erickson Basin, *USDA Forest Service High Uintas*

Wilderness, Trails Illustrated High Uintas Wilderness
Trail contacts: Uinta-Wasatch-Cache National Forest, Forest Supervisor, 857 West South Jordan Pkwy., South Jordan, UT 84095; Kamas Ranger District, 50 East Center St., Kamas, UT 84036, (435) 783-4338

FINDING THE TRAILHEAD

From Kamas, take the Mirror Lake Scenic Byway (Highway 150) about 8.7 miles to Upper Setting Road. Turn left onto the dirt road and twist your way up the mountain until the road ends. Though the road is graded, high-clearance or four-wheel drive may be necessary in some conditions or for a few rough spots.

THE HIKE

North Erickson Lake sits at the head of Smith and Morehouse Creek in Erickson Basin. It can be reached from the Smith and Morehouse trailhead, but it is easier to start hiking from the end of Upper Setting Road in the Provo River Drainage. It is less than 3 miles to North Erickson on a good trail with generally gradual evaluation gain. The 6-mile-long Shingle Creek Trail that begins right off Highway 150 merges with Upper Setting 1.2 miles in, at which point you're only 0.2 mile from East Shingle Creek Lake, an option for camping or fishing for tiger trout. Continuing on, you have to go over the mountain to reach Erickson Basin, but it's not very steep (as mountain passes go). Stay with the trail, or you might walk right past the lake. It is in a bit of a hole surrounded by pines. A

UPPER SETTING ROAD TO EAST SHINGLE CREEK AND ERICKSON LAKES

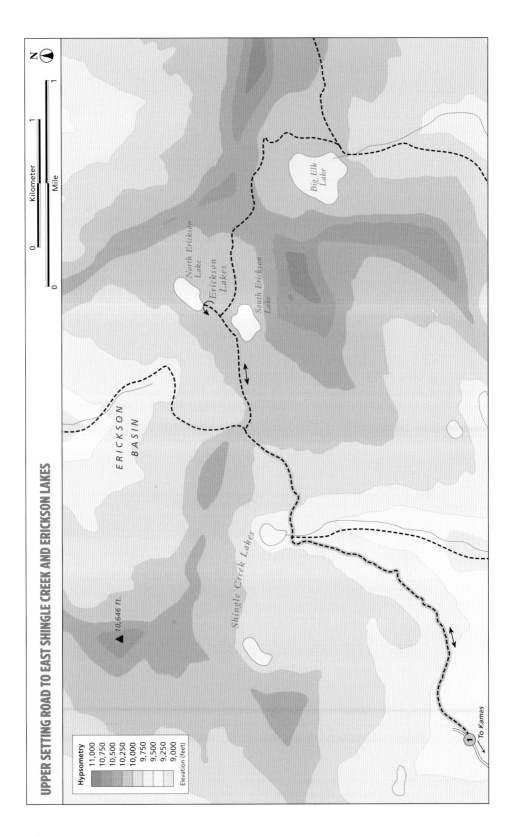

Hypsometry

11,000
10,750
10,500
10,250
10,000
9,750
9,500
9,250
9,000

Elevation (feet)

N

0   Kilometer   1

0   Mile   1

ERICKSON BASIN

▲ 10,646 ft.

North Erickson Lake

Erickson Lakes

South Erickson Lake

Big Elk Lake

Shingle Creek Lakes

To Kamas

Above: View over the slickrock and South Erickson Lake from the pass between Erickson Basin and Big Elk Lake

Though the camping is better at North Erickson, South Erickson is a pretty little lake worth visiting.

mile farther and you'll reach the steep but manageable drop down the ridge to Big Elk Lake—just pay extra attention to the trail and your GPS on the return climb.

The best campsites are on the west side of the lake, just off the trail. Spring water is plentiful around the lake. If you camp on the west side as suggested, an ice-cold spring that feeds into the southwest corner of the lake will serve your water needs nicely. And a quick UV or other filtration process will kill the bugs and keep you hydrated and safe.

South Erickson is just a hop, skip, and a jump to the south (0.25 mile). This pretty alpine lake abuts a talus slope and provides some excellent photo opportunities, but camping and fishing are better at North Erickson Lake. Large slickrock formations are prevalent between the two lakes. It is worth the hike over to South Erickson just to experience the unique terrain.

Back at North Erickson, the fish await. Actually, you'll probably do most of the waiting. The fish seem to feed mostly at dusk and dawn, especially the big ones. Brook trout exceeding 18 inches in length and 2 pounds in weight can be caught if you're patient—and lucky—enough and can cast longer distances.

2 NORWAY FLATS ROAD TO BIG ELK LAKE

If you can get all the way to the proper trailhead in your high-clearance, 4WD vehicle, you can pack extra gear into here. From there, the hike is just a little over 1 mile one way, so bring the camp chairs and float tube. There is a steep incline just before the dam, but otherwise it's a moderate hike. Others may have farther to hike (see "Finding the trailhead" below). If the road makes you nervous, consider the 8-mile round-trip option from Upper Setting trailhead featured in the previous chapter.

Start: Norway Flats
Distance: 3 to 5 miles out and back
Destination elevation: 10,020 feet
Approximate hiking time: 2 to 4 hours
Difficulty: Moderate—one steep section
Usage: Heavy
Nearest town: Kamas, Utah
Drainage: Provo River

Maps: USGS Erickson Basin, *USDA Forest Service High Uintas Wilderness, Trails Illustrated High Uintas Wilderness*
Trail contacts: Uinta-Wasatch-Cache National Forest, Forest Supervisor, 857 West South Jordan Pkwy., South Jordan, UT 84095; Kamas Ranger District, 50 East Center St., Kamas, UT 84036, (435) 783-4338

FINDING THE TRAILHEAD

One of the hardest parts about this trek is finding the right road. From Kamas, go 15 miles west on Highway 150 to FR 035 and turn left. This road climbs onto Norway Flats. Norway Flats Road starts innocently enough as it turns off Highway 150, but it forks several times where there are no markers. Stay with the road that shows the most wear until you are about 6 miles from Highway 150; turn right (east). If you stay on the road most traveled (to the left), you will end up at a beaver pond just below Hourglass Lake. This is the wrong starting place. Go back to the road that turned east and follow it down to the trailhead. You may need a high-clearance, 4WD vehicle with exceptional tires to cover the last couple of miles to the trailhead. Most drivers pull over to park when it gets rough and hike the rest of the way.

THE HIKE

From the end of Norway Flats Road, Little Elk Lake is about 0.3 mile to the west of the trail. Continue another 0.8 mile to a trail junction and Big Elk Lake. The trail itself is often shaded as it rises and falls through the forest. It passes a meadow around 0.5 mile that can fill with wildflowers in the summer.

At Big Elk Lake, fishing is generally good for stocked brook and cutthroat trout. A raft or canoe would be nice to escape the crowds and the bugs, but you can do just fine from shore. When the mosquitoes swarmed at dusk during my visit, the fish rose and flopped all over the lake. I braved the bugs for a few obligatory casts. Fish with a small fly during the morning and evening, and you should have little trouble catching enough for a hearty meal.

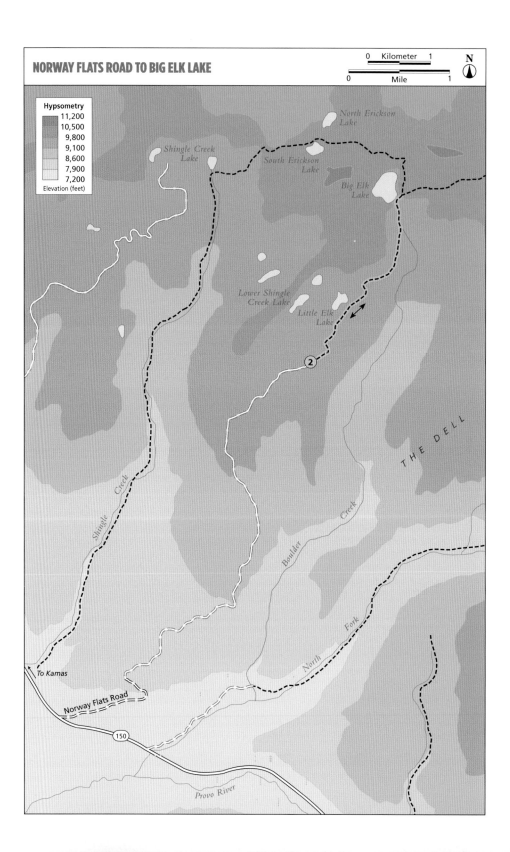

NORWAY FLATS ROAD TO BIG ELK LAKE

0   Kilometer   1

0   Mile   1

N

Hypsometry
11,200
10,500
9,800
9,100
8,600
7,900
7,200
Elevation (feet)

North Erickson Lake

Shingle Creek Lake

South Erickson Lake

Big Elk Lake

Lower Shingle Creek Lake

Little Elk Lake

②

THE DELL

Shingle Creek

Boulder Creek

North Fork

To Kamas

Norway Flats Road

150

Provo River

Daybreak at Big Elk Lake

Campsites are available on the south and east sides of this deep reservoir. Big Elk receives heavy pressure, especially on weekends. If you visit during the week, there might not be anybody else there. Pack out your litter and help keep Big Elk a clean and fun place to explore.

CRYSTAL LAKE TRAILHEAD

Crystal Lake is, simply put, a premier trailhead to the Western Uintas. Accessed via a short, mostly paved, spur off Highway 150, the trailhead is smack in the middle of Washington and Trial Lakes, both classic recreation destinations in the Uintas thanks to their easy access—which also makes them immensely popular. You'd be wise to reserve a campsite in the area or arrive early to get a spot in the parking lot for day hiking or backpacking, even though the Forest Service more than doubled parking in 2021.

From the trailhead, you have miles and miles of trails and cross-country routes to explore on the way to one of a dozen lakes—it's no wonder the Forest Service calls one of the trails "Lakes Country." Peak baggers with sure-footing and solid navigation skills could hop boulders and work their way up the scree of either Haystack Mountain or Mount Watson, though those are not covered in this book. If you're an ambitious day hiker or backpacker with good wayfinding resources, consider continuing from Island Lake to Smith and Morehouse Reservoir.

See trails 3 through 9 for Crystal Lake Trailhead.
Maps: USGS Mirror Lake and USGS Erickson Basin, *USDA Forest Service High Uintas Wilderness*, *Trails Illustrated High Uintas Wilderness*

Trail contacts: Uinta-Wasatch-Cache National Forest, Forest Supervisor, 857 West South Jordan Pkwy., South Jordan, UT 84095; Kamas Ranger District, 50 East Center St., Kamas, UT 84036, (435) 783-4338

FINDING THE TRAILHEAD

From Kamas, take the Mirror Lake Scenic Byway (Highway 150) 27 miles to Trial Lake Campground. Exit left (west) onto a paved road, and travel about a mile to a fork in the road. Turn right (north) for another mile to the trailhead. This is very a popular trailhead, with room for 123 vehicles and nice toilet facilities. Water and other amenities can be found at Trial Lake Campground. Crystal Lake trailhead is the main takeoff point to many lakes only 1 to 5 miles away, including Wall, Ibantik, Meadow, Cliff, Watson, Clyde, Long, Island, Big Elk, Fire, Duck, Weir, and the breathtaking Lovenia.

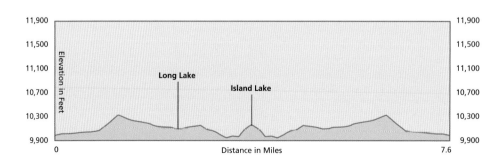

CRYSTAL LAKE TRAILHEAD: LONG POND; ISLAND LAKE;
LAKES COUNTRY; CLIFF LAKE; DIVIDE LAKES; TWIN LAKES; IBANTIK LAKE

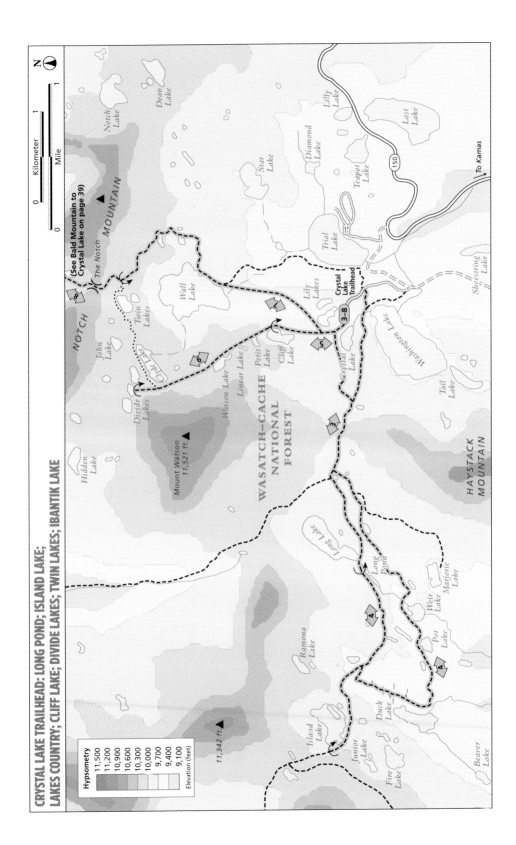

Hypsometry

| 11,500 |
| 11,200 |
| 10,900 |
| 10,600 |
| 10,300 |
| 10,000 |
| 9,700 |
| 9,400 |
| 9,100 |

Elevation (feet)

N

Kilometer

0   1

0   1

Mile

(See Bald Mountain to
Crystal Lake on page 39)

NOTCH

The Notch

NOTCH MOUNTAIN

Notch Lake

Dean Lake

Hidden Lake

John Lake

Twin Lakes

Clyde Lake

Divide Lakes

Wall Lake

Star Lake

Diamond Lake

Lilly Lake

Lost Lake

150

To Kamas

Mount Watson
11,521 ft

Watson Lake

Linear Lake

Petit Lake

Cliff Lake

Lily Lakes

Teapot Lake

Trial Lake

Crystal Lake
Trailhead

Crystal Lake

Shoestring Lake

WASATCH-CACHE
NATIONAL
FOREST

Washington Lake

Tail Lake

HAYSTACK
MOUNTAIN

11,342 ft

Island Lake

Long Lake

Ramona Lake

Long Pond

Weir Lake

Pot Lake

Marjorie Lake

Duck Lake

Junior Lake

Fire Lake

Beaver Lake

3–8

3

4

5

6

7

A

B

The view north across Wall Lake to The Notch, a low pass through Notch Mountain to the North Slope

3 **LONG POND**

Long Pond is just that—a long pond. It is immediately below the outlet of Long Lake. While the lake receives heavy usage, Long Pond is largely ignored, even though it has better fishing and more solitude than the lake. You might also hike around the more popular Long Lake and revel in the views of Mount Watson over the cool, clear waters.

See map and logistics on pages 22–23.
Start: Crystal Lake trailhead
Distance: 4 miles out and back
Destination elevation: 10,100 feet

Approximate hiking time: 2.5 hours
Difficulty: Easy
Usage: Moderate
Nearest town: Kamas, Utah
Drainage: Provo River

THE HIKE

Day hikers should bring their cameras and a picnic and enjoy the stroll. Though rocky at times, there are only a couple hundred feet in elevation gain. Just remember you're starting above 10,000 feet! For anglers, Long Pond has a variety of trout habitat to test your skills. Shallows, pools, rocks, and a few deadfalls combine to give you an array of fishing challenges. Expect the unexpected when exploring Long Pond. The trout you'll likely catch offer variety too. Count on a mixed bag of cutthroat and brook trout, which migrate from Long Lake. Since it has no water flow in winter, Long Pond is not stocked. But enough trout from Long Lake sneak into the pond to make fishing exciting.

From Crystal Lake trailhead parking, take the Lakes Country Trail for about 1.5 miles to a trail junction. On the way, the trail will climb around 300 feet to Watson Pass. At the junction veer right but then stay left: The spur to the right drops into the Middle Fork of the Weber River. Stay left for 0.6 mile to Long Lake. Cross the creek and continue another 0.1 mile to Long Pond.

Good campsites can be found along Long Pond. This is a good spot to camp for a small group (four or fewer). Usually it is a peaceful, serene place, sitting just down the hill from Long Lake—out of sight and out of earshot from the crowds at the lake. It is not a good area for horses to stop, so you will avoid them too.

4 ISLAND LAKE

"Which Island Lake?" you may ask. Just as there are many Hidden Lakes and Lost Lakes, it seems that every other drainage has an Island Lake. This one sits high on the Provo River drainage and can be reached fairly easily. The first mile is steep, and the last 0.5 mile is steep, but sandwiched between these sections is some easy and level hiking. The trail is quite popular among overnighters, so expect to see a few people, especially on weekends.

See map and logistics on pages 22-23.
Start: Crystal Lake trailhead
Distance: 7.6 miles out and back
Destination elevation: 10,140 feet
Approximate hiking time: 4.5 hours

Difficulty: Moderate—some steep sections
Usage: Moderate
Nearest town: Kamas, Utah
Drainage: Provo River

THE HIKE

From Crystal Lake trailhead parking, take the Lakes Country Trail for about 1.5 miles to a trail junction. On the way, the trail will climb around 300 feet to Watson Pass. At the junction veer right but then stay left: The spur to the right drops into the Middle Fork of the Weber River. Stay left for 0.6 mile to Long Lake. Cross the creek and continue another 0.1 mile to Long Pond. Continue another 1.5 miles to Island Lake.

There are sheltered campsites on the east side of the lake. The cleanest source of spring water might be available near the northeast corner—be sure to treat before drinking. Island Lake is picturesque, with its high cliffs dropping straight into deep water along the northern shore. (If you've come for the cliff jumping, be warned: The water is cold.) Whether you are looking at these cliffs from across the lake or standing on top of them, you'll want your camera handy.

Large, wary cutthroat make fishing unpredictable. These fish are well fed by a healthy population of freshwater shrimp, and they don't hit a dry fly as readily as trout do on other backcountry lakes. Try a pink shrimp imitation. You will only need a couple of these trout to fill the frying pan. Faster fishing may be found over the hill about 0.25 mile to Junior Lake. This tiny lake is often overlooked by anglers and usually provides very good fishing for smaller trout. Keep going a little farther and you'll descend to Fire Lake, where fishing can be fast at times. The lake doesn't get too much pressure, since it is situated in steep, rocky terrain; camping opportunities are nearly nonexistent. Other good fishing lakes in the immediate area are Duck and Beaver Lakes.

Back at Island Lake, enjoy a peaceful sunset, or stand atop the cliffs and peer into the depths of the lake for cruising trout. This lake will not satisfy true "solitude seekers," but it is a quick getaway.

The 100-acre Washington Lake sits just to the south of the trailhead for the magnificent Lakes Country loop.

5 LAKES COUNTRY

The Lakes Country trailhead from Crystal Lake offers a variety of hikes of all lengths. A lot of visitors understandably cluster near the trailhead's amenities, but even the farther flung lakes on this trail see some traffic. Why? Reasonable elevation change and the multiple destination lakes that give this trail its name. Even better, Lakes Country offers a rare loop opportunity that isn't solely suitable for overnight backpacking.

See map and logistics on pages 22–23.
Start: Crystal Lake trailhead
Distance: 7.4-mile loop
Destination elevation: 10,325 feet

Approximate hiking time: 4.5 hours
Difficulty: Moderate
Usage: Heavy
Nearest town: Kamas, Utah
Drainage: Provo River

THE HIKE

From Crystal Lake trailhead parking, take the Lakes Country Trail for about 1.5 miles to a trail junction. Veer right but then stay left: The spur to the right drops into the Middle Fork of the Weber River. Stay left for 0.6 mile to Long Lake. Continue for about 1 mile beyond Long Lake, where you'll arrive at the fork that will begin the loop with a quick switchback north then south to Duck Lake.

At around 9,800 feet, Duck Lake is the lowest elevation spot on the loop, which means a climb of about 500 feet on the lower branch of the loop before the final 1-mile descent back to the trailhead. For backpackers, there are excellent dispersed camp options at both Duck and Wier Lakes, and a great spring near Duck. A 0.5-mile loop around Weir Lake accesses ideal camp options. The whole of the Lakes Country loop is family and scout friendly, so summer weekends may present a shared outdoor experience.

This description of Lakes Country follows the loop counterclockwise from the first trail junction above. A clockwise loop works just as well! From that same junction, turning left to the southwest it's 0.3 mile to pick up the loop trail. Alternatively, many have found solitude by taking the left fork south to Marjorie Lake. It's 1 mile through lush forest and green meadows. Overnighters can hike around the lake to find the perfect spot. Anglers can fish for brook trout or arctic grayling.

6 CLIFF LAKE

You couldn't ask for a prettier setting. The stage is set with picture-perfect campsites and rock-climbing routes that overlook a small lake dimpled by feeding fish. A stately cliff serves as a backdrop, with Mount Watson rising beyond. Grassy campsites are just off the trail on the eastern shore, providing an ideal place to watch the sunset and reflect on the finer things of life. The whole scene mirrors off the clear water.

See map and logistics on pages 22–23.
Start: Crystal Lake trailhead
Distance: 1 mile out and back
Destination elevation: 10,230 feet

Approximate hiking time: 1 hour
Difficulty: Easy
Usage: Heavy
Nearest town: Kamas, Utah
Drainage: Provo River

THE HIKE

Cliff Lake is close enough to the trailhead that you should have plenty of time to watch the sunset and still make it back to the car before dark. It's also a great place to try out some new gear before taking on a more serious hike.

From Crystal Lake trailhead, take the Lakes Country Trail 0.4 mile to the Clyde Lake Trail at a signed junction. It's only another 0.4 mile to Cliff Lake. (The trail to the right from the parking lot goes to Wall Lake and the Notch, or serves as the return trail on a 5.4-mile loop.)

Expect to see a fair amount of foot traffic pass this lake. Anglers and day hikers have to pass by to get to the many lakes above. Cliff Lake is obviously not for loners, but if you're the friendly type and enjoy a quaint little spot with a gorgeous view, then this may be for you.

A small population of cutthroat trout will keep you company. However, the fishing is likely to be only fair due to the easy access and the wary nature of these trout. Better fishing can be found by continuing up the trail another mile to Clyde Lake. Most hikers don't stop at Cliff Lake very long, but almost all remember the pleasant scenery. Try this trail on a weekday, and you might have it all to yourself.

7 DIVIDE LAKES

Here's a backpacking campout to take the kids on. You'll see plenty of small lakes along the way, and the trail has a good mix of uphill and level stretches. They're fairly easy to find, but the spur trail is easy to miss if your attention is on Clyde Lake. The trail is well marked from regular foot traffic all the way to Clyde. From the west side of Clyde, head due north to reach Divide Lakes.

See map and logistics on pages 22-23.
Start: Crystal Lake trailhead
Distance: 5 miles out and back
Destination elevation: 10,460 feet
Approximate hiking time: 3 hours

Difficulty: Moderate—some steep sections
Usage: Moderate
Nearest town: Kamas, Utah
Drainage: Provo River

THE HIKE

This hike is a great overnighter for small groups—or a wonderful escape if you are camped at Trial Lake and want to get away from camp for a spell. You couldn't ask for a better nature trail; it offers a wide variety of scenery, complete with fishing holes.

From Crystal Lake trailhead, take the Lakes Country Trail 0.4 mile to the Clyde Lake Trail at a signed junction. On your hike, you'll pass Cliff, Petit, Linear, and Watson Lakes, all west of the trail. At about 2 miles, you will pass Clyde Lake on the right and Mount Watson on the left. It's another 0.3 mile to the Divide Lakes.

The best places to camp are at the west end of Divide Lake 2 and between Divide Lake 1 and Divide Lake 2. Choose the latter site if the weather looks to be fair; otherwise seek the safety of the pines at Divide Lake 2. Although these lakes are less than 100 yards apart, Divide Lake 1 is on the Provo River drainage (part of the South Slope), and Divide Lake 2 is on the Weber River drainage (North Slope). There is a large rock between the two lakes—when rain falls on the rock, half the water heads toward the Provo River and half toward the Weber.

Several springs are located on the west end of Divide Lake 2. They are conveniently close to camp, easy to treat, and ice cold. Small lakes abound, and there is plenty to do and see without wandering too far. Nearby Booker Lake offers fair fishing, but you'll probably do better right at Divide Lake 1, which has a nice population of smallish brook trout. For best results, try the deeper southwest corner of the lake with a tiny fly.

If you're after bigger fish, try Little Hidden Lake on the Weber drainage. You'll want a topographical map and a compass to find it. There is no trail, but stay close to the mountain to the east, and head north about 0.5 mile. This lake has brookies ranging from 0.5 pound to well over 1 pound. A #16 Renegade fly, cast in the northwest end of the lake, should put a few nicer trout in the creel. Be quiet here—the fish have learned to disappear when noisy visitors appear. As long as you're quiet, they'll keep biting. If you prefer filtering from springs, there is one to the northeast.

From Divide Lakes notice "The Notch" in the mountains to the northeast. This well-known pass is a thing of beauty, especially when you're on it. From the top of Notch Pass is a spectacular view right down into Lovenia Lake. It's worth the mile trip over; or

Clyde Lake sits just below the three Divide Lakes—all four are pictured in the foreground on the cover. PHOTO COURTESY UTAH OFFICE OF TOURISM/MORE THAN JUST PARKS

you could go there on your way back to the trailhead. The Notch Pass Trail returns to Crystal Lake trailhead too.

8 TWIN LAKES

Most people proceed unknowingly right past these lakes. It seems everyone makes the extra effort to hike over Notch Pass to see the beautiful scenery that Ibantik Lake offers. And rightly so. From Notch Pass, the country is amazing. On the other hand, Twin Lakes may make a good base camp that gives you the serenity no other lakes in this area can provide. Don't get us wrong; Twin Lakes get their fair share of attention, but they are often overlooked.

See map and logistics on pages 22–23.
Start: Crystal Lake trailhead
Distance: 5.4 miles out and back or loop
Destination elevation: 10,410 feet

Approximate hiking time: 3 hours
Difficulty: Easy—one steep section
Usage: Moderate
Nearest town: Kamas, Utah
Drainage: Provo River

THE HIKE

It's much easier to find Twin Lakes than it used to be. A low-slung metal sign and well-tread trail replaced the rock piles that once marked the way. Begin your journey at the Crystal Lake trailhead, from the northeast Wall Lake Trail. Follow the trail 1.1 miles to Wall Lake. There is a trail junction here with the trail coming from Trial Lake. Continue to the left (north) up some steep rocky switchbacks. Just past the top of all the switchbacks, before the base of Notch Mountain, turn at the sign and follower the trail west to Lower Twin Lake.

Twin Lakes offer a number of natural amenities. The vista is pretty and only a short distance from the trailhead. Fishing is good for 9- to 15-inch brook trout, and other exciting excursions lie just beyond the immediate. Spring water is only found in the early summer months, and camping areas are only fair due to rocky terrain. However, there is one excellent campsite near the northwest end of Upper Twin. This site sits on a bench overlooking the lakes.

Another option for visiting Twin Lakes is on the loop that follows the Divide Lakes Trail, turning east on the north side of Clyde Lake. It's 0.5 mile to North Twin Lake and the whole loop is about the same distance as the out-and-back approach.

The view from Notch Pass to the south over Wall and Twin Lakes (at right), Haystack Mountain at center

9 IBANTIK LAKE

The trail goes right over Notch Pass. Even if you don't visit Ibantik Lake, you should hike to the top of Notch Pass and gaze into the deep turquoise depths of Lovenia Lake directly below. Absolutely gorgeous! Words cannot describe its beauty. Pictures cannot depict its depth, nor the feeling you get at the top of a cliff looking down. The view is a must for hikers searching for awesome alpine scenery.

See map on page 39 and logistics on page 22.
Start: Crystal Lake trailhead
Distance: 8.4 miles out and back
Destination elevation: 10,100 feet
Approximate hiking time: 5.5 hours

Difficulty: Moderate—steep over Notch Pass
Usage: Heavy
Nearest town: Kamas, Utah
Drainage: Weber River

THE HIKE

The trail from Crystal Lake trailhead goes north 1.1 miles to Wall Lake. There is a trail junction here with the trail coming from Trial Lake. Continue to the left (north) 1.6 miles past Lovenia Lake on the west side of the trail to the notch in Notch Mountain. Ibantik Lake is 0.6 mile northeast of the Notch.

Campsites exist at Lovenia Lake, but there are better ones and fewer people at Ibantik. There is more room for the crowds to disperse once you reach Ibantik Lake. It is well suited for a half-day hike or a quick overnighter. Some backpackers can't get to the trailhead until evening. Ibantik might be ideal for someone getting a late start—strong hikers could reached the site within 2 to 2.5 hours of Crystal Lake trailhead.

Day anglers frequently try their luck in this area. Lovenia, Ibantik, and Meadow Lakes to the north all receive frequent plants of brook and cutthroat trout. The fishing may be good or poor, depending on the time of year, the time of day, or your own fishing skill. Keep in mind that these lakes get heavy pressure, so don't be surprised if many of the fish are wary—or have already been caught.

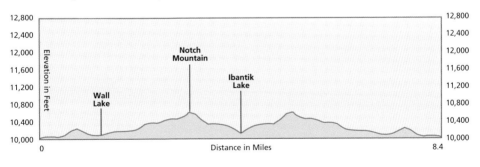

On the North Slope of the Uintas, the lovely Lovenia Lake, seen here from Notch Pass, sits just southwest of Ibantik.

BALD MOUNTAIN PASS

For peak baggers, the Uinta Mountains present an array of remote, rocky scrambles that are slow-going and simply not advisable for many casual hikers. While Bald Mountain has its fair share of loose scree and ankle-twisting potential, it is one peak many visitors to Utah's Uintas can bag. One reason is access: The beautiful, paved Mirror Lake Scenic Byway climbs Bald Mountain Pass, taking drivers above 10,700 feet. That leaves barely 1,200 feet for the hike itself. From the same trailhead, hikers can descend the North Slope to Notch Lake or drive about 1 mile over the pass to the Fehr Lake trailhead for another popular, family-friendly option.

See trails 10 through 12 for Bald Mountain Pass.
Maps: USGS Mirror Lake, *USDA Forest Service High Uintas Wilderness*, *Trails Illustrated High Uintas Wilderness*

Trail contacts: Uinta-Wasatch-Cache National Forest, Forest Supervisor, 857 West South Jordan Pkwy., South Jordan, UT 84095; Kamas Ranger District, 50 East Center St., Kamas, UT 84036, (435) 783-4338

FINDING THE TRAILHEAD

From Kamas, take the Mirror Lake Scenic Byway (Highway 150) 30 miles to Bald Mountain overlook. About 0.5 mile north of the overlook is the left turn to Bald Mountain. Bald Mountain has space for twenty-five cars and offers picnic tables and toilets. No water is available. Bald Mountain trailhead is heavily used by hikers making the 2.5-mile trek to the top of Bald Mountain, where you can peer into four major drainages. For Fehr Lake, continue 1.3 miles over the pass to the trailhead parking lot on the right. If you pass Moosehorn Lake, you've gone a little too far.

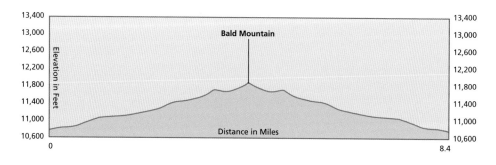

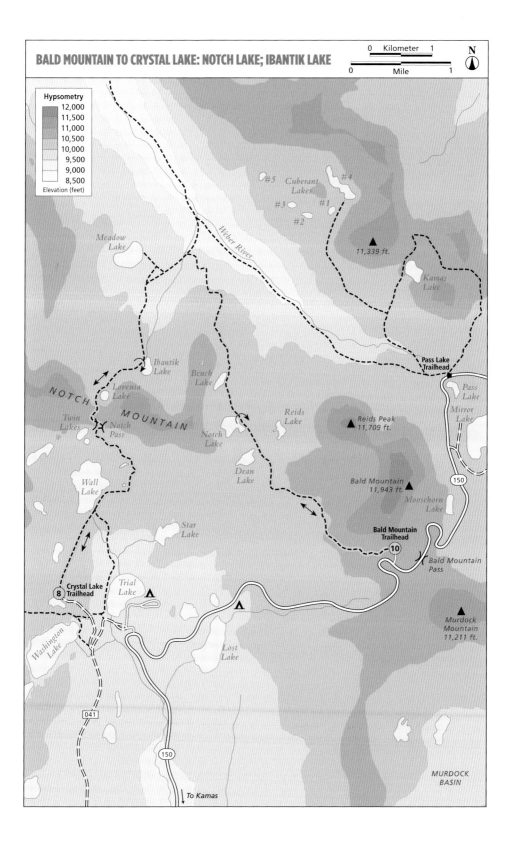

BALD MOUNTAIN TO CRYSTAL LAKE: NOTCH LAKE; IBANTIK LAKE

0   Kilometer   1

0   Mile   1

N

Hypsometry

12,000
11,500
11,000
10,500
10,000
9,500
9,000
8,500
Elevation (feet)

#5   Cuberant
Lakes   #4

#3   #1

#2

11,339 ft.

Kamas
Lake

Meadow
Lake

Weber River

Pass Lake
Trailhead

Pass
Lake

Ibantik
Lake

Bench
Lake

Mirror
Lake

N O T C H

Lovenia
Lake

Twin
Lakes

M O U N T A I N

Notch
Pass

Notch
Lake

Reids
Lake

Reids Peak
11,709 ft.

150

Dean
Lake

Bald Mountain
11,943 ft.

Wall
Lake

Moosehorn
Lake

Star
Lake

Bald Mountain
Trailhead

10

Bald Mountain
Pass

Crystal Lake
Trailhead

8

Trial
Lake

Washington
Lake

Lost
Lake

Murdock
Mountain
11,211 ft.

041

150

To Kamas

MURDOCK
BASIN

Bald Mountain Pass is the highest point on the Mirror Lake Scenic Byway and the highest paved road in Utah.

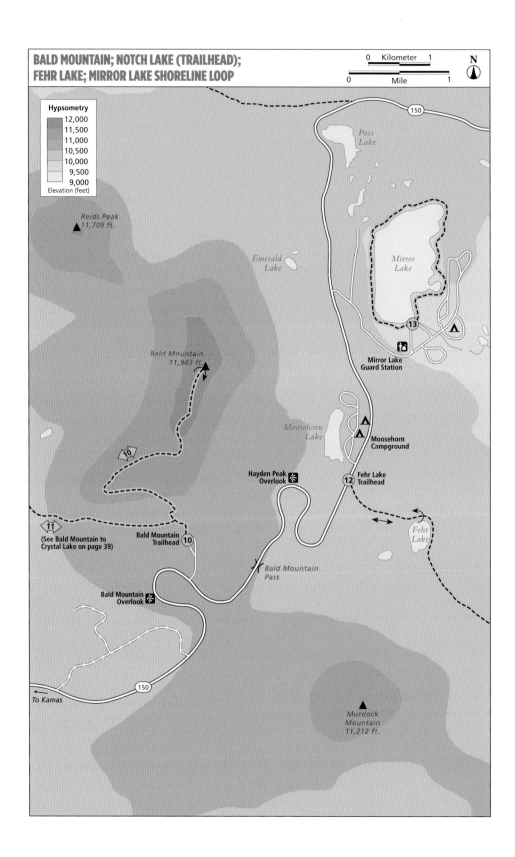

0   Kilometer   1

0   Mile   1

N

Hypsometry

12,000
11,500
11,000
10,500
10,000
9,500
9,000

Elevation (feet)

150

Pass Lake

Reids Peak
▲11,709 ft.

Emerald Lake

Mirror Lake

Bald Mountain
11,943 ft.

13

Mirror Lake
Guard Station

10

Moosehorn Lake

Moosehorn Campground

Hayden Peak Overlook

Fehr Lake
Trailhead
12

11

(See Bald Mountain to
Crystal Lake on page 39)

Bald Mountain
Trailhead   10

Fehr Lake

Bald Mountain
Pass

Bald Mountain
Overlook

150

To Kamas

▲
Murdock
Mountain
11,212 ft.

10 BALD MOUNTAIN

Bald Mountain—the best time investment you can make in the High Uintas. If you only have a few hours to spend and want to experience some grand vistas, then this is the place. Just 1.4 miles of steep hiking puts you atop this well-known peak, where you'll have a bird's-eye view of four of Utah's major watersheds. Scan the cliffs and debris fields of Bald Mountain for moving white spots; there is a high chance of spotting mountain goats.

See map and logistics on pages 38 and 42.
Start: Bald Mountain trailhead
Distance: 2.8 miles out and back
Destination elevation: 11,943 feet
Approximate hiking time: 2.5 hours

Difficulty: Moderate—steady climbing
Usage: Heavy
Nearest town: Kamas, Utah
Drainage: Duchesne River

THE HIKE

The Weber, Provo, Duchesne, and Bear Rivers all begin near here. Looking to the west, you can spot a couple dozen lakes that speckle the upper regions of the Provo and Weber Rivers. Turn around to the east and enjoy a spectacular view of the Mirror Lake Scenic Byway winding its way through heavy timber, past Mirror Lake, and on toward Mount Agassiz and Hayden Peak.

This hike begins at the well-marked Bald Mountain trailhead, located at the base of Bald Mountain. You start climbing immediately and will soon find yourself traversing a series of switchbacks on the western slope. The view is great all the way, and it somehow manages to improve with every step. Listen for and then look for the unique small mammals known as pikas along the way. Near the summit, the trail follows a thin ridge with steep drops off either side. There's really no danger if you stick with the trail, but a person with acrophobia might feel uncomfortable. Then take a natural rock stairway to what feels like the top of the world.

Take your time on this hike. It is steep. Mind your steps. Allow about three hours for a round-trip, which should give you plenty of time at the top to appreciate the views in every direction. Remember:

1. Stay off Bald Mountain when lightning is possible.
2. Don't get too close to the cliff edges on the east side—they can break away.

Follow these rules on Bald Mountain and any other exposed trail or summit you attempt. And certainly don't let this scare you away. This hike is time well spent.

Smoke from the East Fork Fire created a hazy atmosphere atop Bald Mountain.

11 NOTCH LAKE

Going down anyone? Boy, you sure don't find many hikes like this one in the High Uintas. You actually get to hike downhill on the hike in. A fast hiker should be able to cover the entire distance to the lake in an hour. But coming back out may be a bit slower, as you'll have to make up 500 feet of elevation.

See map and logistics on pages 38–39.
Start: Bald Mountain trailhead
Distance: 4.6 miles out and back
Destination elevation: 10,300 feet

Approximate hiking time: 3 hours
Difficulty: Easy
Usage: Heavy
Nearest town: Kamas, Utah
Drainage: Weber River

THE HIKE

Notch Lake lies at the east base of Notch Mountain and is visible from the trail. From Bald Mountain trailhead, the trail goes west and then northwest 2.3 miles to the lake. It is actually a reservoir that fluctuates quite a bit as the summer progresses. Notch usually drops more than 20 feet and loses about half its surface size. Campsites are abundant and spacious, so don't worry about a place to stay, although you might have some company on this popular backpacking route. Good spring water for filtering flows just west of the lake.

Notch is stocked with brook trout, but heavy pressure is to blame for only fair fishing. Bait anglers can expect to have some luck here, as well as fly fishers. Many high-country lakes offer poor fishing for bait anglers, but Notch is one of the exceptions.

There are a couple of other lakes nearby. Give them a try if Notch doesn't fill your needs. Bench Lake is just 0.5 mile north, and Dean Lake is 0.5 mile south of Notch Lake. Bench Lake often experiences winterkills but receives far less camping pressure. This scenic alpine lake is a great place for a small party to camp if you don't care if you catch fish.

If you don't want to hike back up to the trailhead, then park another vehicle at the Crystal Lake trailhead near Trial Lake. From Notch Lake, follow the trail north a couple of miles around the mountain, then south over Notch Pass (gorgeous), and then down to the Crystal Lake trailhead. The entire route, from Bald Mountain trailhead to Crystal Lake trailhead, is just under 10 miles and makes an easy and scenic day hike. After all, except for the rise over Notch Pass, it's downhill almost all the way.

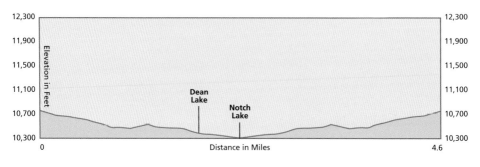

12 FEHR LAKE

Even small kids can enjoy this hike. You don't have to be in good shape either. This is a mini hike. If you only have a couple of hours to spend, you could take a leisurely stroll down to Fehr Lake, fish a bit, and still make it back in time for lunch.

See map and logistics on pages 38 and 42.
Start: Fehr Lake trailhead
Distance: 1 mile out and back
Destination elevation: 10,260 feet

Approximate hiking time: 1 hour
Difficulty: Easy
Usage: Heavy
Nearest town: Kamas, Utah
Drainage: Duchesne River

THE HIKE

The only thing difficult about this hike is spotting the trailhead. There is a nice large sign indicating where to begin your hike, but some people drive right past it after descending the scenic S-curve from Bald Mountain Pass.

The hike to Fehr is gentle and provides a variety of scenery in its short distance. You'll pass through cool groves of pines and mountain meadows and stroll past a small waterfall or two. It's a great place to get away from busy campgrounds. You'll feel more removed than you really are. Notice the quiet. Fehr is a natural lake (6 acres) in a picture-book setting. It is surrounded on three sides by pines and bounded by a meadow on the south. Beyond the meadow are more pines, backed by a stately mountain.

Fishing at Fehr is only fair, which is probably as good as you'll find at any of the road-side lakes. But you won't be crowded here. Move around and try various lures and flies, or just sit on the bank and drown a worm. The odds are you will catch a few fat brook trout—maybe even a nap. This is a great little body of water to portage a canoe into where you can fish in the middle of the lake or simply paddle around.

The trail continues past Fehr Lake, going down to Shepard, Maba, Hoover, and Marshall Lakes. Many people using this trail are just out for a hike because you could drive to these lakes on the unimproved, high-clearance Murdock Basin Road. Try it for a relaxing day hike. It may seem a little steep on the return trip though.

Wildflowers at Fehr Lake, a short, family-friendly hike below Bald Mountain Pass

MIRROR LAKE AREA

One can argue that any tour of the Mirror Lake Scenic Byway (Highway 150) should include a stop at its namesake. It's a good argument: The 53-acre Mirror Lake is the largest natural lake along the highway and attracts hikers, campers, anglers, and equestrians to its shores, trails, and campground and kayakers, paddle boarders, and other non-motorized boaters to its waters. On a calm day, its glassy waters reflect nearby Bald Mountain and painterly clusters of evergreen trees. It's no wonder families return annually, and reservations may be necessary to grab a campsite. If not staying overnight, pack a picnic and find a spot along the shore to relax and enjoy the cool mountain air. Otherwise, see you out on the trails.

See trails 13 and 14 for Mirror Lake Area.
Maps: USGS Mirror Lake, USGS Hayden Peak, and USGS Iron Mine Mountain; *USDA Forest Service High Uintas Wilderness*; *Trails Illustrated High Uintas Wilderness*
Trail contacts: Uinta-Wasatch-Cache National Forest, Forest Supervisor, 857 West South Jordan Pkwy., South Jordan, UT 84095; Kamas Ranger District, 50 East Center St., Kamas, UT 84036, (435) 783-4338; Ashley National Forest, Forest Supervisor, 355 North Vernal Ave., Vernal, UT 84078, (435) 781-1181; Duchesne Ranger District, 85 West Main, Duchesne, UT 84021, (435) 738-2482

FINDING THE TRAILHEAD

From Kamas, take the Mirror Lake Scenic Byway (Highway 150) 31 miles to Mirror Lake. There are two trailheads. The first is a large day-use area with more than fifty parking spots, restrooms, and a boat ramp. You will find a second trailhead about 0.25 mile east of the Mirror Lake entrance. This trailhead has eighteen parking places and offers a very popular and well-maintained campground with water, toilets, and a stock-unloading ramp. (A northbound trail departing from here, also called Mirror Lake, is a connector trail to Highline.)

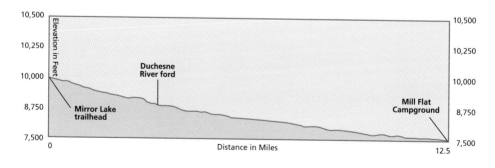

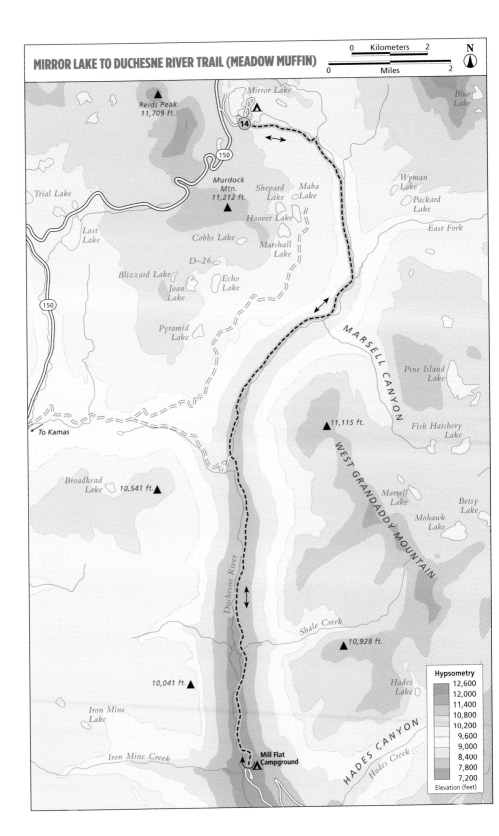

MIRROR LAKE TO DUCHESNE RIVER TRAIL (MEADOW MUFFIN)

0 Kilometers 2
0 Miles 2

N

Reids Peak
11,709 ft.

Mirror Lake

Blue
Lake

14

150

Murdock
Mtn.
11,212 ft.

Shepard
Lake

Maba
Lake

Wyman
Lake

Packard
Lake

Trial Lake

Hoover Lake

East Fork

Lost
Lake

Cobbs Lake

Marshall
Lake

D–26

Blizzard Lake

Joan
Lake

Echo
Lake

150

Pyramid
Lake

MARSELL CANYON

Pine Island
Lake

To Kamas

Fish Hatchery
Lake

11,115 ft.

WEST GRANDADDY MOUNTAIN

Marsell
Lake

Betsy
Lake

Broadhead
Lake

10,541 ft.

Mohawk
Lake

Duchesne River

Shale Creek

10,928 ft.

10,041 ft.

Hades
Lake

Iron Mine
Lake

HADES CANYON

Iron Mine Creek

Mill Flat
Campground

Hades Creek

Hypsometry

	12,600
	12,000
	11,400
	10,800
	10,200
	9,600
	9,000
	8,400
	7,800
	7,200

Elevation (feet)

Bald Mountain overlooks the popular Mirror Lake area of the Mirror Lake Scenic Byway.

The boardwalk on the south side of the Mirror Lake Shoreline Loop offers a view northeast to Hayden Peak.

13 MIRROR LAKE SHORELINE LOOP

The gently rolling shoreline trail of Mirror Lake never climbs more than about 25 feet above the starting elevation, making this trail a wonderful way to stretch your legs without a lot of extra exertion—being mindful of the possibility of altitude sickness that can occur at 10,000 feet above sea level, of course. Whether you're scouting a spot to have a picnic or from which to cast a line, this is a perfect introduction to the High Uintas landscape.

See map and logistics on pages 42 and 48.
Start: Mirror Lake trailhead
Distance: 1.5-mile loop
Destination elevation: 10,025 feet

Approximate hiking time: 45 mins
Difficulty: Easy
Usage: High
Nearest town: Kamas, Utah
Drainage: Duchesne River

THE HIKE

Mirror Lake Shoreline Loop begins from a picnic area and day-use area (which includes a boat ramp) that is well marked on the lefthand side of the road. There are Mirror Lake Campground sites on the right and beyond the picnic area.

It's easy to orient yourself here with Bald Mountain rising directly to the west beyond a screen of trees. It's worth noting that the Duchesne River begins in the Mirror Lake area and flows to the southeast on a 115-mile journey to the Green River (which, in turn, flows into the mighty Colorado River), a reminder of the interconnectedness of the geography of the Uinta Mountains to the western United States. More on the Duchesne in the next chapter.

If going counterclockwise, you'll set out across a boardwalk in the direction of Bald Mountain. (If you haven't yet hiked Bald, you may find it calling to you.) But as you leave the boardwalk and round the bend heading north, the taller Mount Agassiz and Hayden Peak are sure to catch your eye, about 3.5 miles to the east and northeast.

After 0.5 mile, the trail veers to the northeast and, just past 0.75 mile, back south, following the eastern contours of the lake. As with all "popular" destinations, the size of the crowds can depend on your timing. Either way, you'll be glad for this chance to get to know Mirror Lake.

14 DUCHESNE RIVER TRAIL (MEADOW MUFFIN)

Most people use the Mirror Lake entryway instead of Mill Flat on the South Slope and the Ashley National Forest side, solely because the trail loses elevation starting from Mirror Lake. Usually, two vehicles are used to support this trip. One vehicle transports the trekkers to Mirror Lake, while the other is left behind at Mill Flat (about 0.25 mile north of Iron Mine Campground). Another alternate route can be made via a branch off the Murdock Basin Road. This 4WD road takes you to the east portal of the Duchesne Tunnel.

See map and logistics on pages 48 and 49.
Start: Mirror Lake trailhead
Distance: 12.5-mile one-way shuttle
Destination elevation: 7,520 feet
Approximate hiking time: 8 hours

Difficulty: Moderate—some steep sections
Usage: Moderate
Nearest town: Kamas, Utah
Drainage: Duchesne River

THE HIKE

The trailhead is the second one described in "Mirror Lake Area," above, about 0.25 mile east of Mirror Lake. The adventure begins on the North Fork Trail 086 of the Duchesne River drainage. After a slight incline, the trail descends rapidly to the Pinto Lake–Mill Flat junction 2.5 miles from the trailhead. Following the trail to Mill Flat, a deep river gorge begins to emerge. Spectacular views of plummeting cliffs soon appear, as mystic scenery stimulates the soul—although exposed areas from a 2018 fire can make for hot afternoon hiking.

About 7.5 miles from the trailhead, near the east portal of the Duchesne Tunnel, the gorge widens to a ford. This is also where the trail crosses the river. Due to high water, it is not feasible—or safe—to cross the river until after the month of July. The gate of the east portal remains closed until water is needed downstream in the Provo River. Water is then diverted through the Duchesne Tunnel, dropping the Duchesne River to expose a makeshift trail, which runs along the top of a dike.

Excellent campsites can be found before and after the ford, and spring water is available all along the trail. However, the presence of cows makes drinking water hard to find—and serves as a reminder of the importance of treating all water before drinking. Angling is best upstream from the portal. The fish are small, but they can prove to be exciting. (That's if you don't mind stepping in a cow pie or two.) The trail upstream from the portal is plagued with cow-tainted mud holes. If you're not careful, one of these stench-pots can suck your boot right off.

After the portal, the trail becomes rather relaxing. Vistas of a deep river gorge are nearby, and an excellent trail reclines on down the mountain. The last couple of miles of this trek can be a little confusing. A hit-or-miss trail winds through dense vegetation as it crosses lots of tiny streams. In any case, you'll soon know when you are on the right track. The friendly service of our courteous cows will leave a trail of meadow muffins for you to follow.

15 BUTTERFLY LAKE TO CASTLE LAKE

This hike is for the roadside camper looking for a short diversion. Castle Lake is less than half a mile west of Butterfly Lake. Butterfly Lake has excellent campground facilities, as well as a parking area for day-use anglers. It's a rugged "route" rather than a clear trail to Castle Lake, but just head due west, stay close to the base of the cliffs and you can't miss it. There are several small ponds on the way. Don't mistake one of them for Castle Lake.

Start: Butterfly Lake
Distance: 0.8 mile out and back
Destination elevation: 10,300 feet
Approximate hiking time: 1 hour
Difficulty: Moderate—cross country hiking
Usage: Moderate
Nearest town: Kamas, Utah
Drainage: Duchesne River

Maps: USGS Hayden Peak, *USDA Forest Service High Uintas Wilderness, Trails Illustrated High Uintas Wilderness*
Trail contacts: Uinta-Wasatch-Cache National Forest, Forest Supervisor, 857 West South Jordan Pkwy., South Jordan, UT 84095; Kamas Ranger District, 50 East Center St., Kamas, UT 84036, (435) 783-4338

FINDING THE TRAILHEAD

Start at Butterfly Lake. From Kamas, take the Mirror Lake Scenic Byway (Highway 150) for about 33 miles. The trailhead is on the west side of the road.

THE HIKE

Cliffs parallel Castle Lake just beyond its northern shore. This is a quiet little place (1 acre) that can be a welcome reprieve from the public campground scene. A round-trip from Butterfly Lake to beautiful Castle Lake makes a wonderful evening stroll that should only take an hour, unless you stop to sit awhile, do some birdwatching, or try the fishing. There is no trail to Castle Lake from Butterfly Lake, but with a good sense of direction and navigation skills through the forest, it's relatively easy to reach by going west from the inlet of Butterfly Lake near the campground. Another bonus are the views back to Bald Mountain and Reid Peak during the hike.

Open shorelines make casting easy, but also make for wary trout; Castle Lake has both. Cutthroat trout are the fish of the day at Castle. This is a good second option if the shores at Butterfly are crowded, which is usually the case. There are a few moist areas around the lake, so mosquitoes can be a nuisance. Give yourself a good dose of insect repellent, and you'll breathe easier while enjoying this secluded spot. It seems farther away than it is from the crowded campgrounds and the highway.

BUTTERFLY LAKE TO CASTLE LAKE

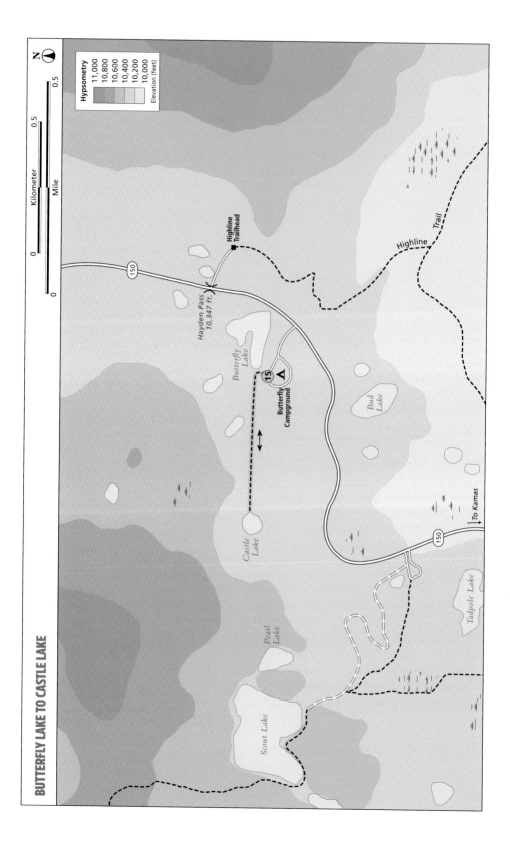

N

Hypsometry

11,000
10,800
10,600
10,400
10,200
10,000

Elevation (feet)

Kilometer

0   0.5

Mile

0   0.5

150

Hayden Pass
10,347 ft.

Highline
Trailhead

Highline   Trail

Butterfly
Lake

15

Butterfly
Campground

Bud
Lake

Castle
Lake

Pearl
Lake

Scout Lake

Tadpole Lake

150

To Kamas

HIGHLINE TRAILHEAD (WEST)

For many, hiking in Utah's High Uintas all begins (or ends) right here. That's because the Highline trailhead off Highway 150 is either the enthusiastic launch of a 10- to 100-mile trek or the exuberant conclusion of one (see the Highline Trail on page 187). Outside of the 3-mile hike to Mirror Lake or the strenuous 3.5-mile scramble to Hayden Peak (head due east from the trailhead and expect 2,000 feet in careful, rock-hopping elevation gain), Highline is all about distance. Most day hikes begin at 7 or 8 miles, round-trip, and continue up to 23 miles complete with mountain passes—doable on foot, of course, but easy to see why someone might bring a horse.

If you're just getting started hiking at 10,000 feet, you might consider these hikes part of a more advanced class. Oh, and, at just about 1.1 miles into these hikes, you'll pass into the designated High Uintas Wilderness Area. Remind your group of the power of Leave No Trace principles to help you and others who follow to fully enjoy the gift of America's protected outdoor places.

See trails 16 through 21 for Highline Trailhead (West).
Maps: USGS Hayden Peak and USGS Explorer Peak, *USDA Forest Service High Uintas Wilderness*, *Trails Illustrated High Uintas Wilderness*
Trail contacts: Uinta-Wasatch-Cache National Forest, Forest Supervisor, 857 West South Jordan Pkwy., South Jordan, UT 84095; Kamas Ranger District, 50 East Center St., Kamas, UT 84036, (435) 783-4338; Ashley National Forest, Forest Supervisor, 355 North Vernal Ave., Vernal, UT 84078, (435) 781-1181; Duchesne Ranger District, 85 West Main, Duchesne, UT 84021, (435) 738-2482

FINDING THE TRAILHEAD

The Highline is the most popular trailhead of the High Uintas. From Kamas, take the Mirror Lake Scenic Byway (Highway 150) 34 miles to a large sign on the east side of the road that says "Highline Trail." You can't get lost finding this one.

This trailhead has a listed capacity of twenty-four vehicles, but there are often considerably more parked here on busy weekends. The overcrowded trailhead is equipped with toilets, water, stock ramp, and nearby campsites.

HIGHLINE TRAILHEAD (WEST): PACKARD AND WYMAN LAKES; JORDAN LAKE; MORAT AND BLUE LAKES; CAROLYN LAKE; FOUR LAKES BASIN; OURAY LAKE

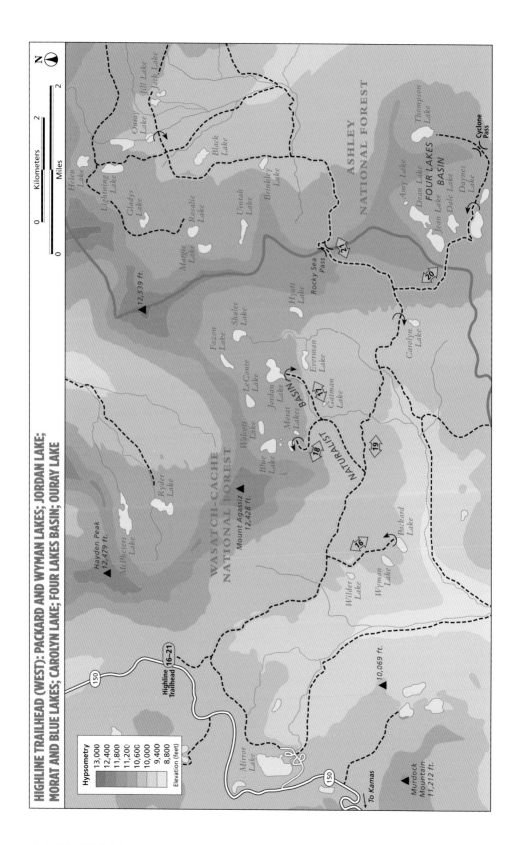

Hayden Peak stands watch over the western edge of the Highline Trail, whose trailhead is popular among hikers and horse packers.

16 WILDER, WYMAN, AND PACKARD LAKES

Wilder, Wyman, and Packard Lakes make a great day hike for kids and adults alike. Some people begin their adventure from Mirror Lake rather than the Highline trailhead because better accommodations are found at Mirror Lake, but that will add about a mile to the trip in each direction. (Scudder Lake is only 2 miles along this same trail but may still be unsuitable for camping after the 2018 Mirror Lake Complex fire.)

See map and logistics on pages 55–56.
Start: Highline trailhead
Distance: 6.5 to 8.5 miles out and back
Destination elevation: 9,980 feet

Approximate hiking time: 4 to 6 hours
Difficulty: Easy to moderate—some steep sections
Usage: Moderate
Nearest town: Kamas, Utah
Drainage: Duchesne River

THE HIKE

Wyman Lake features heavy timber and pretty lily pads clinging to the shore. Campsites are plentiful, as are the bugs. This area is not on the campfire restrictions map, but the burn areas from the 2018 fire—though started by lightning—may have you practicing Leave No Trace by bringing a stove to cook meals. Wyman receives heavy camping and angling use and frequently experiences winterkill, which usually means only fair fishing. Surrounded by heavy timber, Wilder has nice camping, horse pasture, and willing grayling and brook trout.

From the Highline trailhead, the trail descends about 300 feet to the Mirror Lake Trail junction. Access from Mirror Lake begins near the east side of the lake at the north end of the campgrounds. The Mirror Lake Trail makes its way 2 miles northeast, then connects with the Highline Trail. From this junction, follow the Highline Trail 2 miles southeast to a posted sign on the eastern top of a ravine. Follow the Packard Lake Trail 1 mile south down a steep and rocky slope, where you'll have the option to stop at Wilder Lake or continue up and down a hill to Wyman Lake. Packard Lake is another 0.5 mile of hiking to the southeast of Wyman Lake. To get there, follow Wyman's east shore and continue south about 0.3 mile. Turn east and hike 0.2 mile.

Packard is a pretty lake located on a high ledge with a view of the East Fork of the Duchesne River drainage. Good campsites are available, but horse pasture is limited. This lake receives heavy fishing pressure, but a good supply of brook trout inhabits the lake. All lakes in this area receive heavy usage and are prone to litter. Help keep them clean.

Packard Lake is a popular Uinta Mountains destination accessed from either the Highline trailhead or Mirror Lake. PHOTO BY MATT MCKELL/UTAH DIVISION OF WILDLIFE RESOURCES

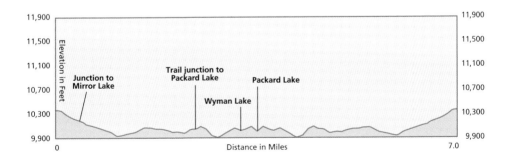

17 JORDAN LAKE

Considering the heavy usage thrown upon this area, Naturalist Basin remains remarkably clean. Thoughtful hikers and the Forest Service deserve kudos for keeping this beautiful wilderness free of debris and litter. To ensure this mountain range remains unscarred, fire restrictions are in effect throughout Naturalist Basin. Gas stoves will be necessary for cooking.

See map and logistics on pages 55–56.
Start: Highline trailhead
Distance: 13 miles out and back
Destination elevation: 10,660 feet
Approximate hiking time: 8 hours

Difficulty: Moderate—some steep sections
Usage: Heavy
Nearest town: Kamas, Utah
Drainage: Duchesne River

THE HIKE

In scenic timbered terrain, a steep boulder slope, pickled with pine trees on the northwest side, identifies Jordan Lake. Excellent posted campsites are located west of the lake. Other camping areas can be found along the east side of the outlet. This wide outlet is composed of several small ponds connected by a meandering stream. A small source of spring water might be found trickling into the northwest side of the lake. During dry years, the lake will be the only water source.

A large population of brook trout inhabits the outlet, making fly fishing a pleasure. The lake is stocked regularly. Angling can be kind of slow until dusk. Then they're jumping like popcorn.

The only lakes that have campsites in the Jordan Lake vicinity are Jordan, Hyatt, and Everman. Shaler Lake can be found on the Naturalist Basin Trail 0.75 mile northeast of Jordan Lake. Hyatt is located on a scenic rocky shelf 0.5 mile east of Everman. Everman is in a small meadow 0.75 mile east of the Blue-Jordan Trail junction and just 200 yards east of the Naturalist Basin Trail. LeConte is situated above timberline, 0.5 mile northwest of Jordan, over steep and rocky terrain. Faxon and Gatman Lakes do not sustain fish life.

From the Highline trailhead, descend on the trail about 300 feet to the Mirror Lake Trail junction. Then follow the Highline Trail 4 miles southeast across several gentle ravines and around the southern foot of the 12,433-foot Mount Agassiz to a posted sign at the Naturalist Basin turnoff. Proceed 1.8 miles northeast to the Blue-Jordan Trail junction. At this point the Jordan Lake Trail crosses the river and heads east through a scenic meadow. Then it turns north up a couple of rocky switchbacks, leveling out at the lake. North of Faxon Lake, the col (lowest point of a ridge) is the best access point to the ridgeline that reaches the 12,540-foot Spread Eagle Peak. It's more than 5 miles round-trip between Jordan and Spread Eagle.

Jordan Lake is a good place to camp while exploring the Naturalist Basin. PHOTO BY MATT MCKELL/UTAH DIVISION OF WILDLIFE RESOURCES

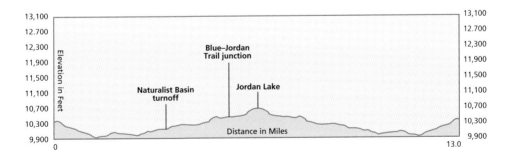

18 MORAT AND BLUE LAKES (AND MOUNT AGASSIZ)

The Morat Lakes receive heavy usage from both backpackers and day hikers. For anglers, fishing pressure remains somewhat moderate at these lakes because many anglers bypass the Morat Lakes and begin to fish at Blue Lake. However, large cutthroat trout can often be netted at Morat #1. This trail also grabs the attention of peak baggers eyeing the strenuous scramble up Mount Agassiz. Its challenging, but the most popular way up.

See map and logistics on pages 55–56.
Start: Highline trailhead
Distance: 11 to 14 miles out and back
Destination elevation: 10,740 feet
Approximate hiking time: 8.5 to 12 hours

Difficulty: Moderate—some steep sections
Usage: Moderate
Nearest town: Kamas, Utah
Drainage: Duchesne River

THE HIKE

From the Highline trailhead, descend on the trail about 300 feet to the Mirror Lake Trail junction. Then follow the Highline Trail 4 miles southeast across several gentle ravines to a posted sign at the Naturalist Basin turnoff. Proceed 1.8 miles northeast to the Blue-Jordan Trail junction.

From the Blue-Jordan Trail junction, follow the Blue Lake Trail 0.5 mile west then north to Morat Lakes. The last 0.125 mile is excessively rocky and almost vertical—a couple hundred feet of elevation change with grades of 5 to 20 percent. Above 10,750 feet, Blue and Morat Lakes also sit in the cooler part of Naturalist Basin and are usually not free of ice until mid-July.

The deeper Morat #1 (West Morat) is at the base of Blue Lake Ridge next to a talus slope interspersed with conifers. Morat #2 (East Morat) is located just east of Morat #1. Even though these lakes sit in rocky, timbered terrain, several good camping areas can be found. But remember, a fire restriction is often in effect at Naturalist Basin, so gas stoves will be necessary for cooking. If on horseback and you can make it up the hill to Morat Lakes, bring along some oats. Only limited feed is available. If you prefer springs for treating, the only dependable source of spring water in the Morat or Blue Lake area is at Morat #2.

Blue Lake is located over a ridge 0.25 mile north of Morat #1. The steep trail is next to a small waterfall and tricky with heavy backpacks. A steep, rocky basin at the east base of Mount Agassiz characterizes this pretty lake. There is some room for camping in a meadow on the east side of the lake, but little shade. Spring water might be found in early summer. Fishing is usually fast for small brook trout.

If you've come with the intent to tackle Mount Agassiz, then you've come prepared to navigate without a defined trail. Continuing north from the east side of Blue Lake, seek out a visible shoulder along the westbound ridge. You'll be working your way around

The Morat Lakes in the Naturalist Basin hold cutthroat trout and are a good place to set up a camp. PHOTO BY MATT MCKELL/UTAH DIVISION OF WILDLIFE RESOURCES

boulders and up loose rocky slopes, all of which can shift beneath your weight. Though the summit only adds around 1 mile one-way, take your time—in both directions. At 12,433 feet, you'll have views north into Middle Basin and South all the way to the backside of the Wasatch Mountains.

Near the Blue-Jordan Trail junction, there are a couple of nice campsites near the main stream. This might be a good place to stay if you wanted to fish deep, slow waters flowing through open meadows.

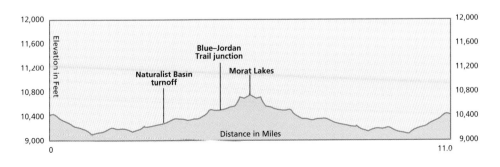

19 CAROLYN LAKE

Although Carolyn Lake is in a popular area, it is most often passed by. This small lake is in timbered country characterized by boggy shorelines and a small, wet meadow. Spring water is somewhat limited, but good running water can be found on the southeast side of the lake—it's a pro tip to start with the cleanest water source possible when treating!

See map and logistics on pages 55–56.
Start: Highline trailhead
Distance: 13 miles out and back
Destination elevation: 10,460 feet
Approximate hiking time: 9 hours

Difficulty: Moderate—some steep sections
Usage: Moderate
Nearest town: Kamas, Utah
Drainage: Duchesne River

THE HIKE

There are plenty of good camping areas at Carolyn Lake. However, a fire restriction is in effect in this area, and only posted campsites may be used. These designated sites are located on the west side of the lake, 50 yards from shore. Unposted camping areas exist near the south end of the lake on a little plateau. About 100 feet south of these campsites is an awesome view of the West Fork Rock Creek drainage.

Access is 6.5 miles south then east on the Highline Trail. From the Highline Trail, look for a deeply rutted trail that takes off to the south and across an open meadow. About 200 yards down this trail lies Carolyn Lake. No posted signs point the direction to the lake, but the trail can be clearly seen if you're watching for it.

This is a great place for an overnighter that will seem more remote than it is, and it's a centrally located base camp for day trips to Naturalist and Four Lakes Basins. One reason this lake is overlooked is because Carolyn contains a large population of arctic grayling. This is no problem if you know how to prepare them (e.g., cleaning like a brook trout and then descaling or a clever fillet), but most anglers prefer high-mountain trout. If grayling are on your menu, you should have no problem limiting out. The fish seem to

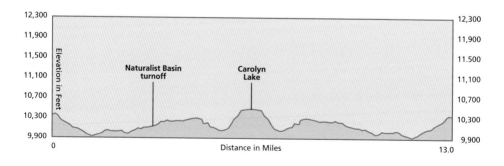

be jumping all day long and will smack a small, colorful fly or flashy spinner.

20 FOUR LAKES BASIN

Jean, Dean, Dale, and Daynes Lakes make up Four Lakes Basin. The best places to stay are at Dale or Daynes Lake. Campsites, horse pasture, space for horses, and spring water are plentiful at both lakes. Backpackers might opt for a little more solitude at Dean Lake, which is not as suitable for horses. There is spring water at Dean Lake, but it is on the extreme northern shore (a long walk from the campsites).

See map and logistics on pages 55–56.
Start: Highline trailhead
Distance: 18 miles out and back
Destination elevation: 10,700 feet

Approximate hiking time: 12 hours
Difficulty: Moderate
Usage: Heavy
Nearest town: Kamas, Utah
Drainage: Rock Creek

THE HIKE

Four Lakes Basin is about 9 miles from either the Highline or Grandview trailhead. Consider using the Highline trailhead, since the hike has less than half the elevation gain as the hike from the Grandview trailhead. The Highline trailhead is also closer and easier to reach if you are coming from the population centers of Utah (Salt Lake City, Provo, and Ogden).

From the Highline trailhead, descend 300 feet over a mile to the Mirror Lake Trail junction. Stay left and follow the Highline Trail 4 miles southeast across several gentle ravines to a posted sign at the Naturalist Basin turnoff. Stay right (east) at this junction, continuing on the Highline Trail. Go about 1 mile to another junction with the trail heading into the East Fork of the Duchesne River. Stay right (south then east) at another junction about 1 mile farther (at around 6.8 miles) with the trail heading over the high pass and down into the Four Lakes Basin.

Fishing pressure is heavy at all four lakes except Dean Lake, which receives moderate pressure. If you take the time to walk to the back side of Dean Lake, you'll find that hardly anyone else has been there. You might have your best success there. The predominant species in these lakes is brook trout. An occasional cutthroat may be caught, and Daynes Lake has a few arctic grayling to spice up your fishing. Fly fishing works best, but a surprising number of anglers use worms here. You don't find many lakes in the High Uintas where bait anglers are as successful as they are in the Four Lakes Basin.

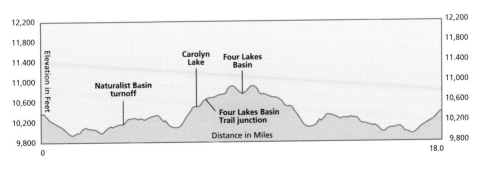

Photographers can find plenty of subject matter in this basin. Jean and Dean Lakes provide spectacular alpine scenery. Keep your camera handy as you ride or hike around. For a breathtaking view, hike to the top of Cyclone Pass, where you can see the vast regions of the Rock Creek drainage on either side of the pass. Daynes Lake is especially pretty from Cyclone Pass.

Many visitors to the Uinta Mountains use horses to cover more ground while exploring the country. This pack train was spotted on the Highline Trail. PHOTO BY MATT MCKELL/UTAH DIVISION OF WILDLIFE RESOURCES

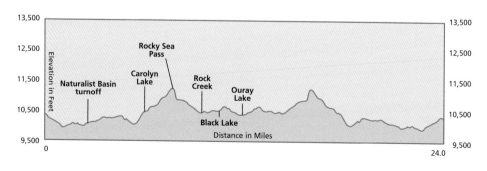

21 OURAY LAKE

It doesn't look like much at first glance but give it a chance. For long-distance hikers or equestrians, Ouray Lake in the remote Rock Creek Basin is a good place to establish a base camp, or just hide out. Thanks to its distance and the "distraction" of Naturalist Basin, fewer backpackers make it here. At the north end of the lake is a great little campsite, complete with rock tables; nearby, a couple of springs enter the small streams that feed Ouray Lake. Equestrians particularly like this spot because it is situated in a box canyon with plenty of horse pasture.

See map and logistics on pages 55–56.
Start: Highline trailhead
Distance: 24 miles out and back
Destination elevation: 10,380 feet

Approximate hiking time: 15 hours
Difficulty: Moderate—mountain pass
Usage: Light
Nearest town: Kamas, Utah
Drainage: Rock Creek

THE HIKE

The quickest way to reach this area is over the 11,300-foot Rocky Sea Pass that marks the boundary between the Uinta-Wasatch-Cache and Ashley National Forests—though a web of trails converge here from both the North and South Slope.

From the Highline trailhead, descend 300 feet over a mile to the Mirror Lake Trail junction. Stay left and follow the Highline Trail 4 miles southeast across several gentle ravines to a posted sign at the Naturalist Basin turnoff. Stay right (east) at this junction, continuing on the Highline Trail. Go about 1 mile to another junction with the trail heading into the East Fork of the Duchesne River. Stay left (east). At another junction about 1 mile farther on with the trail heading south toward Four Lakes Basin, stay left (east) on the trail going over Rocky Sea Pass. The view of the Rock Creek drainage is awesome from atop the pass. Descend the trail to Rock Creek and another trail junction. Stay left. It's another mile to Black Lake. About 0.5 mile from Black Lake, turn right onto a cutoff trail toward Ouray Lake. The lake is about 0.5 mile from the turnoff.

Fishing at Ouray is excellent at times and good most any time. The east side of the lake is the deepest and harbors most of the fish. Flies or a small spinner will take a limit of brookies and cutthroat in short time. Don't forget to fish the main stream that flows into Ouray. The fish are there if you're cautious and lucky enough.

If you are up to some hearty day hikes, there are plenty of other fishing opportunities in the area. Lightning Lake to the northwest is fun. It's not lightning fast, but there are enough feisty fish to keep you interested for quite a while. If it's fast fishing you want, try Doug Lake to the northeast. Small brook trout will smack a fly on just about every cast. Next to Doug Lake is Boot Lake. It is much larger and deeper and is a good place to experiment with various lures and flies.

If you like the area but have a large group, try camping at Black Lake. Both Black and Ouray Lakes are down from the trail and sheltered by pines—an important factor in this windswept region of upper Rock Creek.

GARDNERS FORK AREA

This book highlights three broad regions of Utah's High Uintas based on the major roads that access them. Gardners Fork is an outlier. Weber Canyon Road heads east into the Uintas from the town of Oakley, which is 5.5 miles north of the Kamas turnoff to Highway 150. Weber Canyon Road accesses the stunning and popular Smith and Morehouse Reservoir. Trails leading from there also reach Erickson Basin and Lakes Country, previously covered. The area is some of the lowest-elevation terrain in the Uintas, at least at the starting point—and that's still around 8,000 feet. Both trails covered here have around 2,300 feet in elevation gain.

See trails 22 and 23 for Gardners Fork Area.
Maps: USGS Erickson Basin and USGS Whitney Reservoir, *USDA Forest Service High Uintas Wilderness, Trails Illustrated High Uintas Wilderness*

Trail contacts: Uinta-Wasatch-Cache National Forest, Forest Supervisor, 857 West South Jordan Pkwy., South Jordan, UT 84095; Kamas Ranger District, 50 East Center St., Kamas, UT 84036, (435) 783-4338

FINDING THE TRAILHEAD

From Oakley, head east on Weber River Road. Follow it about 11.7 miles until the pavement ends. The road forks there, and the main road swings to the right (south) toward Smith-Morehouse Reservoir. Don't go that way. Stay on the dirt road that goes east through Thousand Peaks Ranch (the home of the 15,000-acre Park City Powder Cats). The Dry Fork trailhead is around the 7-mile mark of the dirt road; Gardners Fork trailhead will be on the left at around 8.4 miles.

To achieve Utah's "Cutthroat Slam"—a fishing challenge to support conservation projects—anglers can pursue native Bonneville cutthroat trout in the Western Uintas. PHOTO BY MATT MCKELL/UTAH DIVISION OF WILDLIFE RESOURCES

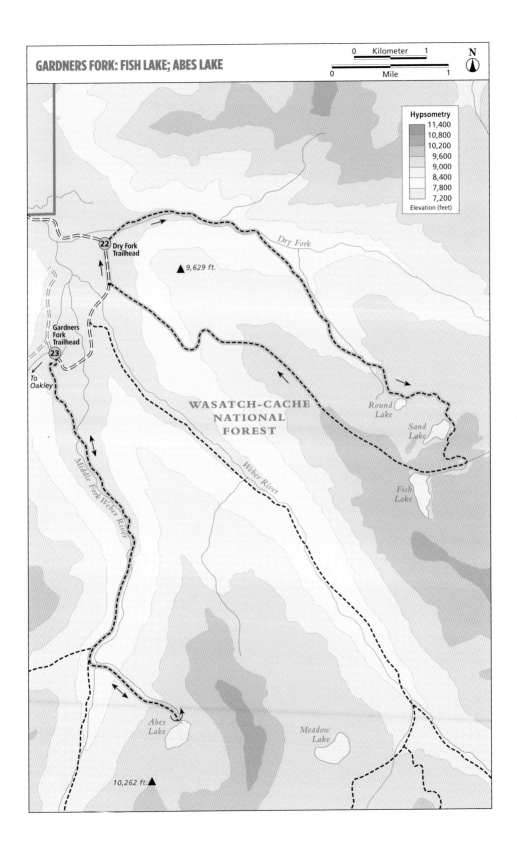

GARDNERS FORK: FISH LAKE; ABES LAKE

0   Kilometer   1

0   Mile   1

N

Hypsometry
11,400
10,800
10,200
9,600
9,000
8,400
7,800
7,200
Elevation (feet)

Dry Fork

22 Dry Fork
Trailhead

▲ 9,629 ft.

Gardners
Fork
Trailhead
23

To
Oakley

WASATCH-CACHE
NATIONAL
FOREST

Round
Lake

Sand
Lake

Middle Fork Weber River

Weber River

Fish
Lake

Abes
Lake

Meadow
Lake

10,262 ft. ▲

22 DRY FORK TRAILHEAD TO FISH LAKE

Many enthusiastic people find the Dry Fork Loop Trail a rewarding day hike, despite the elevation gain—especially those on horseback. Backpackers with heavy loads usually avoid this steep, rugged trail, opting instead for an out-and-back hike.

See map and logistics on pages 68–69.
Start: Gardners Fork area (Dry Fork trailhead)
Distance: 9.4-mile loop
Destination elevation: 10,180 feet

Approximate hiking time: 6 hours
Difficulty: Moderate—some steep sections
Usage: Heavy
Nearest town: Oakley, Utah
Drainage: Weber River

THE HIKE

The main starting point is located on the east side of Holiday Park at the Dry Fork trailhead. The other connecting trail begins 0.5 mile south of the Dry Fork trailhead, but it is hard to locate unless you've made this trip before. From the Dry Fork trailhead, follow a well-marked trail 2 miles east to a shallow river crossing. At this point, the trail twists another 1.5 miles southeast up a 1,300-foot incline to Round Lake. A large outlet releases a good supply of water that provides a wannabe waterfall that crosses the trail just before arrival. This small lake has good campsites all around it, but it's heavily used and degraded.

Following the loop trail 0.5 mile east to Sand Lake, you'll obtain the privilege of being hosted by righteous scenery comprising beautiful, timbered mountains and distant peaks. Sand Lake has only a couple of good campsites and no spring water, but fishing is fast.

Arctic grayling and brook trout inhabit Fish Lake too. This lake sits another 0.5 mile south on the loop trail. Fish Lake is surrounded by alpine mountains and pretty talus slopes on the west. Camping areas are limited due to rocky terrain and water level can vary dramatically from year to year. Angling is only fair but could be better from an inflatable raft.

Many hikers return the way they came. That means GPS data online may be scarce for the loop portion. But with a little will and wayfinding ability, the loop is worth it. Leaving Fish Lake, the loop trail proceeds west and up across a steep incline to the top of a scenic ridge. From here a hit-or-miss trail gradually declines down the ridgetop for about 3 miles. A well-defined trail then drops off the south side of the ridge and down a steep incline, intersecting a logging road that winds down to the Dry Fork trailhead.

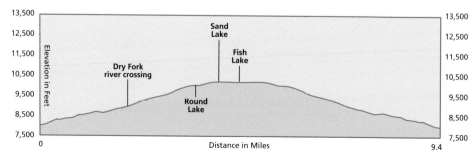

23 **ABES LAKE**

Abes Lake sits all alone, and you might be too, if you take this short, steep hike along the Middle Fork Weber River from Gardners Fork trailhead.

See map and logistics on pages 68–69.	**Approximate hiking time:** 5 hours
Start: Gardners Fork trailhead	**Difficulty:** Moderate
Distance: 7.8 miles out and back	**Usage:** Light
Destination elevation: 9,820 feet	**Nearest town:** Oakley, Utah
	Drainage: Weber River

THE HIKE

This lake can be a little tricky to locate. You have to watch for a side trail that branches away to the left from the main canyon about 2.9 miles up the trail. If you miss the cutoff, you will keep going up the Middle Fork of the Weber River until running into the Lakes Country Trail of Crystal Lake trailhead fame. And that's not to mention three river crossings, two requiring careful wading through water that at times could reach up to your knees or thighs. The last mile to Abes Lake is the steep section, and you should be heading southeast.

Camping at Abes Lake is limited. The terrain is rocky and uneven. Only small camps exist, with perhaps the best one being on the east side of the lake. But it can be quiet here, so it can provide a wilderness experience with lots of firewood at your disposal (for when there are no fire restrictions in place when you visit). There is a small inlet on the south end. This is a good spot to refill water containers, but purifying is always recommended. The inlet is also a good place to find fish.

Cutthroat trout dominate these waters. They reach about 15 inches but can be quite a challenge to catch. As with larger fish, they are particular about the time of day and the offering. If you don't hit it just right, you may come away empty-handed. There are good numbers of trout here, so just keep trying and you will eventually fill the frying pan.

There are not many other angling opportunities nearby. Tiny Neil Lake is 0.5 mile south of Abes Lake and may be good for small brookies.

These lakes are best reached by the trail from Gardners Fork but can also be reached by heading west from Lovenia Lake over a rugged saddle, then descending 600 feet. It is not as easy as it looks on paper, and it's certainly not an option by horseback.

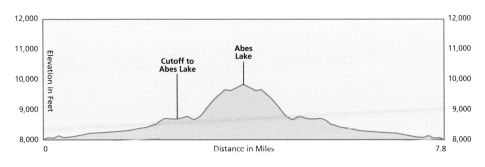

PASS LAKE TRAILHEAD

Back on Highway 150, next up is the immensely popular Pass Lake trailhead. Though Pass Lake is on the east side of the road, this trailhead is just across the highway to the north of Pass Lake. Thanks to relatively short mileage, both of the trails covered here are excellent for families or groups with hikers of varying experience. But don't let the length fool you. Whenever a trek begins above 10,000 feet, even short bursts of elevation gain will leave hikers breathless. Take your time and appreciate the view and benefits of being out in nature, even when the trail is popular and you're sharing that experience with others.

See trails 24 and 25 for Pass Lake Trailhead.
Maps: USGS Mirror Lake, *USDA Forest Service High Uintas Wilderness*, *Trails Illustrated High Uintas Wilderness*

Trail contacts: Uinta-Wasatch-Cache National Forest, Forest Supervisor, 857 West South Jordan Pkwy., South Jordan, UT 84095; Kamas Ranger District, 50 East Center St., Kamas, UT 84036, (435) 783-4338

FINDING THE TRAILHEAD

 From Kamas, take the Mirror Lake Scenic Byway (Highway 150) 32 miles to Pass Lake. The trailhead is on the opposite side of the road from the lake and has a restroom. Two or three dozen cars will fit in the parking area, with overflow along the highway a near guarantee on weekends.

Bald Mountain and Reids Peak from the south side of the excellent Lofty Loop Trail

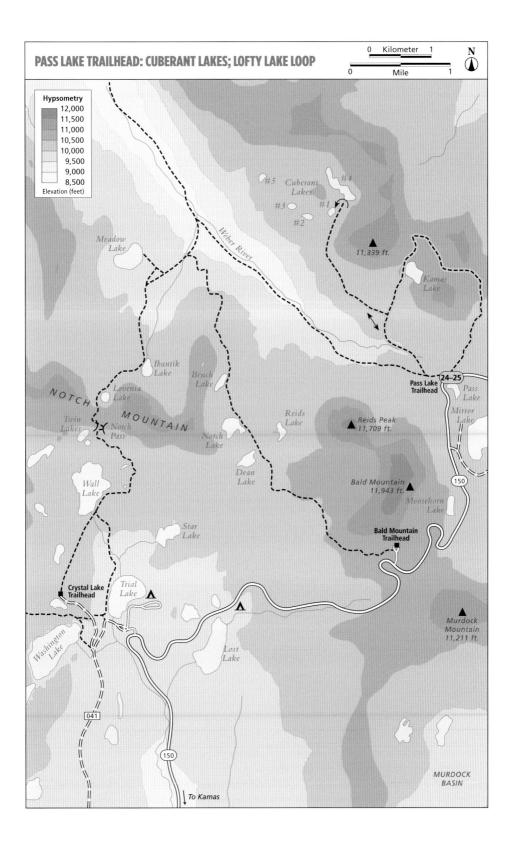

PASS LAKE TRAILHEAD: CUBERANT LAKES; LOFTY LAKE LOOP

0   Kilometer   1

0   Mile   1

N

Hypsometry

12,000
11,500
11,000
10,500
10,000
9,500
9,000
8,500
Elevation (feet)

Meadow
Lake

Weber River

#5   Cuberant
Lakes   #4

#3   #1

#2

▲
11,339 ft.

Kamas
Lake

Ibantik
Lake

Bench
Lake

NOTCH

Lovenia
Lake

MOUNTAIN

Twin
Lakes

Notch
Pass

Notch
Lake

Reids
Lake

▲ Reids Peak
11,709 ft.

24–25

Pass Lake
Trailhead

Pass
Lake

Mirror
Lake

Wall
Lake

Dean
Lake

Bald Mountain
11,943 ft. ▲

Moosehorn
Lake

150

Star
Lake

Bald Mountain
Trailhead

Crystal Lake
Trailhead

Trial
Lake

Washington
Lake

Lost
Lake

Murdock
Mountain
11,211 ft. ▲

041

150

To Kamas

MURDOCK
BASIN

24 CUBERANT LAKES

Most of the Cuberant Lakes are nestled in the pines, except for Cuberant #4, which sits against a talus slope in a picture-book setting. Lake #4 is by far the largest and deepest of the Cuberant Lakes. This is a relatively short and easy hike for these mountains. Please note many online GPS services simply label the largest lake as Cuberant.

See map and logistics on pages 72–73.
Start: Pass Lake trailhead
Distance: 5 miles out and back
Destination elevation: 10,420 feet

Approximate hiking time: 4 hours
Difficulty: Moderate
Usage: Moderate
Nearest town: Kamas, Utah
Drainage: Weber River

THE HIKE

Park at the Pass Lake trailhead, just across the road from Pass Lake. Or park at Pass Lake and catch the trail behind the guardrail where the road makes a ninety-degree turn. Watch the trail signs closely; before long, about 1.2 miles, you'll be branching off the main trail (north) toward Kamas Lake. After another 0.5 mile, take another fork northwest leading to Cuberant Lakes. If all goes according to plan, you will arrive at Cuberant Lake #1 first.

Cuberant Lake #2 is the best place to camp among the five Cuberant Lakes. However, you may want to camp at Cuberant #3. It is the only lake around with possible spring water. These lakes are all a little different from one another, and whether you are on a day hike or an overnighter, it is rewarding to experience each one and enjoy what each has to offer.

Fishing is generally good at these lakes for mostly pan-size cutthroat and brook trout, although a few large fish can occasionally be fooled. Fish are periodically stocked at Cuberants #1, #3, and #4, and Cuberant #2 hosts a natural population of brook and cutthroat. A fly-and-bubble combination is effective around here. The fish like tiny flies, but there isn't much space for traditional fly casting. The conifers surrounding these lakes are notorious for gobbling up ill-presented flies. But the pines offer camouflage that can be used to your advantage when stalking wary trout in these small lakes.

If you like calm, shade, quiet, and lots of pine trees, then you will enjoy the Cuberant Basin. It's a great place to catch a nap and a few trout. Bring along the mosquito repellent, because there won't be much wind to help keep the bugs at bay.

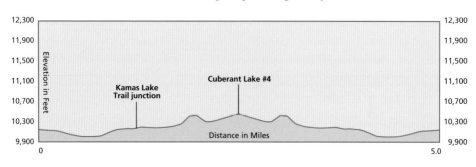

25 LOFTY LAKE LOOP

A short, succinct loop trail with only 1,000 feet in elevation change makes for a rare treat in the vast forested lands of the High Uintas. A couple of trailside lakes make for beautiful picnic stops or campsites—or places simply to catch your breath and enjoy the setting. Extend your exploration with spur trails to Cutthroat Lake, the backway into Ruth, or even a wayfinding scramble up Mount Marsell, Scout Peak, or Lofty Peak.

See map and logistics on pages 72–73.
Start: Pass Lake trailhead
Distance: 4.5-mile loop
Destination elevation: 10,840 feet

Approximate hiking time: 2.5 hours
Difficulty: Moderate
Usage: Heavy
Nearest town: Kamas, Utah
Drainage: Weber River

THE HIKE

The only real decision is whether to hike clockwise or counterclockwise. It's a little steeper going counterclockwise, so consider opting for the more gradual ascent clockwise. While a quick hiker can do the loop in a couple of hours, there are plenty of reasons to take it slow and lots to see off the loop.

Though the trail is named for a smaller lake near the pass between Lofty Peak and Scout Peak, Kamas Lake is the star of Lofty Loop.

At 0.5 mile you'll "bottom out" in elevation a yardstick below 10,000 feet while passing through Reid's meadow, which combines boardwalks across wetlands with a spectacular angle on Bald Mountain and Reids Peak. From there, the gradual climb begins. Bypass the Cuberant Trail at 1.2 miles and continue north on the Lofty Loop Trail toward Kamas Lake, about 0.4 mile farther. The trail had to be rerouted recently, so maps leading up to Kamas may vary. Just stick to the well-marked, well-used trail. There are a few excellent campsites to the west of the lake. From that base camp, whether you're after fish (tiger and cutthroat trout) or just looking to stretch your legs, you can easily work your way around the lake.

From Kamas Lake, the trail crosses another open meadow before tackling a couple of switchbacks up the ridge toward Lofty Lake. That meadow is part of the saddle between Mount Marsell and Lofty Peak, and intrepid peak baggers may wish to size up the slope and veer west. You'll have to pick your route through a boulder field for a while but will eventually find smoother terrain, though it will remain steep on the way to Mount Marsell's summit at 11,340 feet. Alternatively, there's a short downhill to Cutthroat Lake just before the switchbacks.

Lofty Lake itself isn't so much "lofty" as it is . . . higher elevation? The small lake would be good for a cool-down on a hot summer afternoon. Peaks above 11,000 feet stand on either side of the lake, mainly scree fields and boulder-hopping, but excellent side trips for additional views. From Scout Peak, you'll look down onto Kamas Lake and have a fantastic angle south along the Mirror Lake Scenic Byway. The last 1.5 miles from Lofty Lake descend past Scout Lake (once the home of the scout's Camp Steiner) and back to the trailhead.

Backpackers on the north side of Lofty Loop Trail overlook Cutthroat Lake.

26 RUTH LAKE TRAILHEAD TO RUTH LAKE

When you get to Ruth Lake, don't forget to look behind you. Hayden Peak looms larger than life just across the canyon to the west. The view from Ruth Lake is a must for shutterbugs looking for some real photo trophies. You'll want to hang this one on your wall.

Start: Ruth Lake trailhead
Distance: 1.6 miles out and back
Destination elevation: 10,340 feet
Approximate hiking time: 1 hour
Difficulty: Easy
Usage: Heavy
Nearest town: Evanston, Wyoming
Drainage: Bear River
Maps: USGS Mirror Lake, *USDA Forest Service High Uintas*

Wilderness, Trails Illustrated High Uintas Wilderness
Trail contacts: Uinta-Wasatch-Cache National Forest, Forest Supervisor, 857 West South Jordan Pkwy., South Jordan, UT 84095; Bear River Ranger Station, 32 miles south of Evanston, Wyoming, on the Mirror Lake Scenic Byway, (435) 642-6662

FINDING THE TRAILHEAD

From Evanston, take the Mirror Lake Scenic Byway (Highway 150) about 42 miles to the Ruth Lake trailhead, which is a roadside pull-off with a sign pointing to Ruth Lake. There are nice restrooms and paved parking.

Scenes like this one at Ruth Lake are why people return for a lifetime of discovery in the Uinta Mountains. PHOTO BY MATT MCKELL/UTAH DIVISION OF WILDLIFE RESOURCES

RUTH LAKE

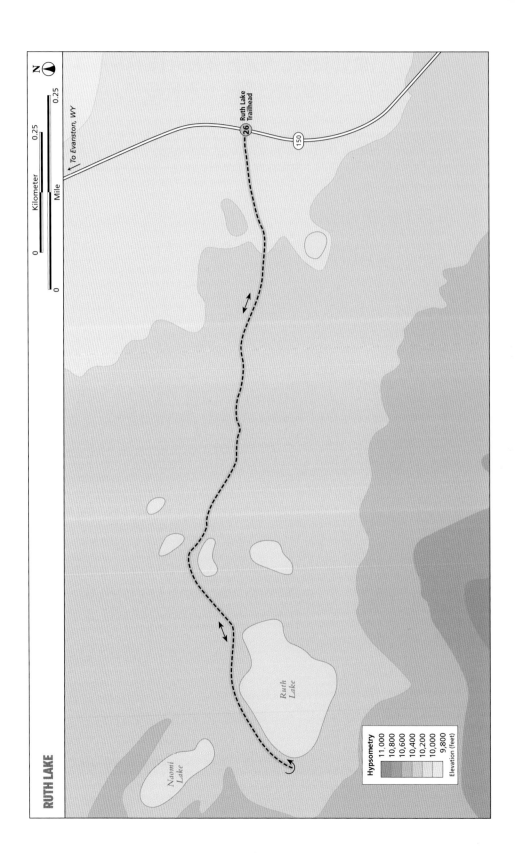

Hypsometry

11,000
10,800
10,600
10,400
10,200
10,000
9,800

Elevation (feet)

Naomi Lake

Ruth Lake

Ruth Lake Trailhead

26

150

To Evanston, WY

Kilometer

0   0.25

Mile

0   0.25

N

THE HIKE

This is a short, easy hike that even young kids enjoy for either a day trip or their first backpacking experience. The Forest Service posted the trail with nature signs, and there are a variety of natural sights along the way. Everything from miniature meadows and waterfalls to playful chipmunks are scattered along this hike that goes only 0.8 mile west of the trailhead and back.

At 0.5 mile the trail forks. Though this hike stays to the right, the left fork is a short spur to the Ruth Lake Cliffs, a set of stunning vertical rock walls that are popular with climbers and feature routes rated from 5.7 to 5.12+. Of course, you can go farther if you like—adding the loop around the lake brings the full hike to 2 miles. There are several other small lakes in the area. You can spend just a couple of hours or a couple of days exploring this basin. The trail dissolves at Ruth Lake though, so have your map and compass handy if you're continuing on.

Camping and fishing pressure is heavy at Ruth Lake, but the crowds fan out past this point. The fish in these parts see mostly day-use anglers. If you are one of them, the most productive fishing times are early morning and late evening. The hike in/out is short enough that you should have no problem managing your hike around prime fishing hours. If it's fish you're after, don't stop at Ruth Lake very long. You will probably have better success at nearby lakes such as Hayden, Cutthroat, Jewel, and Teal.

As with any popular area, litter can be a problem. But this area seems to be well preserved. Let's keep it that way. Pack out what you pack in and avoid building any new fire rings.

A marked trail leads south from Ruth Lake and ties into the trail leading from Scout Lake to Lofty Lake.

27 WHISKEY CREEK TRAIL TO BOURBON LAKE

Everyone says this is an easy hike. Compared to many treks in the High Uintas, it is. But the 675 feet of elevation the trail picks up, although gradual, may catch up with some hikers. So take it easy, don't rush the switchbacks, keep an eye out for moose, and raise a glass to this well-marked trail and gorgeous little lake.

Start: Whiskey Creek Trail
Distance: 2.7 miles out and back
Destination elevation: 9,820 feet
Approximate hiking time: 1.5 to 2 hours
Difficulty: Easy to moderate
Usage: Heavy
Nearest town: Evanston, Wyoming
Drainage: Bear River
Maps: USGS Whitney Reservoir, *USDA Forest Service High Uintas*

Wilderness, Trails Illustrated High Uintas Wilderness
Trail contacts: Uinta-Wasatch-Cache National Forest, Forest Supervisor, 857 West South Jordan Pkwy., South Jordan, UT 84095; Bear River Ranger Station, 32 miles south of Evanston, Wyoming, on the Mirror Lake Scenic Byway, (435) 642-6662

FINDING THE TRAILHEAD

From Evanston (or Kamas—this one's about equidistant), take the Mirror Lake Scenic Byway (Highway 150) about 39 miles to mile marker 39. The beginning of Whiskey Creek Trail is signed alongside a pullout with around a dozen places to park on the west side of the road, directly across the highway from the entrance to Sulphur Campground. Do not confuse the Whiskey Creek Trail to Bourbon Lake with nearby Whiskey Island Lake, which is a 5.4-mile, round-trip hike with two-thirds of its trail on a very rough road followed by cross-country navigating.

THE HIKE

The dotted trail lines for so many High Uintas hikes snake their way deep into wilderness. Those can be daunting or take extra planning. Sometimes, the day calls for a shorter adventure. Though under 1.5 miles out, Whiskey Creek Trail still checks all the boxes for area hikes by furnishing a gentle creek, asking hikers to work a little with some elevation, and landing at a scenic lake at the foot of a jagged peak. Its short length also makes it more attractive for hauling in gear.

The trail starts with a gentle set of switchbacks and some sun-exposed sections of trail. At around 0.3 mile, the trail runs parallel to Whiskey Creek for around 0.3 mile, before climbing a second set of switchbacks to the north and west away from the creek. Be careful not to become too enamored with the creek as the trail comes closest to it or you'll miss the arrow directing you up a switchback.

The trail gets more forested as you hike (which may produce some downed trees), and the combined terrain lends itself to both wildflowers and wildlife—moose have been spotted on this trail (among other wildlife) so keep dogs on leash if they're prone to

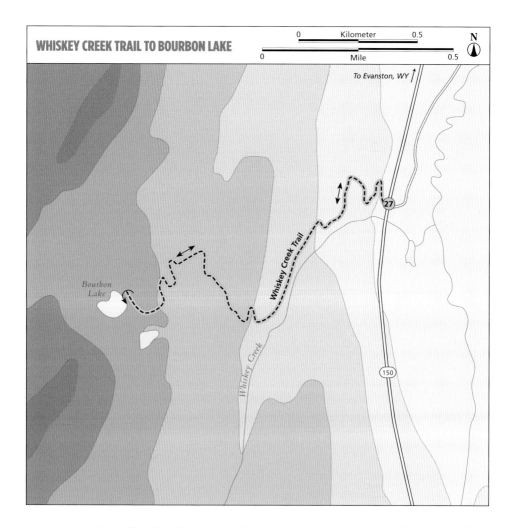

WHISKEY CREEK TRAIL TO BOURBON LAKE

0   Kilometer   0.5

0   Mile   0.5

N

To Evanston, WY

27

Whiskey Creek Trail

Bourbon Lake

Whiskey Creek

150

chasing fauna. Consider this your public service announcement reminding you it's illegal for dogs to chase and harass hoofed wildlife—and some hoofed wildlife may turn aggressive if spooked or threatened, so give them space.

Though the distance may not be "worth it" or far enough for many backpackers to consider hauling in gear (first-timers or those with young kids get all the credit for any distance!), Bourbon Lake is relatively easy to get to and has a few decent campsites established around the lake. Anglers are most likely to encounter brook trout thanks to stocking by the Division of Wildlife Resources every few years. A fishable pond about half the size of Bourbon known as BR-2 can be found in a meadow about 100 yards down the trail. Hiking a loop around Bourbon Lake brings the total trip to around 3 miles.

The spirit is strong at Bourbon, a small, shallow lake up the Whiskey Creek Trail.

28 MAIN FORK TRAILHEAD TO HELL HOLE LAKE (AND A-1 PEAK)

There are faster, more scenic ways to get into the High Uintas Wilderness. But that fact also means you may have more solitude at Hell Hole than other lakes. And from a base camp by the lake, you can have a go at two nearby peaks. As for anglers, Hell Hole is a gamble. Some years it's hot, and some years it's not. It's a relatively small lake and will depend on the planting schedules, winter survival, and catch-and-release rates. Equestrians: There's plenty of feed but watch out for the very rocky second half of the hike. Everyone: The marshlands of Hell Hole are extremely buggy early in the season.

Start: Main Fork trailhead or FR 306
Distance: 10.5 or 12.5 miles out and back
Destination elevation: 10,340 feet
Approximate hiking time: 7 to 8 hours
Difficulty: Moderate
Usage: Moderate
Nearest town: Evanston, Wyoming
Drainage: Bear River

Maps: USGS Christmas Meadows, *USDA Forest Service High Uintas Wilderness*, *Trails Illustrated High Uintas Wilderness*
Trail contacts: Uinta-Wasatch-Cache National Forest, Forest Supervisor, 857 West South Jordan Pkwy., South Jordan, UT 84095; Bear River Ranger Station, 32 miles south of Evanston, Wyoming, on the Mirror Lake Scenic Byway, (435) 642-6662

FINDING THE TRAILHEAD

From Evanston, take the Mirror Lake Scenic Byway (Highway 150) about 34 miles. The unmarked trail starts just off Highway 150. Look right across the road from the Gold Hill turnoff. The other trailhead adds a mile to the hike out but avoids a sometimes-challenging marsh. It begins at a locked gate on FR 306, which is the first right off Christmas Meadows Road.

THE HIKE

From Highway 150, hike the old jeep trail for about 1 mile. There is a river crossing and a marsh that can become very muddy and difficult to pass, but you should find success following GPS routes to the right. Reach a gravel road limited to authorized vehicles only. This is the route along FR 306 followed from the other trailhead described in "Finding the trailhead" above. Follow the road about 1.5 miles to a stream channel. Look for a small trail sign before crossing the bridge and then follow the trail for 2.5 miles to the lake.

Most of the lake is shallow, which makes for good morning and evening fishing for healthy cutthroat trout. During midday the only feasible spot to fish is the deeper northeast corner of the lake. A small rubber raft may be worthwhile here. Maybe there are deeper holes out in the middle that the fish retreat to during the day. No other fishing opportunities exist nearby if Hell Hole doesn't produce.

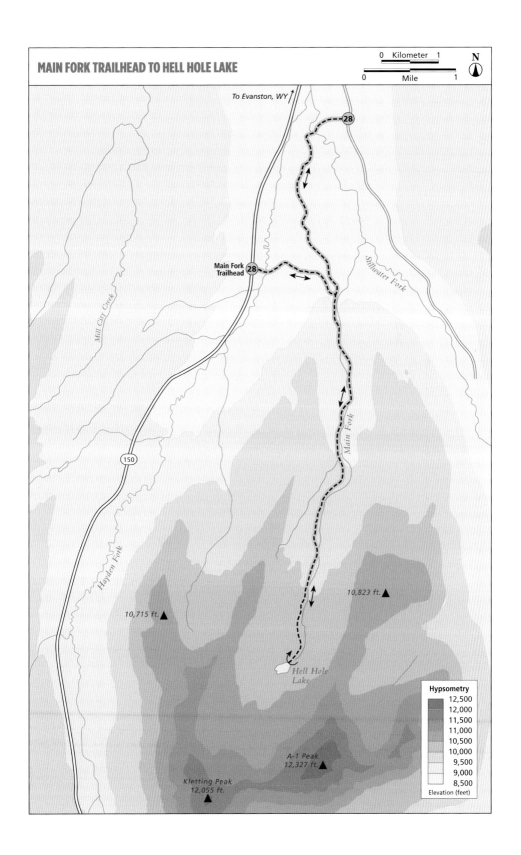

MAIN FORK TRAILHEAD TO HELL HOLE LAKE

0   Kilometer   1

0   Mile   1

N

To Evanston, WY

28

Main Fork
Trailhead   28

Stillwater Fork

Mill City Creek

Main Fork

150

Hayden Fork

10,823 ft. ▲

10,715 ft. ▲

Hell Hole
Lake

A-1 Peak
12,327 ft. ▲

Kletting Peak
12,055 ft.
▲

Hypsometry

Elevation (feet)
12,500
12,000
11,500
11,000
10,500
10,000
9,500
9,000
8,500

The Stillwater Fork of the Bear River near the forest road trailhead

Hell Hole does have a lot to offer, especially if you are looking for a short weekend trip. Excellent campsites are available for backpackers and equestrians. The latter would probably prefer the east side of the lake for horse pasture, while backpackers should like the west side and its pine-sheltered camps. A good spring for filtering flows into the northeast corner of the lake.

Last, but not least, from your base camp at Hell Hole you have the option to bag a couple of 12ers: the 12,327-foot A-1 Peak to the southeast and the 12,041-foot Kletting Peak to the southwest. A-1 is a bit closer but requires tackling an extremely loose and steep field of scree. These loose rocks make for much longer and slower hikes than you might be comfortable tackling, but patience is rewarded with stunning views. It's a little over 1.5 miles to the summit. The ridge between A-1 and Kletting is about 1.25 miles. Return to the saddle to hit Kletting, then return one more time and carefully descend back to Hell Hole. Give yourself a lot of extra time and try to summit earlier in the day to avoid afternoon thunderstorms.

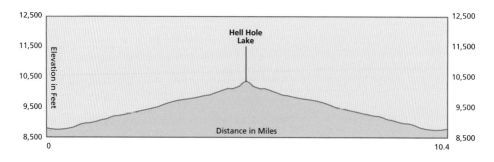

CHRISTMAS MEADOWS TRAILHEAD

Thanks to its glorious setting and access to incredible wilderness hikes, the Christmas Meadows area of the High Uintas inspires wonder and childlike delight in ways that have nothing to do with December 25. (Nor, it can be said, does the California prospector for whom the area was named inspire much either—but one can appreciate why he set up camp here for so long.) Pictures from the area are among the range's most photogenic. The Stillwater Fork of the Bear River traces a sweeping meander through the green meadow of the wide glaciated valley. High mountain ridges run along both sides and appear to converge in the distance at the jagged Ostler Peak, whose 12,718 feet remain capped in snow deep into the year.

A small campground marks the end of the road. If you're lucky enough to snag a campsite at Christmas Meadows, you won't have a lot of company. Just eleven sites dot the small loop. But then, if you've come with a pack equipped for the backcountry (be it backpack or horseback), you won't need a site. But you will need stamina: The hikes up here are long and, from the relatively low starting elevation of 8,800 feet, there's a good amount of climbing.

See trails 29 through 32 for Christmas Meadows Trailhead.
Maps: USGS Christmas Meadows and USGS Hayden Peak, *USDA Forest Service High Uintas Wilderness*, *Trails Illustrated High Uintas Wilderness*

Trail contacts: Uinta-Wasatch-Cache National Forest, Forest Supervisor, 857 West South Jordan Pkwy., South Jordan, UT 84095; Bear River Ranger Station, 32 miles south of Evanston, Wyoming, on the Mirror Lake Scenic Byway, (435) 642-6662

FINDING THE TRAILHEAD

From Evanston, take the Mirror Lake Scenic Byway (Highway 150) south about 33 miles to the Christmas Meadows turnoff. Follow a good dirt road south about 4 miles to the trailhead.

Christmas Meadows has room for a couple dozen vehicles and a stock ramp. The nearby campgrounds have toilets and water. This popular trail leads into some of the most spectacular scenery in the High Uintas.

The Stillwater Fork of the Bear River winds through Christmas Meadows and up into the Middle Basin. PHOTO COURTESY UTAH OFFICE OF TOURISM/MORE THAN JUST PARKS

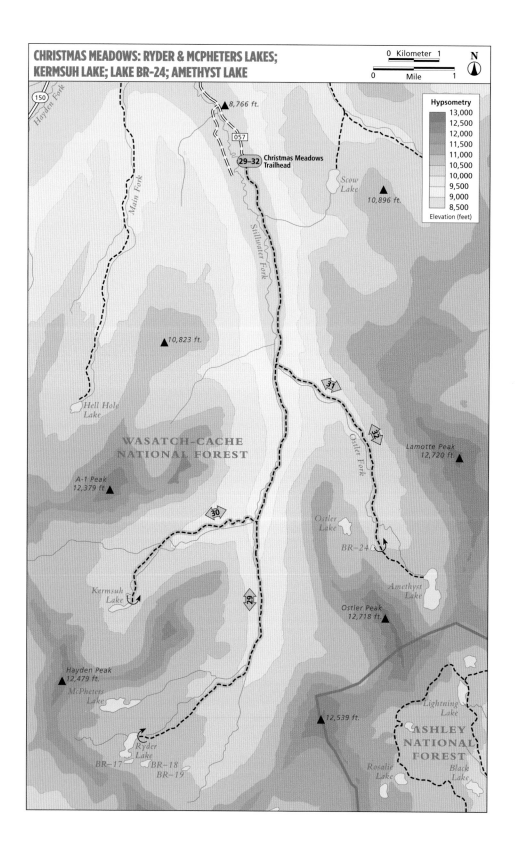

CHRISTMAS MEADOWS: RYDER & MCPHETERS LAKES; KERMSUH LAKE; LAKE BR-24; AMETHYST LAKE

0 Kilometer 1

0 Mile 1

N

Hypsometry

13,000
12,500
12,000
11,500
11,000
10,500
10,000
9,500
9,000
8,500

Elevation (feet)

150

Hayden Fork

Main Fork

057

29–32 Christmas Meadows Trailhead

▲ 8,766 ft.

Scow Lake

▲ 10,896 ft.

Stillwater Fork

▲ 10,823 ft.

Hell Hole Lake

WASATCH-CACHE NATIONAL FOREST

31

32

Ostler Fork

Lamotte Peak 12,720 ft. ▲

A-1 Peak 12,379 ft. ▲

30

Ostler Lake

BR-24

Kermsuh Lake

29

Amethyst Lake

Ostler Peak 12,718 ft. ▲

Hayden Peak 12,479 ft. ▲

McPheters Lake

Lightning Lake

ASHLEY NATIONAL FOREST

▲ 12,539 ft.

Ryder Lake

BR-17   BR-18
BR-19

Rosalie Lake

Black Lake

29 RYDER AND MCPHETERS LAKES

The difficulty of the Stillwater Trail is a little deceiving. It's not the elevation gain. It's the rocks, river crossings, and mud holes that can dampen spirits. The trail picks up some altitude. It's an easy climb until the Kermsuh-Ryder junction. Then the trail proceeds up, up, and up.

See map and logistics on pages 87 and 90.
Start: Christmas Meadows trailhead
Distance: 17 miles out and back
Destination elevation: 10,620 feet
Approximate hiking time: 11 hours

Difficulty: Moderate—one steep section
Usage: Moderate
Nearest town: Evanston, Wyoming
Drainage: Bear River

THE HIKE

Ryder and McPheters Lakes occupy Middle Basin. Mount Agassiz, Spread Eagle, and Hayden are the dominant surrounding peaks. Ryder sits at the foot of three connecting ridges characterized by wind and steep, rocky ledges. Beautiful meadows intersperse the pines, while trickles of water cascade off the cliffs, adding to the aesthetics.

Access begins at the south end of Christmas Meadows Campground. An excellent trail parallels the Stillwater Fork all the way to Middle Basin. The first fork in the trail arrives at around 2.4 miles near the boundary with the Wilderness. For the last 1.5 miles, the trail departs from the river and rock cairns mark the way. Camp on Ryder Lake's east side.

Other lakes in the vicinity are BR–17 and –18. These lakes are located on the south side of Ryder. You'll find good campsites, an abundant supply of spring water for filtering, and good populations of brook trout—and they only receive half the angling pressure of Ryder.

McPheters is another popular fishing hole. This lake is located 0.5 mile north of Ryder on some bedrock shelves next to a talus slope. Campsites are not present in the immediate vicinity but can be found nearby. Due to open terrain, firewood is extremely sparse but can be gathered near the camping areas to the south. Plenty of spring water endows McPheters, along with pan-size cutthroat trout.

If solitude is what you're looking for, Meadow Lake (BR–19) is a good place to visit. Meadow sits 0.5 mile east of BR–18 in rocky, timbered country. This lake plays host to good camping areas and excellent spring water. Deepwater channels circulate through the middle of this shallow lake, which may produce fairly good fishing.

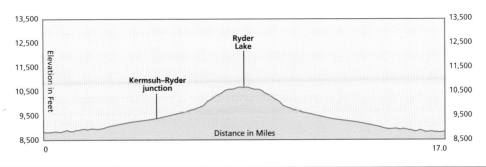

30 **KERMSUH LAKE**

Do you want to get lost? No, this isn't about losing your direction, but about contemplating losing the vast majority of crowds that trample the Stillwater Trail. Kermsuh is a gorgeous, isolated lake situated in rocky, timbered country just inside the Wilderness area. Upon arrival you'll be greeted by several high peaks, including Hayden, Kletting, and A-1. These major peaks have connecting ridges that almost completely enclose the West Basin. This feature, and the fact that Kermsuh is the only lake in the basin, makes the area a remote and peaceful place.

See map and logistics on pages 87 and 90.
Start: Christmas Meadows trailhead
Distance: 13.6 miles out and back
Destination elevation: 10,300 feet
Approximate hiking time: 9 hours

Difficulty: Moderate—one steep section
Usage: Light
Nearest town: Evanston, Wyoming
Drainage: Bear River

THE HIKE

From Christmas Meadows, follow the Stillwater Fork Trail 4.5 miles to a posted sign at the Kermsuh–Ryder junction. The Kermsuh Lake Trail heads southwest to and across a narrow footbridge that scaffolds over the Stillwater Fork River. After the river crossing, you'll encounter several steep switchbacks, and startling scenes of a deep river gorge can be spotted at the end of every other cutback. The trail then gradually climbs to a marshy meadow where rock cairns, tree blazes, and short segments of trail mark the rest of the way.

Kermsuh is mostly visited by day hikers. This trek may be questionable for a day hike, but it is right on the borderline of what is and what isn't. Allow yourself at least 8 hours for a single-day excursion, including half an hour for a shoreline lunch and a couple of 15-minute breaks. A healthy hiker can make the round-trip in 9 hours, but allow extra time for fishing, photography, or relaxing.

Angling pressure is usually very light for cutthroat in the 12-inch class. Fishing is unpredictable but has been known to be good in the early summer months. Due to the rocky terrain that surrounds this lake, no decent campsites exist. Running water is no problem here, and horse pasture can be found at a small meadow to the south.

This one is for the solitude seeker or the explorer. Go seek!

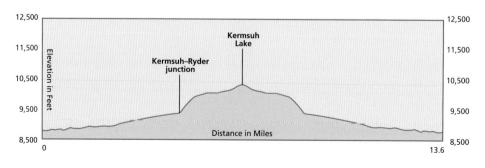

31 LAKE BR-24

In honor of all the great nameless lakes in the High Uintas, this book needed to spotlight one of the best. Some of the lakes without names are the least visited and have become some of the real jewels of the area. If solitude and a chance for some unspoiled fishing rank high on your list, then try the lakes with no names, especially the ones with no trails. That being said, BR-24 is known as Emerald Lake in some hiking circles.

See map and logistics on pages 87 and 90.
Start: Christmas Meadows trailhead
Distance: 11 miles out and back
Destination elevation: 10,460 feet
Approximate hiking time: 7 hours

Difficulty: Moderate—one steep section
Usage: Moderate
Nearest town: Evanston, Wyoming
Drainage: Bear River

Hayden Peak provides a stunning background to Emerald Lake, indicated on many maps as BR-24. PHOTO BY MATT MCKELL/UTAH DIVISION OF WILDLIFE RESOURCES

THE HIKE

From Christmas Meadows trailhead, the trail goes 2.4 miles south along the Stillwater Fork of the Bear River to the turnoff to Lake BR–24 and Amethyst Lake. The trail then follows the Ostler Fork 3.1 miles to Lake BR–24.

When considering what a nameless lake should offer, BR–24 doesn't seem to fit the stereotype. It receives its share of visitors, its few fish are wary, and the main trail passes right by it. But it is still a gem! Its excellent campsites are the best in Amethyst Basin, with spring water for treating at the lake and horse pasture nearby. BR–24 is a great place to camp if you are going to visit Amethyst Lake. Campsites at Amethyst Lake are above timberline and offer little shelter, firewood, spring water, or horse pasture. Staying at BR–24, you'll have all the commodities you need. It's only a brisk 20-minute walk from BR–24 to Amethyst Lake for some grand sightseeing and fast fishing for lots of pan-size brook trout.

Fishing at BR–24 is unpredictable. A few large cutthroat trout patrol these sparkling waters, and they didn't get big by being stupid. You will have to be extremely lucky or tricky to hook one of these spooky lunkers. But you might fool a smaller trout or two. If you would like some trout larger than what Amethyst offers, try Ostler Lake. It is less than 0.5 mile northwest of BR–24 and frequently yields cutthroat in the 1-pound class.

Like Amethyst Lake, BR–24 is emerald green—thus its adopted name—in color due to turbidity. It is fairly shallow and therefore casts its own unique shade of turquoise. It is a great place to sit back and just enjoy the placid scenery while a pan of trout sizzles on the fire. Catch the fish at Amethyst, then retire to BR–24 for the evening.

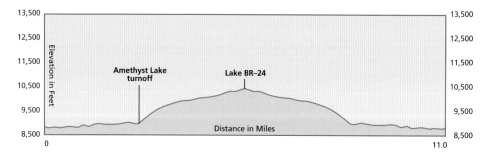

A look at Ostler Peak from Christmas Meadows. Follow the Ostler Fork on the Amethyst Lake Trail to arrive at the foot of this majestic mountain. PHOTO COURTESY UTAH OFFICE OF TOURISM/MORE THAN JUST PARKS

32 AMETHYST LAKE

Set in the top of a glacial cirque, this is one of the prettiest alpine lakes in the High Uintas. A few small pines dot its shores, and the massive cliffs and talus slopes add grandeur to the emerald-green waters. This large lake (42.5 acres) attracts moderate crowds because of its scenery and frequently fast fishing. The hike in is only 6.3 miles each way, but it seems longer. Two thousand feet of elevation is a lot to gain in such a short distance.

See map and logistics on pages 87 and 90.
Start: Christmas Meadows trailhead
Distance: 12.6 miles out and back
Destination elevation: 10,750 feet
Approximate hiking time: 8 hours

Difficulty: Moderate—one steep section
Usage: Moderate
Nearest town: Evanston, Wyoming
Drainage: Bear River

THE HIKE

The trail starts at beautiful Christmas Meadows and is maintained well for the entire hike, though old boardwalks or shaky logs cross some of the mud pit and river crossings. It parallels the Stillwater Fork of the Bear River half of the way, which presents many tempting fishing holes. After 2.4 miles, the trail forks to the left (southeast). Follow the trail up Ostler Fork 3.1 miles to Lake BR–24 and another 0.8 mile to Amethyst Lake. There's a lot to see along the route, so take your time and enjoy the hike.

Brook trout are active all around Amethyst Lake, but the best spots seem to be on the east side or the deeper southwest corner. Small flies draw attention on about every other cast, and even more regularly during the evening. During midday, try small spinners in the deeper sections.

Excellent campsites are available at BR–24 about a mile below Amethyst Lake. This tiny lake is also emerald in color due to turbidity. Several springs emerge here, and a horse pasture is close by in the lower meadows. There is a small population of cutthroat, but don't plan on them for dinner. They are extremely wary. Firewood is limited, unless you care to walk west into the woods a few hundred yards.

Ostler Lake, 0.5 mile to the northwest of BR–24, should have fewer people if you are looking to be alone. It has a few rough campgrounds and several springs. Cutthroat and brookies grow larger at Ostler, so don't be surprised if you hook into one weighing well over a pound. However, fishing is kind of slow, especially when compared to Amethyst Lake.

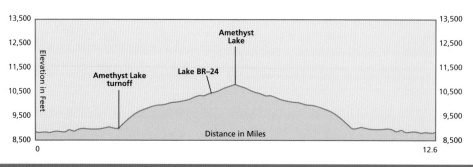

PART 2: U.S. 40 TO THE SOUTH SLOPE

The South Slope is characterized by large, steep drainages that lead to high meadows above timberline. More than two-thirds of the High Uintas lie on the South Slope, so it's only natural that the majority of the lakes are on this side as well. The hikes can be long, if that's what you are looking for. There are many routes that can be combined to make up a 50-mile excursion—these long, long trails are extremely popular for pack trips on horseback, a fact you're sure to notice on the trails.

Access to the South Slope can be tricky. Driving along U.S. 40, the peaks of the High Uintas begin to rise 25 miles or more to the north. The winding, mostly unpaved roads that climb the drainages and canyon slopes range from recently graded routes passable by most vehicles to rocky and rutted paths that will be slow going or require a high-clearance vehicle. And pay attention to your map: GPS may attempt to send you down ATV trails.

While not every trailhead is covered in this section (and certainly not every hike), these chapters will lead you up into the vast South Slope of Utah's High Uintas to access to all the hiking, camping, fishing, and other outdoor recreation you desire.

A lot of water comes off the South Slope of the Uintas, including the Uinta River pictured here. Hikers have the choice of several drainages to follow deep into the wilderness.

GRANDVIEW TRAILHEAD

Other than the westernmost reaches of the Uinta Mountains—the Mirror Lake Scenic Byway or East Weber Canyon Road to Smith and Morehouse—Grandview is the closest trailhead to the populous Wasatch Front and offers some of the best designated Wilderness access around. What does that mean? It means that after parking at the top of the rough Hades Canyon Road (following a short drive north from the beautiful Route 35 rather than U.S. 40), it's only 0.2 mile to the High Uintas Wilderness.

Granted, some "gentle" switchbacks follow and there's still over 900 feet of elevation gain over 2.5 miles, but then it's an easy descent into the massive Grandaddy Basin where you'll have your pick of more than two dozen named lakes near which to spread out, whether you set up a base camp at one lake and explore by day, or move from lake to lake over time. There are multiple loop options that are nearly half the distance of other South Slope loops.

See trails 33 through 37 for Grandview Trailhead.
Maps: USGS Grandaddy Lake and USGS Hayden, *USDA Forest Service High Uintas Wilderness, Trails Illustrated High Uintas Wilderness*

Trail contacts: Ashley National Forest, Forest Supervisor, 355 North Vernal Ave., Vernal, UT 84078, (435) 781-1181; Duchesne Ranger District, 85 West Main, Duchesne, UT 84021, (435) 738-2482

FINDING THE TRAILHEAD

From Heber City, take US 40 east to SR 208, which is about 6 miles east of Fruitland. Head north on SR 208 for 10 miles to SR 35. Follow SR 35 northwest 10 miles to Hanna. From Hanna, follow a dirt road, FR 144, 11 miles northwest to Hades Campground. Stay on the same road another 0.5 mile to a junction. One road takes off to Mill Flat (Iron Mine campground); the other road, FR 315, ventures right (northeast) about 5 steep, rocky miles to Grandview trailhead—it will be slow going for low-clearance vehicles.

Grandview trailhead has at least fifty parking places that, despite the rough road, will fill up on weekends; the amenities here include toilets and a stock-unloading ramp. Sorry, there's no drinking water here. Grandview is the starting point for lakes in the West Fork of the Rock Creek drainage.

The truly grand view from Hades Pass of the 170-acre Grandaddy Lake, the largest natural lake in the Uintas

On the shore of Grandaddy Lake. Campsites must be at least 200 feet from any water source in Wilderness Areas.

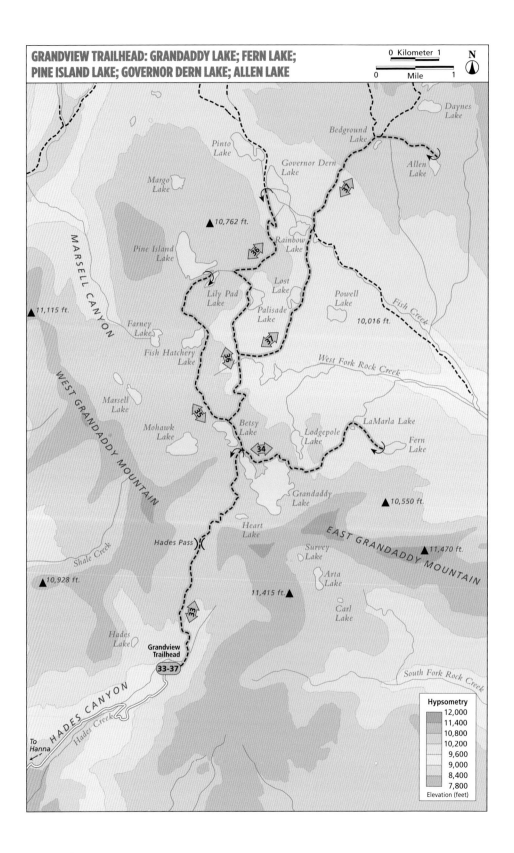

GRANDVIEW TRAILHEAD: GRANDADDY LAKE; FERN LAKE; PINE ISLAND LAKE; GOVERNOR DERN LAKE; ALLEN LAKE

0 Kilometer 1

0 Mile 1

N

Daynes Lake

Bedground Lake

Pinto Lake

Governor Dern Lake

Allen Lake

Margo Lake

37

Pine Island Lake

▲ 10,762 ft.

Rainbow Lake

36

Lost Lake

Powell Lake

▲ 11,115 ft.

Lily Pad Lake

Palisade Lake

Fish Creek

Farney Lake

37

10,016 ft.

MARSELL CANYON

Fish Hatchery Lake

36

West Fork Rock Creek

Marsell Lake

LaMarla Lake

WEST GRANDADDY MOUNTAIN

Mohawk Lake

35

Betsy Lake

Lodgepole Lake

Fern Lake

34

Grandaddy Lake

▲ 10,550 ft.

Heart Lake

EAST GRANDADDY MOUNTAIN

Hades Pass

Survey Lake

▲ 11,470 ft.

Shale Creek

Arta Lake

▲ 10,928 ft.

11,415 ft. ▲

Carl Lake

33

Hades Lake

Grandview Trailhead

33-37

South Fork Rock Creek

HADES CANYON

To Hanna

Hades Creek

Hypsometry

	12,000
	11,400
	10,800
	10,200
	9,600
	9,000
	8,400
	7,800

Elevation (feet)

33 GRANDADDY LAKE

Grandaddy Lake—the name implies it is the largest and best of all the lakes. Is it the largest? Yes, it is easily the largest natural lake in the High Uintas. Is it the best? Judging solely by the number of backcountry visitors, the answer to that question also is yes. Usage is very heavy at this well-known lake that can be extremely busy in July, August, and early September. If you are looking for solitude, a different wilderness destination should be considered. Litter can be a problem, so clean up your mess, leaving a spotless campsite for the next guests.

See map and logistics on pages 98 and 100.
Start: Grandview trailhead
Distance: 7.2 miles out and back
Destination elevation: 10,310 feet
Approximate hiking time: 4.5 hours

Difficulty: Moderate—some steep sections
Usage: Heavy
Nearest town: Hanna, Utah
Drainage: Rock Creek

THE HIKE

It's not a long hike to Grandaddy Lake, but it is a strenuous one. A well-traveled trail climbs more than 900 feet in just 2.4 miles to the top of Hades Pass. There you'll have that "grand view" of Heart Lake, Grandaddy Lake, and countless acres of the pine-covered hills of the Rock Creek drainage. Walk another 1 mile to a trail junction on the narrow piece of land between Betsy and Grandaddy Lakes. Stay right and go another 0.2 mile to a peninsula on the north side of Grandaddy Lake.

When selecting a campsite at Grandaddy, choose one of the existing sites. There are lots of them, and building new camps will only further burden the fragile environment. Be sure to bring along something to purify your drinking water. There is a campfire and firewood gathering restriction in the Grandaddy Basin, making it illegal to have a campfire or gather firewood within 0.25 mile of nearly all the named lakes in the basin.

Cutthroat and brook trout provide fair to good fishing. Catch-and-release angling is encouraged here, especially for larger fish. Many other angling and camping opportunities are nearby. Betsy and Mohawk Lakes are practically right next door, and Lodgepole Lake is just a few hundred yards northeast of Grandaddy. Heart Lake is up a steep hill, just south of Grandaddy. You'll pass it if you hike to Grandaddy Lake via Hades Pass.

There's a lot happening in this basin. Any fan of the High Uintas will enjoy this area, whether you are camping here or just passing through.

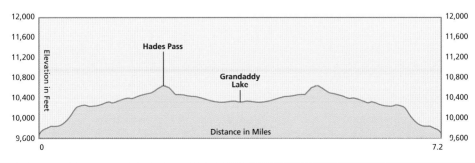

34 FERN LAKE

This hike is a pretty one, but it seems like it's uphill both ways. You'll rise more than 900 feet traversing Hades Pass, and then you'll give almost all that elevation back as you descend to Fern Lake. Even though the elevation gain is a mere 100 feet in less than 6 miles, level ground is unheard of. If you're not forging up, you're headed down.

See map and logistics on pages 98 and 100.
Start: Grandview trailhead
Distance: 11.4 miles out and back
Destination elevation: 9,890 feet

Approximate hiking time: 8 hours
Difficulty: Moderate
Usage: Moderate
Nearest town: Hanna, Utah
Drainage: Rock Creek

THE HIKE

Don't let the destination elevation fool you. From Grandview trailhead, the well-traveled trail climbs more than 900 feet in just 2.4 miles to the top of Hades Pass. There you'll have that "grand view" described on the previous page. Walk another 1 mile to a trail junction in the narrow piece of land between Betsy and Grandaddy Lakes.

Take a right at Betsy Lake and continue your downhill trajectory. Follow the West Fork Rock Creek Trail along the north side of Grandaddy, past Lodgepole Lake a couple of miles to LaMarla Lake, then cut cross-country southeast another 0.5 mile. Fern Lake is nestled at the base of East Grandaddy Mountain below a steep, boulder-strewn slope. The terrain is rough. Rocks and deadfall timber are prevalent, making travel a little slow around the immediate area.

The main attractions at Fern Lake are solitude and fishing. It can be hard to find an unoccupied lake in this basin. Fern may be your best bet if you are searching for a quiet, secluded spot. There are a few comfortable campsites for setting up your wilderness abode. Ice-cold spring water is located on the west side of the lake, ideal for treating before drinking. There are campfire and firewood gathering restrictions within 0.25 mile of the lake. In all, it's a pretty good place to just settle back and let the world pass you by.

Fern Lake has been known for some darn good fishing in the past too. And you might land some big ones. Fat brookies up to 2 pounds have been known to succumb to a well-presented fly or lure. Don't plan solely on fish for your meals though. If they are not biting here, there are no other lakes nearby to count on. Of course, you could plan a trout dinner—but bring some extra nutrient-dense food just in case. You'll have to climb back out a few hundred feet at the beginning of your return hike.

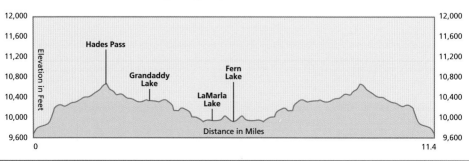

35 PINE ISLAND LAKE

It's no wonder this lake is popular—it is gorgeous. If aesthetics and a nice campsite are important to you, then check out Pine Island Lake. It is the gem of the West Fork of Rock Creek. Small, pine-covered islands rise peacefully out of the clear blue waters of this large natural lake. There is something especially appealing about islands on a wilderness lake. In the background, a steep talus slope adds to the alpine atmosphere. You can easily just sit in camp, munch granola bars, and enjoy the view.

See map and logistics on pages 98 and 100.
Start: Grandview trailhead
Distance: 12.8 miles out and back
Destination elevation: 10,300 feet

Approximate hiking time: 8 hours
Difficulty: Moderate
Usage: Heavy
Nearest town: Hanna, Utah
Drainage: Rock Creek

THE HIKE

From Grandview trailhead, it's a steep 2.4-mile climb to Hades Pass. From the top of the pass, walk another 1 mile to a trail junction in the narrow piece of land between Betsy and Grandaddy Lakes. Turn left (north) and go 0.1 mile to another trail junction on the north end of Betsy Lake. Turn left (northwest) again. It's about 2 miles to Fish Hatchery Lake and another 0.9 mile to Pine Island Lake.

A few spacious campsites are located along the southeast shoreline, just off the main trail. There is plenty of level ground for a large group to set up several tents, and large flat boulders are conveniently located to serve as tables or benches. There are campfire and firewood gathering restrictions within 0.25 mile of the lake. Spring water is nonexistent. As always, be prepared to purify all your drinking water.

Fishing pressure is moderate to heavy—and unpredictable. You may have good luck, but you should have a backup plan if you are planning on fish for dinner. Brook trout are stocked on a regular basis, and a few cutthroat still remain. Lily Pad Lake offers similar angling and is just 200 yards southeast. Give it a try if Pine Island doesn't yield the fishing you want.

If you have horses to carry your load, a rubber raft could be a lot of fun at Pine Island Lake. Paddle out to the islands and fish around them. Remember the life jackets. These icy waters are as dangerous as they are beautiful.

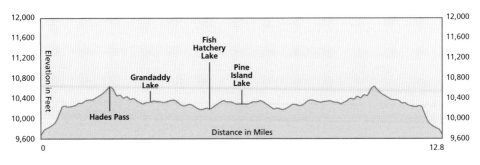

36 GOVERNOR DERN LAKE

A lot of equestrians use this area. Between Governor Dern Lake and the Pinto Lake area there are lots of places to graze your horses and plenty of roomy campsites. Once you get past Hades Pass, the journey is a gentle ride through the pine forests of the West Fork of the Rock Creek drainage. Or you can avoid the steep pass and reach Governor Dern Lake from the Highline trailhead. It is a couple of miles longer this way, but it may be easier on the animals. There are campfire and firewood gathering restrictions within 0.25 mile of Governor Dern, Pinto, and Rainbow Lakes.

See map and logistics on pages 98 and 100.
Start: Grandview trailhead
Distance: 16.4 miles out and back
Destination elevation: 9,990 feet

Approximate hiking time: 10 hours
Difficulty: Moderate
Usage: Moderate
Nearest town: Hanna, Utah
Drainage: Rock Creek

THE HIKE

Another destination lake with a deceptive elevation, the ups and downs of this trail amount to 2,378 feet in elevation gain round-trip. From Grandview trailhead it's a steep 2.4-mile climb to Hades Pass. From the top of the pass, walk another 1 mile to a trail junction in the narrow piece of land between Betsy and Grandaddy Lakes. Turn left (north) and go 0.1 mile to another trail junction on the north end of Betsy Lake. Turn right (northwest) and go about 1.3 miles to the junction with the trail that goes to Powell Lake. Stay left (north) and go past a lake on the right about 0.8 mile from the junction. It's another 0.5 mile to the junction with the trail going to Pine Island Lake. Stay right at this fork and go 2.1 miles to Governor Dern Lake.

Spring water is present on either the north or east shore of Governor Dern Lake. The lake is shallow for its size but is still very pretty and easily fished. It is stocked periodically with brook trout, and a cutthroat may show up in the creel from time to time. Try a small fly in the morning and late evening for best results.

Nearby Pinto Lake is more popular, but it doesn't have any more to offer than Governor Dern Lake. In fact, Governor Dern is more scenic. Given that Pinto Lake is more crowded, Governor Dern seems to be the better choice. Rainbow Lake is less than a mile away (south). It is also worth a look, whether you're looking for a camping spot or a different fishing hole or you're just taking a horse ride.

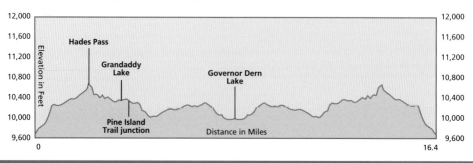

37 ALLEN LAKE

For backpackers arriving via Grandview (or via the Highline Trail to Four Lakes Basin), Allen provides a scenic retreat from the more pressured areas. Anglers seeking large arctic grayling must visit Allen Lake. Grayling over a pound are reported and fishing pressure is light. A few big brook trout inhabit this lake too. You won't catch a lot of fish at Allen Lake, but what you do catch will be sizable.

See map and logistics on pages 98 and 100.
Start: Grandview trailhead
Distance: 18.6 miles out and back
Destination elevation: 10,390 feet

Approximate hiking time: 12 hours
Difficulty: Moderate
Usage: Light
Nearest town: Hanna, Utah
Drainage: Rock Creek

THE HIKE

Allen Lake was named in honor of Floyd Allen, a ranger who was killed by lightning while on duty. A wooden monument still stands as a solemn reminder of the man who lost his life in 1938 and the awesome powers of nature. Remember to check the sky for storm clouds and take them seriously.

After the 2.4-mile ascent to the top of Hades Pass, walk another 1 mile to a trail junction in the narrow piece of land between Betsy and Grandaddy Lakes. Turn left (north) and go 0.1 mile to another trail junction on the north end of Betsy Lake. Turn right (northwest) about 1.3 miles to the junction with the trail that goes past Powell Lake. Stay right and go 1 mile to Lost Lake. The Fish Creek Trail junction is another 1 mile after you cross the creek. Go a short distance and turn right (north), then travel another 1.3 miles to Bedground Lake. Situated in a large, grassy meadow, Allen Lake can be located by traveling due east from Bedground Lake about 0.75 mile. A hit-or-miss game trail takes off from the northeast side of Bedground. Carefully follow your compass or GPS. It is easy to get turned around in this heavily timbered terrain.

Allen Lake is ideal for horses. Horse pasture and water are plentiful, and there are places to picket or hobble the horses. Spacious campsites make it easy to watch your stock from camp while still receiving shelter from large pines. The best camps dot the western side of the lake. There is a campfire and firewood gathering restriction within 0.25 mile of the lake. A small campsite on the eastern side of the lake can accommodate one tent. Good water for treating can be found along the eastern shore, where several springs emerge.

Remember, watch out for lightning.

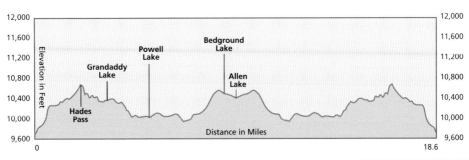

ROCK CREEK TRAILHEAD

Travelers to the Uintas accustomed to the paved access of Highway 150 will appreciate the smooth drive to Rock Creek trailhead. While you could certainly reserve a base camp in the campground among the ponderosa, lodgepole, and aspen forest and fish the stunning Upper Stillwater Reservoir (or, better yet, where Rock Creek enters the reservoir), excellent backpacking routes from Rock Creek trailhead shoot west, north, and east—though the destinations to the west are easier to access from Grandview trailhead.

A few years ago, the lightning-sparked East Fork Fire torched around 90,000 acres on the South Slope including Upper Lake Fork (next chapter) and here in the Rock Creek drainage. After the two-mile hike along the reservoir, you will get a close look at the aftermath of that fire. Parts of the Sinowauvf Basin and east of the East Fork of Rock Creek were severely burned. Also note that signage, guidebooks, and blogs may still refer to several sites in this region by the former name, "Squaw." In consultation with some seventy tribes, the offensive term was removed from nearly 650 place names on U.S. federal land. Updated place names include Sinowauvf Basin, Kyhv Lake, Kweeyahgut Peak, and Nahguch Creek and Pass.

See trails 38 through 40 for Rock Creek Trailhead.
Maps: USGS Explorer Peak, USGS Kidney Lake, and USGS Twooroose Pass; *USDA Forest Service High Uintas Wilderness; Trails Illustrated High Uintas Wilderness*

Trail contacts: Ashley National Forest, Forest Supervisor, 355 North Vernal Ave., Vernal, UT 84078, (435) 781-1181; Duchesne Ranger District, 85 West Main, Duchesne, UT 84021, (435) 738-2482

FINDING THE TRAILHEAD

From Heber City, take US 40 east 69 miles to Duchesne. Then take SR 87 north 14 miles to Mountain Home. Rock Creek trailhead is 22 miles northwest of Mountain Home on the paved FR 134. Turn west (left) on FR 135 and travel for 0.25 mile. The trailhead is on the right (north). There are no campsites, but the Upper Stillwater Campground is just 0.25 mile away on FR 134. There are toilets, water, a stock ramp, and a stock corral at the trailhead. This is a popular takeoff point for equestrians heading into the Fall Creek or Sinowauvf Basin areas. It's a long, steep hike to any lakes from here. Some lakes at the head of the Rock Creek drainage are more easily reached via the Highline Trail over Rocky Sea Pass.

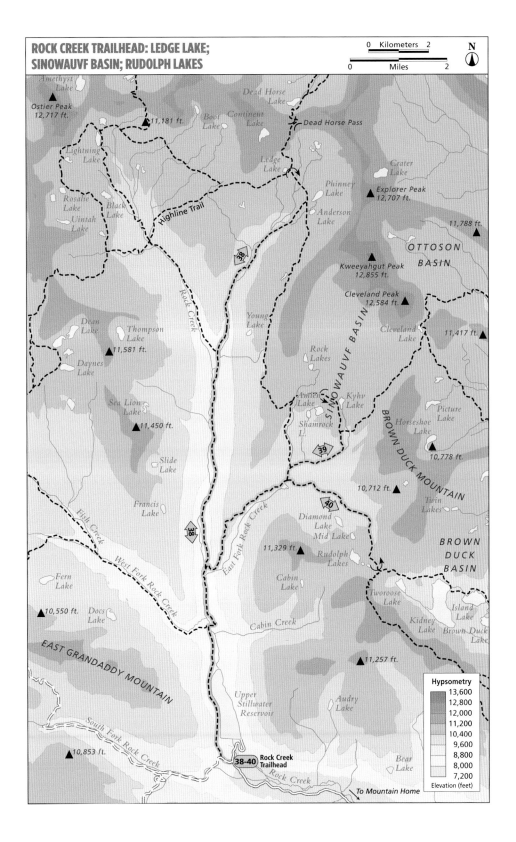

ROCK CREEK TRAILHEAD: LEDGE LAKE;
SINOWAUVF BASIN; RUDOLPH LAKES

0   Kilometers   2

0   Miles   2

N

Amethyst
Lake

Ostier Peak
12,717 ft.

11,181 ft.

Boot
Lake

Continent
Lake

Dead Horse
Lake

Dead Horse Pass

Lightning
Lake

Ledge
Lake

Crater
Lake

Phinney
Lake

Explorer Peak
12,707 ft.

Rosalie
Lake

Black
Lake

Uintah
Lake

Highline Trail

Anderson
Lake

11,788 ft.

OTTOSON
BASIN

38

Kweeyahgut Peak
12,855 ft.

Rock Creek

Young
Lake

Cleveland Peak
12,584 ft.

Cleveland
Lake

11,417 ft.

Dean
Lake

Thompson
Lake

11,581 ft.

Rock
Lakes

SINOWAUVF BASIN

Daynes
Lake

Sea Lion
Lake

11,450 ft.

Antler
Lake

Kyhv
Lake

Picture
Lake

Shamrock
L.

Horseshoe
Lake

BROWN DUCK MOUNTAIN

10,778 ft.

Slide
Lake

39

10,712 ft.

Francis
Lake

40

Diamond
Lake
Mid Lake

Twin
Lakes

Fish Creek

38

West Fork Rock Creek

East Fork Rock Creek

11,329 ft.

Rudolph
Lakes

BROWN
DUCK
BASIN

Fern
Lake

Cabin
Lake

10,550 ft.

Docs
Lake

Tworoose
Lake

Island
Lake

Cabin Creek

Kidney
Lake

Brown Duck
Lake

EAST GRANDADDY MOUNTAIN

11,257 ft.

10,853 ft.

South Fork Rock Creek

Upper
Stillwater
Reservoir

Audry
Lake

Hypsometry

	13,600
	12,800
	12,000
	11,200
	10,400
	9,600
	8,800
	8,000
	7,200

Elevation (feet)

Bear
Lake

38-40 Rock Creek
Trailhead

Rock Creek

To Mountain Home

Rock Creek Road to Upper Stillwater and the Rock Creek trailhead is one of those scenic drives that begs you to pull over to pause and appreciate the view.

38 **LEDGE LAKE**

Geologically, this area is the oldest in the High Uintas. Some refer to it as the backbone of the Uintas, while others call it the heart. After all, the upper basins of Rock Creek are shaped somewhat like a heart. Ledge Lake is a haven in this vast heart, providing everything one could want in a camp. Spring water is abundant, as is horse pasture, but so are mosquitoes around the waterlogged outlet. The fishing may be surprising. Brook trout weigh in at well over a pound and seem to prefer an olive-green scud fly for dinner. The problem is finding out what time dinner is served.

See map and logistics on pages 106–107.
Start: Rock Creek trailhead
Distance: 29 miles out and back
Destination elevation: 10,845 feet

Approximate hiking time: 17 hours
Difficulty: Difficult—long and steep
Usage: Moderate
Nearest town: Duchesne, Utah
Drainage: Rock Creek

THE HIKE

From Rock Creek trailhead the trail climbs up the hill to the west and passes by the Upper Stillwater Dam approximately 0.3 mile from the trailhead. The trail then parallels the Upper Stillwater Reservoir for 1.7 miles, follows Rock Creek for 0.8 mile, then arrives at the junction of the West Fork Rock Creek Trail. Continue up the Rock Creek drainage. After 1 mile, the trail meets the trail from Sinowauvf Basin. (It is also possible to reach Ledge Lake from this junction.) Continue up the valley for another 5.5 miles to another trail junction. The valley splits here. Rock Creek goes to the left; stay right, following Fall Creek another 5 miles to a trail junction. Continue straight for another 1.5 miles to Ledge Lake.

This basin houses some of the best-quality fishing holes in the whole mountain range. Continent Lake, about 2 miles northwest, commonly surrenders brookies in the 2-pound class and cutthroat over 16 inches. But you'll have to work for them. Work a green spinner deep, or a #14 Black Gnat just under the surface. The northeast segment of the lake may be the best place to start. Southeast from Ledge Lake are Phinney and Anderson Lakes. They offer fast fishing for smaller trout. They'll hit anything that moves.

Ledge Lake gets its name from the tall ledges behind its northern shore. It is easy to find, but there is no easy way to it. It's almost 15 miles from the Stillwater Dam trailhead and seems twice that long with the tremendous elevation gain. There are two other trails that may prove less taxing on the body. Both trails start at a higher elevation, but both also require traversing a steep mountain pass. It's about 12 miles to Ledge Lake coming from Blacks Fork over Dead Horse Pass and about 14 hilly miles via the Highline Trail over Rocky Sea Pass. Use Dead Horse if you're traveling by foot, Rocky Sea if by horse.

The impressive concrete Upper Stillwater Dam alongside the trailhead to Rock Creek

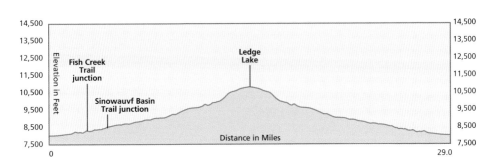

39 SINOWAUVF BASIN

A compass is a must in this heavily timbered area. It's easy to get headed in the wrong direction as the trails twist, turn, intersect, and sometimes disappear in Sinowauvf Basin. Getting into the area is not a problem but finding your way around Sinowauvf Basin can be confusing. Keep your map and compass handy, keep your group together, and keep the insect repellent nearby. There is plenty of spring water, but remember to properly filter water before drinking.

See map and logistics on pages 106–107.
Start: Rock Creek trailhead
Distance: 21 miles out and back
Destination elevation: 10,400 feet
Approximate hiking time: 12 hours

Difficulty: Moderate—some steep sections
Usage: Moderate
Nearest town: Duchesne, Utah
Drainage: Rock Creek

THE HIKE

From Rock Creek trailhead the trail climbs up the hill to the west and then passes by the Upper Stillwater Dam approximately 0.3 mile from the trailhead. The trail then parallels the Upper Stillwater Reservoir for 1.7 miles. The trail then follows Rock Creek for 0.8 mile until meeting the junction of the West Fork Rock Creek Trail. Continue up the Rock Creek drainage. After 1 mile, the trail meets the trail from Sinowauvf Basin. Veer right and work your way up a series of switchbacks on the Ottoson Trail overlooking the East Fork Rock Creek drainage. At about 8 miles turn north. There will be another junction with the trail coming down East Fork. Stay right (east) here and continue to the junction with the Kyhv Lake Trail a couple miles farther and turn north. It's about 2.5 miles to Kyhv Lake in the middle of Sinowauvf Basin.

Kyhv Lake is a popular camping location, featuring plenty of spring water and horse pasture. From a base camp at Kyhv Lake, consider a trip up Cleveland Pass if you have the time. It offers an unsurpassed view of the upper regions of the Lake Fork drainage and is well worth the extra effort.

If you are looking for a little more solitude, pitch your tent at Amlen or Shamrock Lake. These lakes are only a few hundred yards apart, and between the two you should find excellent campsites and spring water but only fair horse pasture. There is no trail to these lakes for the last 0.5 mile. Cross-country access is easiest from the southwest.

Fishing prospects are good to excellent throughout this large basin. Take a short hike up to Rock Lakes. These lakes see few visitors and house large populations of brook trout. Peak baggers might give the 12,708-foot Explorer Peak a look from Rock Lakes by heading north about 1.5 miles cross-country to a saddle and carefully ascending talus fields to a ridge with access to both Explorer and the 12,855-foot Kweeyahgut Peak.

The southern section of Sinowauvf Basin could have some real fishing holes too. Diamond, Mid, and Rudolph Lakes are just far enough off the beaten path to sustain good fisheries, with only light to moderate pressure.

A look over Upper Stillwater Reservoir into the Rock Creek drainage and Wilderness, the 12,706-foot Yard Peak about 12 miles north

Sinowauvf Basin is a good area for equestrians. The elevation gain is huge if you're starting at the Rock Creek trailhead and can quickly turn legs into rubber. Letting a horse do the heavy work is a great idea. Once into Sinowauvf Basin, there is lots of room to roam and explore, and a good steed can be a real leg and time saver. Horse pasture is abundant near most suitable campsites, and of course water is everywhere. The East Fork Fire of 2020 affected the southern portion of Sinowauvf Basin.

There are campfire and firewood gathering restrictions within 0.25 mile of Rock Lakes, Shamrock Lake, and Kyhv Lake.

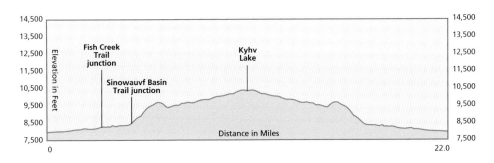

40 **RUDOLPH LAKES**

There are three different routes to Rudolph Lakes #1, #2, and #3. One trail begins at Moon Lake via Brown Duck Trail; total distance 9.5 miles one way. Another starts at the end of the challenging ATV Dry Ridge Road. Perhaps the most popular of the three begins right here at the Rock Creek trailhead.

See map and logistics on pages 106–107.
Start: Rock Creek trailhead
Distance: 24 miles out and back
Destination elevation: 10,470 feet
Approximate hiking time: 14 hours

Difficulty: Moderate—some steep sections
Usage: Moderate
Nearest town: Duchesne, Utah
Drainage: Rock Creek

THE HIKE

From Rock Creek trailhead the trail climbs up the hill to the west and then passes by the Upper Stillwater Dam approximately 0.3 mile from the trailhead. The trail then parallels the Upper Stillwater Reservoir for 1.7 miles. The trail then follows Rock Creek for 0.8 mile until meeting the junction of the West Fork Rock Creek Trail. Continue up the Rock Creek drainage. After 1 mile, the trail meets the trail from Sinowauvf Basin. It's 3.5 miles to the junction with the trail from Rudolph Lakes. Stay right and travel 6 miles.

Rudolph Lakes lie in an alpine ravine at the base of several talus slopes. No permanent trail exists to the lakes, but a posted sign clearly points the way. Campsites can be found on the east side of Rudolph Lakes #2 and #3, while spring water ready to be treated is located on the south side of Rudolph #1. There are campfire and firewood gathering restrictions within 0.25 mile of the lakes. These lakes receive light to moderate usage, and anglers should have no problem limiting. If by chance Rudolph Lakes don't produce, try Mid or Diamond. These small lakes sit in heavy timber and are off the beaten path.

Another angling trip worth checking out is Cabin Lake. It is located 1 mile southwest of Rudolph #1. Follow an old sheep trail over the saddle of Rudolph Mountain, then on through several boulder fields. The saddle creates no difficult problems, but afterward, rugged boulder fields make travel tiring and time-consuming.

Cabin Lake gets very little usage. This isolated lake sits all by its lonesome in its own little basin. Campsites are undesirable due to rocky and heavily timbered terrain. However, camping areas can be found near the open meadows to the north. Tall tales of this lake speak of big, healthy brook trout.

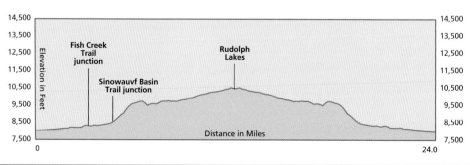

END OF FR 143 TO ARTA LAKE

Long drive, short hike, and solitude pretty well sum up this day trip. No matter which way you come from, you will probably be in for a long drive before you start hiking. But if you would rather spend more time driving through scenic country than hiking it, then this hike may interest you, especially if you're looking to get away from other people.

Start: End of the road
Distance: 1.5 mile out and back
Destination elevation: 10,450 feet
Approximate hiking time: 1.5 hours
Difficulty: Moderate—cross-country
Usage: Light
Nearest town: Duchesne, Utah
Drainage: Rock Creek
Maps: USGS Grandaddy Lake, *USDA Forest Service High Uintas*

Wilderness, Trails Illustrated High Uintas Wilderness
Trail contacts: Ashley National Forest, Forest Supervisor, 355 North Vernal Ave., Vernal, UT 84078, (435) 781-1181; Duchesne Ranger District, 85 West Main, Duchesne, UT 84021, (435) 738-2482

FINDING THE TRAILHEAD

From Heber City, take US 40 east 69 miles to Duchesne. Then take SR 87 north 14 miles to Mountain Home. Rock Creek trailhead is 22 miles northwest of Mountain Home on FR 134; the road is paved to Upper Stillwater Reservoir. Turn west on FR 135 and continue past the Rock Creek trailhead. After 2 miles, at the junction of FR 135 and FR 143, turn right and continue about 4.5 miles to the end of FR 143.

Here's what to expect on the very rough route to Arta Lake.

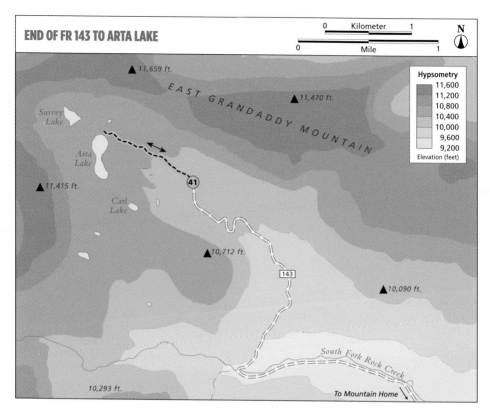

0   Kilometer   1

0   Mile   1

N

Hypsometry

	11,600
	11,200
	10,800
	10,400
	10,000
	9,600
	9,200

Elevation (feet)

▲ 11,659 ft.

EAST GRANDADDY MOUNTAIN

▲ 11,470 ft.

Survey Lake

Arta Lake

▲ 11,415 ft.

Carl Lake

41

▲ 10,712 ft.

143

▲ 10,090 ft.

South Fork Rock Creek

10,293 ft.

To Mountain Home

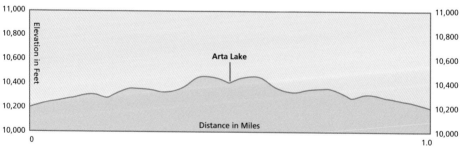

THE HIKE

It is only a 0.75-mile trek to Arta Lake from the end of FR 143, but it seems longer. A faint trail begins where the road ends but disappears after a couple hundred yards. Then you are left to pick your own route around lots of deadfall timber. Just keep heading due west and you will soon run into Arta Lake. Although attractive and quiet, this lake doesn't offer much in the way of good overnight campsites. The ground is strewn with boulders and pines. Water can be found on the northwest side, where it drains down a steep hill from Survey Lake, but you will need to purify it.

If you've come as far as Arta Lake, consider making the extra effort to hike the short, steep hill up to Survey Lake. The vista from the top of the hill overlooking Arta is magnificent, and on the other side of the hill Survey Lake lies in a great little alpine cirque (more pristine solitude). If you're really feeling ambitious, trek up the mountain behind Survey Lake and look down on Grandaddy Lake—what a view!

These lakes may experience winterkill, limiting your catch. You never know, though—fishing could improve after periodic stocking, or as the thousands of minnows observable early in the season grow up. It would at least be worth a try if you were making the trip anyway. Regardless, it's fun to go beyond the paved road. Unmarked routes from Arta to nearby East Grandaddy Mountain's 11,659-foot summit might be possible to locate, but they are described as Class 3 and Class 4, meaning scrambles with some exposed areas that should not be taken casually.

LAKE FORK TRAILHEAD

Like Rock Creek, Lake Fork also sits at the end of a paved road. Of course, the nearby reservoir plus the deluxe cabins and paved RV sites of Moon Lake Resort are among the main reasons for this luxury. But for those seeking quick access to the High Uintas Wilderness and the increased solitude of the backcountry, it can be nice having the red carpet rolled up to the trailhead.

Though there's a comparatively more leisurely stroll through the forest up the Fish Creek National Recreation Trail, the trails covered here are all about distance and solitude. A few years ago, the lightning-sparked East Fork Fire torched around 90,000 acres on the South Slope and caused some damage to the resort, so expect to see the aftermath of the fire along portions of the trails.

See trails 42 through 46 for Lake Fork Trailhead.
Maps: USGS Kidney Lake, USGS Oweep Creek, and USGS Explorer Peak; *USDA Forest Service High Uintas Wilderness*; *Trails Illustrated High Uintas Wilderness*

Trail contacts: Ashley National Forest, Forest Supervisor, 355 North Vernal Ave., Vernal, UT 84078, (435) 781-1181; Duchesne Ranger District, 85 West Main, Duchesne, UT 84021, (435) 738-2482

FINDING THE TRAILHEAD

From Heber City, take US 40 east 69 miles to Duchesne. Turn north onto SR 87 and travel 14 miles to Mountain Home. Take the Moon Lake Road north about 15 miles to the Lake Fork trailhead.

The trailhead has forty vehicle parking places with water and toilets. The Moon Lake Campground is 0.25 mile past the Lake Fork trailhead. Lake Fork is the main takeoff point for Brown Duck, East, and Ottoson Basins and is an optional trailhead for Sinowauvf Basin.

Mountain Home, Utah, stakes its claim as "The Gateway to the High Uintas," thanks to two paved access roads, one to Rock Creek (previous chapter), and the other to Lake Fork, near Moon Lake.

LAKE FORK TRAILHEAD: KIDNEY LAKE; CLEMENTS RESERVOIR; PICTURE LAKE AND THREE LAKES

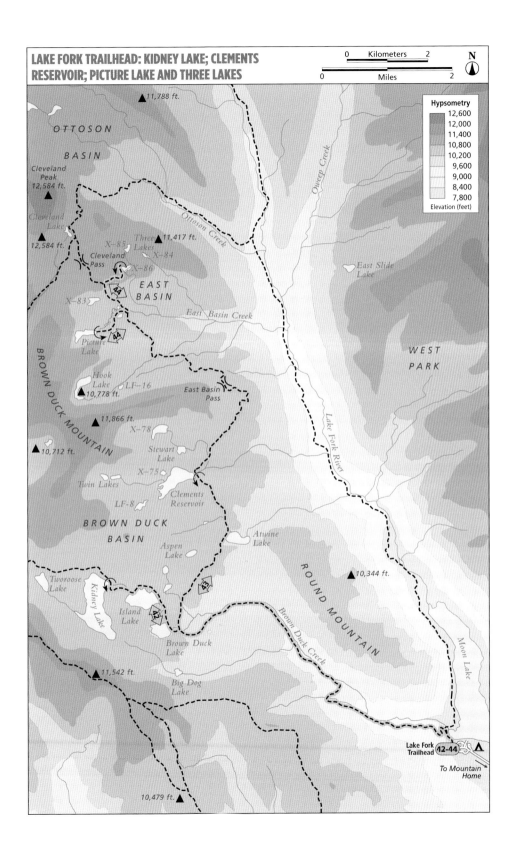

0 Kilometers 2
0 Miles 2

N

Hypsometry
12,600
12,000
11,400
10,800
10,200
9,600
9,000
8,400
7,800
Elevation (feet)

▲ 11,788 ft.

OTTOSON

BASIN

Cleveland
Peak
12,584 ft.
▲

Cleveland
Lake

Owweep Creek

▲ 12,584 ft.

Ottoson Creek

X–85
Three
Lakes ▲ 11,417 ft.
Cleveland
Pass
X–84
X–86

East Slide
Lake

EAST
BASIN

X–83

East Basin Creek

WEST

PARK

44

Picture
Lake

Hook
Lake
▲ 10,778 ft.

LF–16

East Basin
Pass

▲ 11,866 ft.

X–78

BROWN DUCK MOUNTAIN

Lake Fork River

Stewart
Lake

▲ 10,712 ft.

X–75

Twin Lakes

Clements
Reservoir

LF–8

BROWN DUCK

BASIN

Atwine
Lake

Aspen
Lake

ROUND MOUNTAIN

▲ 10,344 ft.

Twooroose
Lake

43

Kidney Lake

Island
Lake

42

Brown Duck
Lake

Brown Duck Creek

Moon Lake

▲ 11,542 ft.

Big Dog
Lake

Lake Fork
Trailhead 12-44

△

To Mountain
Home

10,479 ft. ▲

42 KIDNEY LAKE

Topping out at 190 acres, Kidney Lake is one of the largest reservoirs in the High Uintas backcountry. Just try walking around it, and you'll become a believer. Because of its "kidney" shape, you don't really see all of it at any one time, so it is even bigger than it looks.

See map and logistics on pages 118–119.
Start: Lake Fork trailhead before Moon Lake Campground
Distance: 15 miles out and back
Destination elevation: 10,267 feet

Approximate hiking time: 10 hours
Difficulty: Moderate
Usage: Heavy
Nearest town: Duchesne, Utah
Drainage: Lake Fork

THE HIKE

From Lake Fork trailhead, the trail is wide and clear for the first few miles, following Brown Duck Creek on the west side of Round Mountain. After about 6 miles, there is a trail junction with the trail going to Clements Reservoir. Shortly after this junction, the trail passes Brown Duck Lake and, in 0.5 mile, Island Lake (yes, another one). Kidney Lake is 1 mile from the first glimpse of Island Lake.

There's a lot of room to spread out, so despite heavy pressure you should still find some solitude. This area is attractive to equestrians because of the large campsites that are available and a good supply of horse pasture. The eastern shoreline has the best accommodations, including a limited supply of spring water. The area is popular with backpackers too, but they might be happier at more isolated nearby lakes, like Tworoose.

The streams linking Kidney, Island, and Brown Duck Lakes have good flow and should provide an opportunity for some good stream fishing. Try a flashy spinner in the ripples and pools. These lakes and streams are fun to fish because of the variety of opportunities that exist. Cutthroat are stocked, but an occasional brook trout may show up.

Kidney Lake is also a convenient stopover for hikers continuing on into the Rock Creek drainage. Spend a night near the trail at Kidney Lake, then you'll be fresh the next day to tackle Tworoose Pass (about 2 miles west). Hikers can also turn northeast on the Ottoson Trail for a loop around Brown Duck Mountain and return via Cleveland Pass to East Basin past Picture, Three Lakes, and Clements Reservoir for a 32-mile loop. (See map in next chapter.)

There are campfire and firewood gathering restrictions within 0.25 mile of Kidney, Island, Tworoose, Brown Duck, Big Dog, and Dog Lakes.

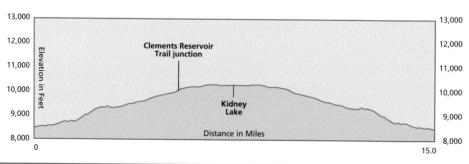

43 CLEMENTS RESERVOIR

After a long, steep climb, Clements Reservoir will look mighty good. Sheltered campsites are abundant along the northern shoreline, and you can easily imagine what it would be like to have a cabin overlooking the lake. The setting is rustic and peaceful.

See map and logistics on pages 118–119.
Start: Lake Fork trailhead before Moon Lake Campground
Distance: 18 miles out and back
Destination elevation: 10,444 feet

Approximate hiking time: 11 hours
Difficulty: Moderate—some steep sections
Usage: Heavy
Nearest town: Duchesne, Utah
Drainage: Lake Fork

THE HIKE

The trail from Moon Lake starts out easy. An old road is now a wide, clear trail for the first few miles. Then the going gets tough as the trail rears its ugly head and you find yourself picking your way through the steep and rocky path. After 6 miles, there is a junction with the trail that goes to Kidney Lake, just before reaching Brown Duck Lake. Stay to the right here. The cursed rocks are relentless and don't give you a break until you reach Clements Reservoir. Level ground never looked as good as it does here.

Be prepared to purify water from the lake or the spring on the back side of the lake. Because of heavy use, firewood is scarce near the campsites. You'll have to walk a little for this commodity as well. (And there are campfire and firewood gathering restrictions within 0.25 mile of Clements, Mud, Stewart, Atwine, and Aspen Lakes.)

Clements can withstand heavy pressure and frequently provides fast fishing for fat cutthroat from 13 to 17 inches. Fly-fish right off the dam about an hour before sunset, and you'll likely catch all you want. If you want to get away from the people at Clements, there are three other small lakes nearby. Southwest of Clements is LF–8. Head west to X–75 or another mile to Twin Lakes. A short journey north to Stewart Lake may prove rewarding. Any of these lakes might produce the "mother lode" of fish. But expect rough cross-country travel that includes hopping over deadfall and boulders.

For spectacular scenery, hike up the trail 1 mile to East Basin Pass. From there you can view the entire upper region of the Lake Fork drainage, including such sights as Mount Lovenia and Nahguch Pass. Although East Basin Pass isn't as high as most other passes, it provides one of the most panoramic vistas in the High Uintas.

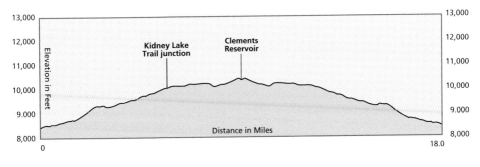

44 PICTURE LAKE AND THREE LAKES

Your arrival at East Basin Pass may lead you to believe that no one has ever been here before. An expanse of wilderness spreads out in front of your eyes, with Lambert Meadow at the base of the ridgeline 6 miles distant. It's an inspirational view of the whole Upper Lake Fork drainage. It's a lot of mileage whether on foot or on horseback, and your effort is sure to be rewarded.

See map and logistics on pages 118–119
Start: Lake Fork trailhead before Moon Lake Campground
Distance: 34 miles out and back
Destination elevation: 10,731 feet

Approximate hiking time: 22 hours
Difficulty: Moderate—some steep sections
Usage: Moderate
Nearest town: Duchesne, Utah
Drainage: Lake Fork

THE HIKE

From Lake Fork trailhead, the trail is wide and clear for the first few miles, following Brown Duck Creek on the west side of Round Mountain. After about 7 miles, there is a junction with the trail going to Clements Reservoir. Stay to the right here and go 3.5 miles to the reservoir. The trail continues another 6 miles to two small lakes. The trail forks here to Picture Lake or Three Lakes. For Picture, follow the creek southwest another 0.5 mile to the lake.

Most groups make their base camp at the three small lakes that lie below Picture Lake. Several good camping areas exist near these lakes, and others can be found along the inlet streams. These lakes receive moderate to heavy angling pressure but can still be hot at times. Try a small spinner or fly. With a little skill, brook trout can be hooked throughout the deepwater channels. Two major inlets feed these lakes. By following the southwest inlet 0.5 mile up a timbered slope, you'll find a beautiful lake called Picture.

Picture Lake fits its name perfectly. This lake has a pretty talus slope as a backdrop, with timber-mirrored waters and a large outlet cascading down the mountainside. Rocky, timbered terrain surrounds the lake on three sides, adding to its artistic value. Due to this same fact, campsites are poorly defined.

Hook Lake is located 1 mile south of Picture. There is no trail from Picture to Hook, and the terrain is consistently rough, rocky, and filled with deadfalls. A horse will not make it through here. However, an alternate route starting from LF–16 is much easier. From LF–16, follow the inlet stream 0.5 mile west along the base of a ridge to the lake. Hook is situated in the southwest corner of East Basin next to a glacial talus slope. Huge boulders interspersed with heavy timber make camping poor, but spring water can be found near the outlet.

Three Lakes are not to be confused with the three lakes that lie just below Picture Lake. Three Lakes are in a remote area 1 mile north of the three smaller lakes next to the East Basin Trail. From the fork mentioned above, follow the East Basin Trail north about

200 yards to where the trail levels out a bit. At this point, cut cross-country 1 mile northeast to the outlet of X–86.

Lake X–86 is the first of the Three Lakes you'll reach. Due to the rocky nature of this terrain, only one decent campsite exists. This campsite is found near the outlet, where you'll find good running water as well.

X–85 is the place to stay. This lake plays host to several good camping areas on the southwest side. It is also equipped with a superb spring that flows into the lake from the north. X–85 should produce some fairly good fishing for fat brook trout. Access the lake by following the inlet of X–86 0.25 mile to the north.

Like the other lakes, X–84 is in a rough alpine setting that may remind you of a desolate and faraway place. Campsites and spring water are not available. Angling usage is quite light, which means fishing prospects may be worthwhile. Reach X–84 by following a couple of ponds that lie northeast of X–86.

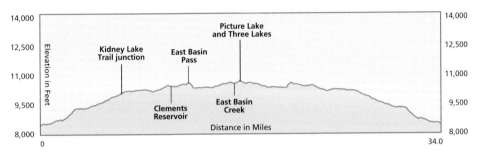

45 **OTTOSON BASIN**

Ottoson Basin offers one of the grandest views in the High Uintas, especially when viewed from the top of Cleveland Pass. Shutterbugs will want to be on the pass in early morning when the sun illuminates the peaks. Mornings are also very good for fishing, but you can always find fast fishing in the evening. If you want superb photos, choose the early hike up Cleveland Pass.

See map on page 125 and logistics on page 118
Start: Lake Fork trailhead before Moon Lake Campground
Distance: 30.4 miles out and back
Destination elevation: 11,075 feet

Approximate hiking time: 18 hours
Difficulty: Moderate
Usage: Light
Nearest town: Duchesne, Utah
Drainage: Lake Fork

THE HIKE

The easiest access to Ottoson Basin is the Lake Fork River Trail. (The most scenic route, however, is via the Brown Duck Trail, then through East Basin and over Cleveland Pass.) From Moon Lake, follow the Lake Fork River Trail 9 miles north to the Ottoson Basin Trail junction. From here go 3 miles northwest up a 1,200-foot incline to the base of Cleveland Peak. Then cut across rugged country 1.2 miles northwest to Lower Ottoson Lake.

Upper and Lower Ottoson Lakes are in open terrain in the upper west portion of Ottoson Basin. These lakes lie at the base of a talus ridge that connects Explorer and Kweeyahgut Peaks. There are no decent campsites at these lakes, but good camping areas and horse pasture can be found 0.5 mile southeast of Lower Ottoson. Both lakes contain healthy populations of cutthroat trout, and fishing pressure remains mostly light. During the late summer months, sheep grazing takes place in the whole upper part of Ottoson Basin. This activity depreciates the glamour of this beautiful basin and adds the need for extra caution where drinking water is concerned.

There are additional lakes in Ottoson Basin that may make for ideal campsites. The meadow provides good campsites, horse pasture, and hot fishing for cutthroat trout. You're already hovering in the neighborhood of 11,000 feet in parts of the Ottoson Basin, so continuing south over the pass to Cleveland Lake doesn't add a lot of climbing. From the lake there's a recorded route up to the top of Cleveland Peak, but as with most mountains in the High Uintas, you'll be carefully choosing your way across rocks and boulders.

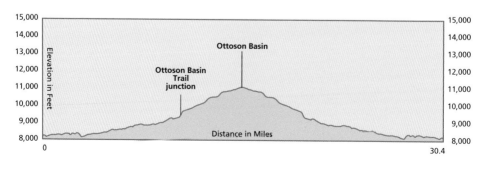

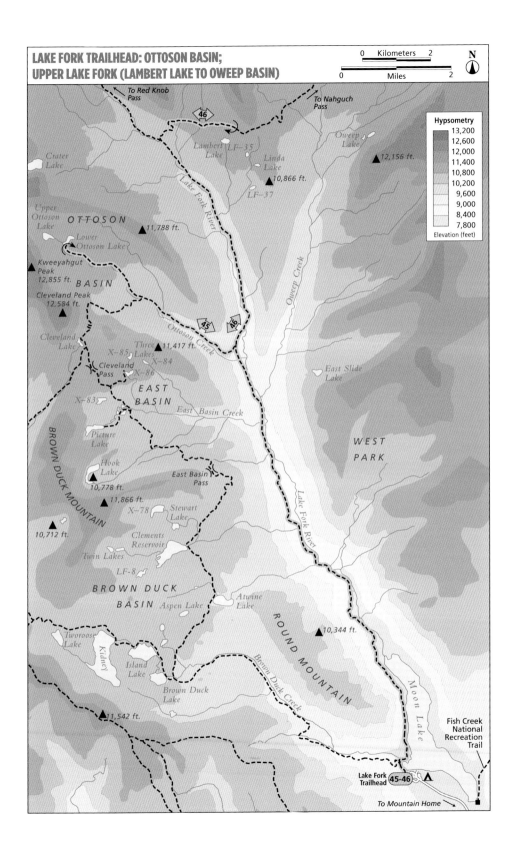

LAKE FORK TRAILHEAD: OTTOSON BASIN;
UPPER LAKE FORK (LAMBERT LAKE TO OWEEP BASIN)

0   Kilometers   2

0   Miles   2

N

Hypsometry

	13,200
	12,600
	12,000
	11,400
	10,800
	10,200
	9,600
	9,000
	8,400
	7,800

Elevation (feet)

To Red Knob Pass

To Nahguch Pass

46

Oweep Lake

Lambert Lake

LF–35

Linda Lake

▲ 12,156 ft.

Crater Lake

▲ 10,866 ft.

LF–37

Lake Fork River

Upper Ottoson Lake

OTTOSON

▲ 11,788 ft.

Lower Ottoson Lake

Kweeyahgut Peak
12,855 ft.

BASIN

Oweep Creek

Cleveland Peak
12,584 ft.

Ottoson Creek

45

46

Cleveland Lake

Three Lakes ▲ 11,417 ft.

X–85

X–84

East Slide Lake

Cleveland Pass

X–86

EAST BASIN

X–83

East Basin Creek

BROWN DUCK MOUNTAIN

Picture Lake

WEST PARK

Hook Lake

10,778 ft.

East Basin Pass

▲ 11,866 ft.

X–78

Stewart Lake

Lake Fork River

▲ 10,712 ft.

Clements Reservoir

Twin Lakes

LF–8

BROWN DUCK

BASIN

Aspen Lake

Atunne Lake

▲ 10,344 ft.

Tworoose Lake

Kidney

Island Lake

ROUND MOUNTAIN

Moon Lake

Brown Duck Lake

Brown Duck Creek

▲ 11,542 ft.

Fish Creek National Recreation Trail

Lake Fork Trailhead

45-46

To Mountain Home

UPPER LAKE FORK (LAMBERT LAKE TO OWEEP BASIN)

The upper regions of the Lake Fork drainage display some of the finest scenery in the High Uintas. From one pass to another, grand panoramas seem to enchant the mind. Red Knob Pass grants access to two other beautiful drainages, while Nahguch and Porcupine Passes branch into others. To say the least, this area is a gold mine for photographers. However, the Lake Fork Trail from Moon Lake is not as seductive as it winds through a 14-mile corridor of tall standing pines. Not much else can be seen until you get to the upper basins. If you prefer filtering spring water to drink, make a note of which lakes in the area have a supply.

See map on page 125 and logistics on page 118.
Start: Lake Fork trailhead before Moon Lake Campground
Distance: 30 miles out and back
Destination elevation: 11,200 feet

Approximate hiking time: 19 hours
Difficulty: Moderate to difficult
Usage: Light
Nearest town: Duchesne, Utah
Drainage: Lake Fork

THE HIKE

Although Crater, Lambert, and Oweep Lakes are located in the Lake Fork River drainage, they might be easier reached from East Fork Blacks Fork by way of Red Knob or Nahguch Pass—if the passes are free of snow. You may find the northern route to be more scenic and it supports a loop trail. But be prepared for some hard work going over Red Knob Pass.

From Moon Lake, follow the Lake Fork River Trail 9 miles north to the Ottoson Basin Trail junction. From here go 5.2 miles to the junction with the Highline Trail and follow the right fork north and then east. In the middle of the Upper Lake Fork drainage lies Lambert Lake. Find this alpine water by following the Highline Trail about 2 miles. If you're coming from the west, keep to the trail until you get above timberline. Once you exit the pines, the lake should be south of the trail just a few hundred yards. Lambert offers good campsites and horse pasture, but spring water is limited. It receives moderate usage from those hiking the Highline Trail. Fly fishing is often great for feisty, fat brook

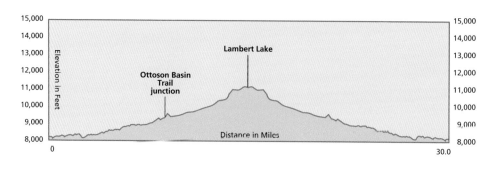

Wilson Peak, from East Oweep Creek in the Upper Lake Fork Drainage. PHOTO BY MATT MCKELL/ UTAH DIVISION OF WILDLIFE RESOURCES

trout. The best campsite at Lambert Lake is located just above the cliffs overlooking the lake. It includes a small spring that emerges from the rocks and rolls down to the lake.

Nearby Linda Lake sits in a boggy meadow 0.5 mile east on the Highline Trail from Lambert, then 0.25 mile south from the trail. Campsites and spring water are limited, but a wary population of brook trout await your offerings. LF–35 is right next to Linda Lake and may provide faster fishing.

In the eastern portion of the Upper Lake Fork drainage lies the fantastically remote Oweep Creek Basin. This scenic area is at the base of a long talus slope bordering the Lake Fork and Yellowstone drainages. Surrounded by rocky terrain, camping areas are limited. Spring water is abundant, and usage by anglers is considered light. In late summer, sheep grazing occurs in the whole Upper Lake Fork drainage. Highliners approaching from the east get the best view of Oweep Creek Basin from Porcupine Pass.

Crater Lake lies at the northeast base of Explorer Peak and is encased by a spectacular cirque basin. Steep cliffs and talus slopes abut the water from the north, west, and south. Crater is known to be a mystifying lake. Some say that brook trout rise to the surface

A view from Porcupine Pass into the remote Oweep Basin of the Upper Lake Fork Drainage.
PHOTO BY MATT MCKELL/UTAH DIVISION OF WILDLIFE RESOURCES

all at once, then mysteriously disappear for the rest of the day. "Where do they go?" you ask. Who knows? This lake has a depth of at least 150 feet, and no one really knows if anybody has found the bottom yet.

If you are planning to stay at Crater Lake to see if these stories are true, good luck. Due to open, rocky terrain, campsites are poorly defined. Camping areas and spring water for treating can be found 1 mile to the east. Access to Crater is 16 miles north on the Lake Fork River Trail, then cross-country 2 miles west.

CENTER PARK TRAILHEAD

If trucks hauling fifth wheels and horse trailers can navigate the narrow, rocky road called Hells Canyon to Center Park trailhead, surely anyone can make it, right? Not so fast. Literally, don't go fast if you're in a lower-clearance vehicle or there is any doubt about the condition of your tires.

Once at the trailhead, enjoy a wide-open parking area (where I left a Redington fly rod) and your choice of a couple of unique out-and-back trail options: the rolling terrain of Spider Lake or the down-then-up and varied terrain of Toquer. Fish Creek National Recreation Trail also branches off from Center Park, though it's more commonly explored from the Moon Lake Dam side, near Lake Fork trailhead.

See trails 47 and 48 for Center Park Trailhead.
Maps: USGS Garfield Basin, *USDA Forest Service High Uintas Wilderness*, *Trails Illustrated High Uintas Wilderness*

Trail contacts: Ashley National Forest, Forest Supervisor, 355 North Vernal Ave., Vernal, UT 84078, (435) 781-1181; Duchesne Ranger District, 85 West Main, Duchesne, UT 84021, (435) 738-2482

FINDING THE TRAILHEAD

From Heber City, take US 40 east 69 miles to Duchesne. Turn north on SR 87 and travel 14 miles to Mountain Home. Follow Moon Lake Road north 4 miles to where Yellowstone River Road intersects on the east side. From this point, follow Yellowstone River Road another 4 miles to Hells Canyon Road. Center Park trailhead is 7 miles northwest up Hells Canyon Road.

Center Park has room for fifteen vehicles to park and has an information board and a vault toilet. Hells Canyon Road fits its name perfectly—it is a road from hell. It is well defined but steep and very rocky. A high-clearance vehicle is recommended, and the road may require four-wheel drive when wet. But Subaru and other passenger vehicles with good tires should be able to make the trip much of the time.

The trail to Fish Creek also leads to the fork to Toquer Lake. A separate trail heads due north to Spider Lake.

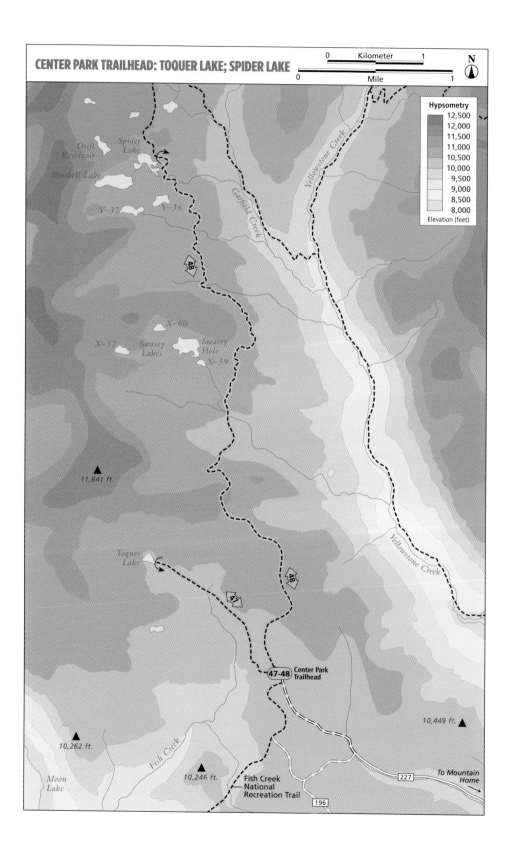

CENTER PARK TRAILHEAD: TOQUER LAKE; SPIDER LAKE

47 TOQUER LAKE

This is one of those places where you go to be alone. Toquer Lake is the only body of water in the area deserving of the designation "lake." It's not on the way to anywhere else, so very few hikers bother checking it out. But if you're looking for a short, mild hike that leads to serene scenery and a great chance for some genuine solitude, then look no further.

See map and logistics on pages 129–130.
Start: Center Park trailhead
Distance: 5.5 miles out and back
Destination elevation: 10,470 feet

Approximate hiking time: 4 hours
Difficulty: Easy
Usage: Light
Nearest town: Duchesne, Utah
Drainage: Lake Fork

THE HIKE

Toquer Lake offers an exquisite setting, but better campsites can be found about 0.25 mile below the lake. Everything you need is found near the lake. A cold, free-flowing spring on the north side provides a good source of water for treating, and firewood is pretty much everywhere throughout the heavily timbered terrain. If you're lucky, the lake will even yield a few of its brook trout for your evening meal. But don't expect great fishing. An avid angler would probably be happier somewhere else, and that's okay. That means there will be even fewer visitors here.

The trail from the Center Park trailhead is a tough one to follow. It frequently disappears, and you may find yourself picking through the many fallen trees. Cairns are present

The small but peaceful Toquer Lake

An example of deadfall that can easily overtake a trail in the Uintas

but infrequent. About 2 miles in there's a creek crossing after emerging from the forest into a meadow. It's a quick turn northwest out of the forest and way too easy to make the mistake of following that creek west. Keep your map handy while hiking and keep bearing northwest. You can always just find Fish Creek and then follow it up to Toquer Lake.

If you are camped at Toquer Lake, try hiking to the top of the ridge about 1 mile to the northeast. From there you'll witness one of the finest vistas of Swasey Hole and the upper regions of the Yellowstone drainage. On a clear day you can see all the way to Kings Peak. Take your camera.

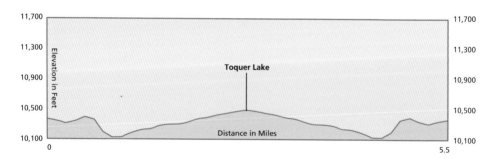

48 SPIDER LAKE

This unique trail pairs 3,600 feet in elevation gain from one of the Uintas most dramatic up-and-down hikes with a plethora of outstanding lakes. Acclimated distance hikers comfortable on rocky trails should give this route a close look. Spider is named for its many elongated bays that can offer interesting fishing for cutthroat and brook trout. And it's just one of many fishing holes in the Garfield Basin. Depending on your tolerance for elevation and distance, this hike may become a favorite you return to or the one you're glad you did once.

See map and logistics on pages 129–130.
Start: Center Park trailhead
Distance: 17.6 miles out and back
Destination elevation: 10,876 feet
Approximate hiking time: 13 hours

Difficulty: Difficult—up and down many times
Usage: Heavy
Nearest town: Duchesne, Utah
Drainage: Yellowstone River

THE HIKE

This is a tiring hike, but availability of water from roughly 2.5 miles on means backpackers can treat rather than haul their water. And, for the most part, it's a straight shot without any forks. On paper the terrain doesn't look that bad, but you'll feel like a yo-yo upon arrival. The trail seems to go up and down endlessly. Allow yourself extra hiking time to make up for the rest stops you're bound to need. Take your time and enjoy the scenery. It is a pretty hike. You may have a tough time remembering any level ground until you reach Spider Lake. Then things get much better. The camping sites are plentiful all around the lake, and that's good, because this aesthetic lake sees lots of pressure on the weekends. Be sure to clean up after yourself, practice low-impact camping, and pack out all your trash.

Bluebell Lake has some nice-size brooks and cutthroat. A small fly should yield fish. Or try Y–36 and Y–37 just to the south. These lakes are stocked with brook trout and receive little attention. Head northwest from Spider Lake about 0.5 mile, and you'll run into Drift Reservoir. Who knows what you will find here. It is out of the way just enough to keep a few secrets.

Take plenty of mosquito repellent if you are traveling during bug season. There are several moist areas that produce some fair-size clouds of mosquitoes. Take that into consideration when selecting your campsite, and you'll breathe easier.

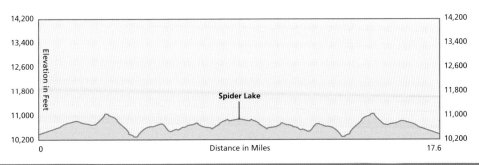

The 0.25-mile campfire restriction applies to Spider, Bluebell, Drift, Gem, Five Point, Doll, Superior, and Little Superior Lakes—and many hikers on this trail do continue to the lovely Five Point Lake, about 1.5 miles farther north at the junction with a spur from the Yellowstone Trail out of Swift Creek.

SWIFT CREEK TRAILHEAD

It can be easy to forget that the U.S. Forest Service is part of the U. S. Department of Agriculture until you wake up in your tent surrounded by a herd of mooing cattle, open-range grazing through the campground. But pay them no mind. If you're camping below the trailhead at one of multiple campgrounds, your biggest challenge may be finding a large enough area free from cow pies to stake your tent. Otherwise, there are decent amenities (vault toilets, picnic tables, water) and plenty of fish in the river.

From the trailhead, most hikers and equestrians climb the ridgeline dividing Swift Creek and Yellowstone drainages and then continue the ascent up into the Swift Creek Basin. The rocky, tree-covered route along the Yellowstone would add variety to a loop hike.

See trails 49 through 54 for Swift Creek Trailhead.
Maps: USGS Burnt Mill Spring, USGS Mount Emmons, USGS Garfield Basin, USGS Mount Powell, and USGS Kings Peak; *USDA Forest Service High Uintas Wilderness*; *Trails Illustrated High Uintas Wilderness*

Trail contacts: Ashley National Forest, Forest Supervisor, 355 North Vernal Ave., Vernal, UT 84078, (435) 781-1181; Duchesne Ranger District, 85 West Main, Duchesne, UT 84021, (435) 738-2482

FINDING THE TRAILHEAD

From Heber City, take US 40 east 69 miles to Duchesne. Turn north onto SR 87 and travel 14 miles to Mountain Home. Follow Moon Lake Road north 4 miles to where Yellowstone River Road intersects on the east side. Follow Yellowstone River Road another 4 miles past the rough and tumble Hells Canyon Road. Stay on Yellowstone River Road another 6 miles to the Swift Creek trailhead.

The Swift Creek trailhead can handle parking for twenty-five vehicles and is equipped with campsites, toilets, water, and a stock ramp. Many of the high lakes are 10 to 15 miles away, up steep and rocky terrain. Swift Creek also serves as an optional trailhead for the Yellowstone River drainage.

The Swift Creek trailhead branches northwest along Yellowstone Creek and north along Swift Creek, traveling several miles into Timothy Basin, as seen from this ridge.

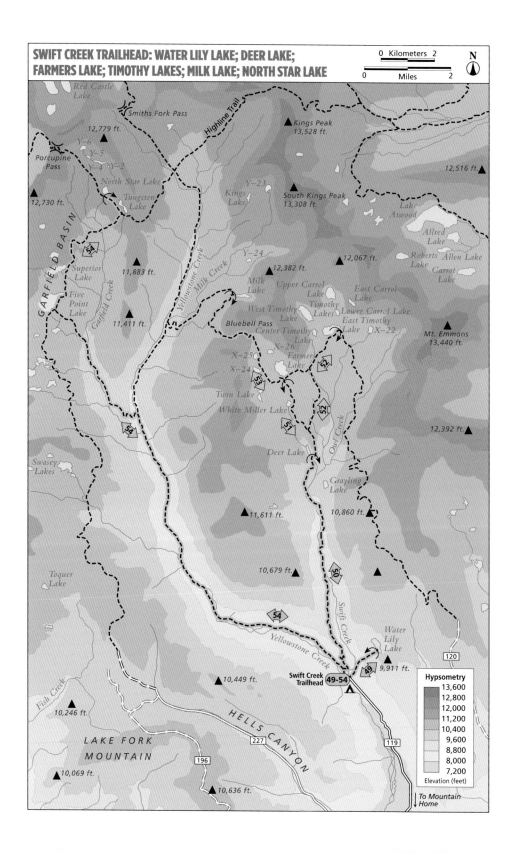

SWIFT CREEK TRAILHEAD: WATER LILY LAKE; DEER LAKE;
FARMERS LAKE; TIMOTHY LAKES; MILK LAKE; NORTH STAR LAKE

0   Kilometers   2

0   Miles   2

N

Red Castle Lake

Smiths Fork Pass

Highline Trail

Kings Peak
13,528 ft.

12,779 ft.

Porcupine Pass

Y-6
Y-5
Y-4 Y-2

12,516 ft.

North Star Lake

Y-23

12,730 ft.

Tungsten Lake

Kings Lake

South Kings Peak
13,308 ft.

Lake Atwood

Allred Lake

GARFIELD BASIN

54

Superior Lake

11,883 ft.

Yellowstone Milk Creek

Y-24

12,382 ft.

12,067 ft.

Roberts Lake

Allen Lake

Carrot Lake

Milk Lake

Upper Carrol Lake

East Carrol Lake

Five Point Lake

Garfield Creek

11,411 ft.

Bluebell Pass

West Timothy Lake

Center Timothy Lake

Timothy Lakes

Lower Carrol Lake

East Timothy Lake

Mt. Emmons
13,440 ft.

X-26

X-22

X-25

Farmers Lake

52

X-24

53

Twin Lake

White Miller Lake

52

12,392 ft.

51

Swasey Lakes

Deer Lake

Owl Creek

Grayling Lake

10,860 ft.

54

11,611 ft.

10,679 ft.

50

Toquer Lake

Swift Creek

Water Lily Lake

120

54

9,911 ft.

Yellowstone Creek

49

10,449 ft.

Swift Creek Trailhead
49-54

Fish Creek

HELLS CANYON

227

119

Hypsometry

13,600
12,800
12,000
11,200
10,400
9,600
8,800
8,000
7,200

Elevation (feet)

10,246 ft.

LAKE FORK MOUNTAIN

196

10,069 ft.

10,636 ft.

To Mountain Home

49 WATER LILY LAKE

A short but strenuous day hike can put you at beautiful Lily Lake, surrounded by pines and quaking aspens that hiss in the breeze. The lake is clear and deep except for the southern end, where numerous aquatic plants grow in the shallows. If Swift Creek Campground is your base camp, Lily Lake is an excellent place to escape the crowds and find some peace and quiet.

See map and logistics on pages 135–136.
Start: Swift Creek trailhead
Distance: 2 miles out and back
Destination elevation: 9,346 feet
Approximate hiking time: 2 hours

Difficulty: Moderate—some steep sections
Usage: Moderate
Nearest town: Duchesne, Utah
Drainage: Swift Creek

THE HIKE

From Swift Creek trailhead, go back down Yellowstone River Road about 0.5 mile to FR 403 at Grant Springs. From there, a trail will lead you up the mountainside northeast to Lily Lake. It is quite steep—you'll pick up more than 1,200 feet of elevation in just 1 mile. It may seem farther than a mile. Mountain miles usually do. But don't give up; you should complete the trek in 30 to 45 minutes. The walk back down should be a lot quicker.

Anglers like to venture to Lily Lake in hopes of finding faster fishing than near the campgrounds. This may or may not happen. Lily Lake is stocked with brook trout, but stocking schedules, angling pressure, and the mood of the fish will determine your fishing luck. Try to be at the lake in early morning or late evening. This should be feasible because of the short hike. Try a small fly (#16) around the inlet and outlet, and don't overlook the lily pads. Brook trout like to hang around these looking for bugs. Lily Lake is just close enough to camp that you won't mind toting a few fish back for dinner.

Lily Lake doesn't sport good camping facilities. It is not a good place to spend the night. Don't make any new camping areas or fire pits. This area is more suitable for day use and probably should remain that way.

50 DEER LAKE

Early in the summer season, before the higher country opens up, you may find yourself wanting some alpine adventure. Here's a lake that just might provide some early relief from cabin fever; that is, if you call mid-June early. Pack some warm clothes. The temperatures can still be pretty brisk during June. Much of the hike is steep, but it's not very far. Deer Lake makes an excellent primer hike that can easily fit into a weekend.

See map and logistics on pages 135–136.
Start: Swift Creek trailhead
Distance: 11.2 miles out and back
Destination elevation: 10,240 feet

Approximate hiking time: 6.5 hours
Difficulty: Moderate
Usage: Moderate
Nearest town: Duchesne, Utah
Drainage: Swift Creek

THE HIKE

From Swift Creek trailhead, it's a short distance to where the trail forks left to Yellowstone River or right to Swift Creek. Stay right and climb 5.6 miles to Deer Lake—with multiple stream crossings on shaky logs over the aptly named creek that will check the balance of hikers with heavy backpacks.

Deer Lake is probably at its best early in the season. Later on, the lake becomes less attractive as the water level drops, leaving a muddy, rocky shoreline. If you can get there just after "ice-off," you could experience some fast fishing for pan-size brook and cutthroat trout. Other fishing opportunities include Grayling Lake (about 1 mile southeast) and Swift Creek. The outlet from Deer Lake joins Swift Creek about 0.5 mile below. Hardly anyone fishes the creek. Try it with a small spinner and you might be pleasantly surprised.

Fair campsites can be found near the outlet. They are not top-quality camping spots, but they will suffice. Spring water to be treated is available at the inlet, as is a small amount of horse pasture. There is a campfire restriction within 0.25 mile of Deer Lake. Most travelers—including extensive usage by horse packs—only stop for lunch on their way to more popular lakes. You should have it all to yourself during the evening hours.

Shutterbugs will enjoy the view back down Swift Creek drainage, as well as the setting around Deer Lake. Deer Lake lies in a narrow valley, surrounded by pines on its long sides, with a picturesque cliff sealing off the back end.

Follow Swift Creek north to Deer Lake

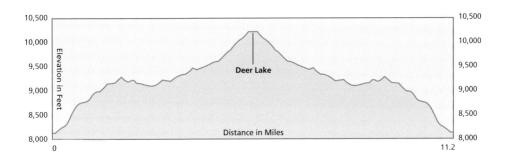

51 FARMERS LAKE

If you like to get a lot of elevation gain out of the way early, then this hike is for you. Right from the start, you'll traverse a long series of switchbacks that pick up 1,000 feet in 1.5 miles. Then the trail levels off for a few miles before another steep ascent to Deer Lake. Deer Lake is a great place to stop for lunch, and maybe catch a few neglected brook trout.

See map and logistics on pages 135–136.
Start: Swift Creek trailhead
Distance: 15.8 miles out and back
Destination elevation: 10,990 feet
Approximate hiking time: 10 hours

Difficulty: Moderate—some steep sections
Usage: Moderate
Nearest town: Duchesne, Utah
Drainage: Swift Creek

THE HIKE

From Swift Creek trailhead, it's a short distance to where the trail forks left to Yellowstone River or right to Swift Creek. Stay right and climb 5.6 miles to Deer Lake. Though easier said than done, given the multiple stream crossings on shaky logs that will check the balance of hikers with heavy backpacks. Farmers Lake is another 2.3 miles up the valley.

You will pass White Miller Lake on the way. This is a tempting place to camp and fish but push on another mile to Farmers Lake. Farmers is a better base camp. It sits in the middle of several good fishing lakes and has excellent horse pasture nearby to the west. The best campsite is about 0.25 mile below Farmers Lake. Just follow the outlet stream and you can't miss it.

Fishing at Farmers Lake varies greatly from year to year. Some years you can catch eager brook trout on every other cast. At other times, the lake seems empty. If it doesn't produce for you, then head north over the hill to X–26. It frequently has fast fishing for pan-size brookies. The lakes west of Farmers hold a few surprises too. Large cutthroat roam these lakes. Try the inlets with a salmon-egg fly and look out. You won't catch too many, but you'll only need a couple to make a hearty meal.

Timothy and Carrol Lakes are not far from Farmers. A short day hike of 2 to 4 miles northeast will put you right in the middle of this open basin. Cattle graze up here, which detracts from the aesthetics of the vast tundra, but it's still worth seeing—and definitely worth fishing. Plenty of open shoreline exists for the fly fisher.

Campfires are not allowed within 0.25 mile of Farmers, White Miller, or Timothy and Carrol Lakes. The same campfire restrictions apply to lakes or areas with no name to the southwest and northwest of Farmers Lake.

A fully loaded pack train during archery season on the Swift Creek Trail heading north to Farmers Lake and beyond

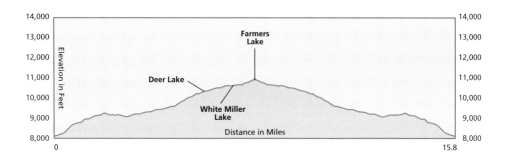

52 TIMOTHY LAKES

Timothy Lakes offer an excellent chance for an "above timberline" experience. A grueling 9-mile hike places you in an open basin where Swift Creek originates. Equestrians and fly fishers adore this area because of the wide-open tundra. Horses have plenty of room to roam, and anglers have plenty of room for back casting. Fishing is a primary reason for coming here. Combine the three Timothy Lakes with the three Carrol Lakes, and you have some of the finest fishing you can find packed into 2 miles.

See map and logistics on pages 135–136.
Start: Swift Creek trailhead
Distance: 18.4 miles out and back
Destination elevation: 11,000 feet

Approximate hiking time: 12 hours
Difficulty: Moderate
Usage: Moderate
Nearest town: Duchesne, Utah
Drainage: Swift Creek

THE HIKE

From Swift Creek trailhead, it's a short distance to where the trail forks left to Yellowstone River or right to Swift Creek. Stay right and climb 5.6 miles to Deer Lake. One option is to continue to Farmers Lake, another 2.3 miles up the valley. From Farmers Lake turn right (east) and go 1.6 mile to the lower Timothy Lake. If skipping Farmers Lake, take the Swift Creek Trail about 1 mile after Deer Lake. This route is 18.4 miles, round-trip.

Good camps can be set up at East Timothy or Center Timothy. At the latter you'll probably see fewer people and will also stand a better chance of locating some spring water. But either place is a good choice. Sometimes cattle range up here, so don't be surprised if you wake up in the morning to the sound of mooing. The 0.25-mile campfire restriction applies to West, Center, and East Timothy, Upper (West) Carrol, East Carrol, and Lower Carrol Lakes. A gas stove is a worthwhile investment if you are planning on cooking some trout.

The trout should cooperate here. Brook trout are in all of these lakes, and cutthroat will appear from time to time. It's hard to recommend the best fishing hole. Try them all. If one lake doesn't produce, scoot over to the next one. You're bound to find at least one lake that will yield some lightning-fast fishing. Check the connecting streams too. Many trout migrate from lake to lake or simply prefer to spend their summer in the creeks. A small spinner can produce some fun action on the streams when your arms tire of fly-casting on the lakes.

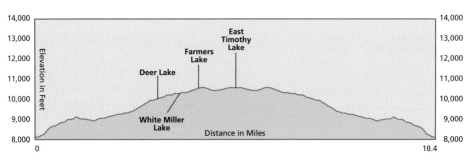

53 MILK LAKE

Milk Lake is for loners. In fact, Milk Lake is a loner itself. Situated high on the east side of the Yellowstone drainage, there are no other lakes for miles in any direction. It's a long, steep hike whether you're following Yellowstone Creek or coming over Bluebell Pass from the Swift Creek drainage. The Swift Creek route is shorter by 3 miles and is the suggested route. You'll need to traverse Bluebell Pass, but it is not bad as mountain passes go, even by horseback.

See map and logistics on pages 135–136.
Start: Swift Creek trailhead
Distance: 24 miles out and back
Destination elevation: 10,983 feet

Approximate hiking time: 15 hours
Difficulty: Moderate to difficult
Usage: Light
Nearest town: Duchesne, Utah
Drainage: Yellowstone River

THE HIKE

If you feel alone and remote at Milk Lake, it's because, well, you are. It's a great feeling. You might feel almost like an explorer in this vast country that rarely sees visitors of the human kind. This is a true wilderness experience. You should be in great physical shape and confident of your skills before coming out here.

From Swift Creek trailhead, it's a short distance to where the trail forks left to Yellowstone River or right to Swift Creek. Stay right and climb 5.5 miles to Deer Lake. Farmers Lake is another 2 miles up the valley. At Farmers Lake turn left (west) past a few small lakes and over Bluebell Pass. The trail descends then turns to the right (north) and follows the small creek up to Milk Lake.

The best camping and horse pastures are located just west or south of the lake. Remember that microscopic parasites can be found anywhere in the High Uintas, even in high, remote alpine lakes. There was a time when people could safely drink from lakes and springs, but filtration systems are easy to carry and a worthwhile precaution.

As for fishing, who knows what to expect. This is the type of water that could produce some quality fishing time. Stocked brook trout can live many seasons without seeing an artificial lure and may have the chance to reach large proportions. If the fish aren't cooperating at Milk, you are out of luck. There's no place else nearby.

Perhaps here it is better to just relax and enjoy the quiet space. You will most certainly have earned it.

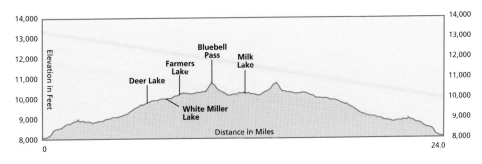

54 NORTH STAR LAKE

Of all the lakes in the High Uintas, North Star is considered to be closest to the exact center of this mountain range. Due to this fact, access is possible from several locations.

See map and logistics on pages 135–136.
Start: Swift Creek trailhead
Distance: 34.8 miles out and back
Destination elevation: 11,395 feet
Approximate hiking time: Variable

Difficulty: Moderate—some steep sections
Usage: Light
Nearest town: Duchesne, Utah
Drainage: Yellowstone River

THE HIKE

The shortest route to North Star is found at Center Park trailhead, but a nicer road and better trailhead amenities launch more treks to North Star from the Swift Creek trailhead. From Swift Creek follow the Yellowstone Creek Trail 9.3 miles to the Garfield Basin junction, then proceed 4 miles northwest up a 1,600-foot incline to Five Point Lake. Past Five Point, keep following the Garfield Basin Trail 3.5 miles north then northeast to the Highline Trail. Then follow the Highline Trail another 0.75 mile north to North Star Lake. Other starting points are at China Meadows, East Fork Blacks Fork, and the Highline trailhead. A slightly longer route is also possible following Yellowstone Creek all the way to Highline.

North Star is a popular stopping point for backpackers making the Highline trek. Although only a few mediocre campsites exist, it is the only decent place to make camp in the area. If you are traveling via the Garfield Basin route, you may want to pitch your tent at Five Point Lake and save North Star Lake as an exciting day hike. The upper portion of Garfield Basin is characterized by rocky, windswept tundra. There is little or no horse pasture, and firewood is extremely scarce.

North Star and Tungsten Lakes receive moderate angling pressure for brook and cutthroat trout. If you are looking for more solitude and more remote fishing possibilities, try lakes Y–2, Y–4, and Y–5. These lakes receive little attention and harbor an excellent supply of pan-size brook trout. Find these lakes by following the inlet of North Star Lake 1 mile north to Y–2. Then just follow a string of lakes to Y–4, Y-5, and Y-6. Sorry, there are no fish at Y–6.

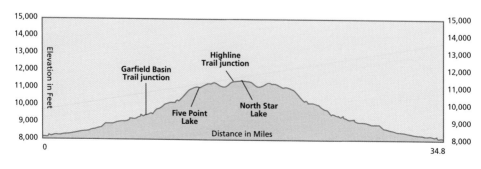

A look at Garfield Basin from Porcupine Pass, with North Star Lake at center above the shadow line. PHOTO BY MATT MCKELL/UTAH DIVISION OF WILDLIFE RESOURCES

55 KINGS PEAK VIA THE SOUTH SLOPE (SWIFT CREEK OR UINTA)

Kings Peak, the highest point in the state of Utah, is the most popular destination of peak baggers in the High Uintas and in the entire Beehive State. Novice mountaineers with no special equipment can even reach it. However, it is a long, steep hike to the top of the 13,528-foot summit. Good health and conditioning are a must.

More than 10,000 people attempt to reach the top of Utah each year according to the nonprofit group Friends of Kings Peak.

There are several routes to the top of Kings Peak, all of them long and each providing a different backcountry hiking experience. This chapter describes two approaches from the South Slope. No matter the route, hikers should plan to head to the top early in the morning and return by early afternoon to avoid the trademark afternoon thunderstorms on the High Uintas. These summer storms frequently include lightning, and the highest point in Utah is the last place you want to be when the electrified bolts are coming from the sky. To time this correctly, most hikers plan at least one overnight at a nearby lake, basin, or pass—although from the south you'll likely need two or more nights of backpacking preparedness.

See map on pages 147 and 149 and logistics on pages 135 and 151.
Start: Swift Creek or Uinta trailhead
Distance: 39.6 to 49 miles out and back
Destination elevation: 13,528 feet

Approximate hiking time: Variable
Difficulty: Difficult—steep sections
Usage: Light
Nearest town: Duchesne, Utah
Drainage: Yellowstone River or Uinta River

THE HIKES

In addition to increased distance, South Slope trails to Kings Peak also add 2,000 feet (or much, much more) of elevation change. The Swift Creek Trail starts at the Swift Creek campground, which serves as the access point to the Swift Creek and Yellowstone drainages. From the Swift Creek trailhead, it is 0.4 mile until the trail splits at the junction of Trails 057 and 056. Trail 056 climbs up the ridge and into the Swift Creek drainage, past Farmers Lake, and over Bluebell Pass before dropping back down into the Yellowstone drainage and rejoining Trail 057 at around 14 miles. Because of the extra pass, this route adds another 1,200 feet in elevation gain and around 2.5 miles one way, but it has more mountain views. It's 4 miles to the junction with Highline 025. Turn right onto Trail 025 and continue for 3.5 miles through the alpine and scrub forest to the cirque basin below Kings Peak. Here the trail climbs up Anderson Pass below Kings Peak. Then turn right for the last 0.6 mile of careful boulder hopping. Traveling to Kings Peak and back on the same path you'll hit 45 miles.

For the "shorter," nearly 40-mile round-trip route from Swift Creek, turn left onto Trail 057; the trail parallels the Yellowstone River for 15.2 miles until reaching the

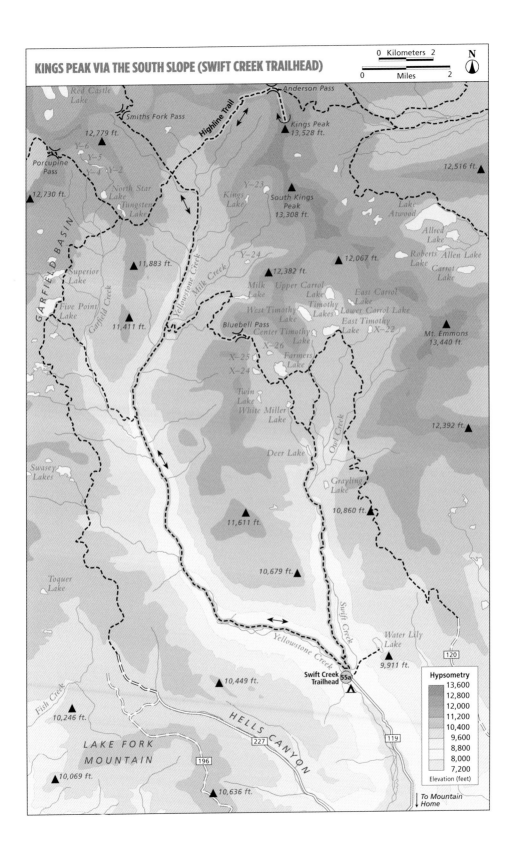

0   Kilometers   2

0   Miles   2

N

Red Castle
Lake

Smiths Fork Pass

Highline Trail

Anderson Pass

Kings Peak
13,528 ft.

12,779 ft.

12,516 ft.

Y-6
Y-5
Porcupine
Pass
Y-4 Y-2

North Star
Lake
Tungsten
Lake

Kings
Lake

Y-23

South Kings
Peak
13,308 ft.

Lake
Atwood

12,730 ft.

GARFIELD BASIN

Superior
Lake

11,883 ft.

Y-24

12,067 ft.

Allred
Lake

Roberts Allen Lake
Lake   Carrot
Lake

12,382 ft.

Milk
Lake

Upper Carrol
Lake

East Carrol
Lake
Timothy   Lower Carrol Lake
Lakes
East Timothy
Lake   X-22

Mt. Emmons
13,440 ft.

Five Point
Lake

11,411 ft.

Yellowstone Creek

Milk Creek

Garfield Creek

West Timothy
Lake
Bluebell Pass
Center Timothy
Lake

X-26

X-25
X-24

Farmers
Lake

Twin
Lake
White Miller
Lake

Deer Lake

Owl Creek

12,392 ft.

Swasey
Lakes

11,611 ft.

Grayling
Lake

10,860 ft.

Toquer
Lake

10,679 ft.

Swift Creek

Water Lily
Lake

9,911 ft.

120

10,449 ft.

Swift Creek
Trailhead 65a

Yellowstone Creek

Fish Creek

10,246 ft.

HELLS CANYON

227

119

LAKE FORK
MOUNTAIN

196

10,069 ft.

10,636 ft.

Hypsometry

	13,600
	12,800
	12,000
	11,200
	10,400
	9,600
	8,800
	8,000
	7,200

Elevation (feet)

↓ To Mountain
Home

The view from the top of Utah in the direction of nearby South Kings Peak. PHOTO BY MATT MCKELL/UTAH DIVISION OF WILDLIFE RESOURCES

Hikers enter designated Wilderness at around 6 miles from the Uinta trailhead, the longest but very scenic route to Kings Peak.

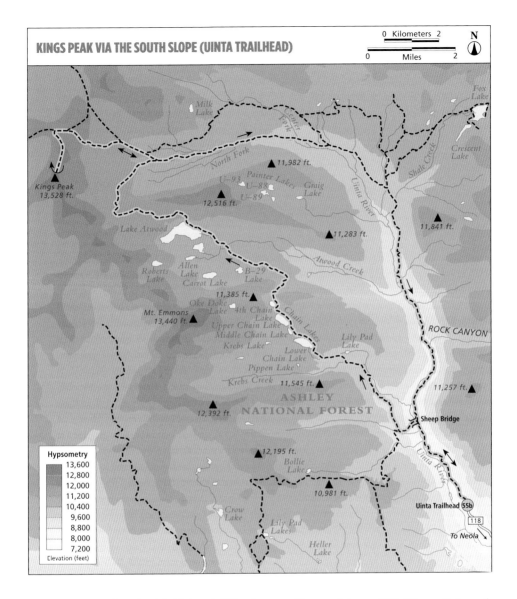

junction of Trails 025, 054, and 057 where you'll turn right on 025. The trail through the Yellowstone drainage combines the Uinta's signature rocky trails with marshes and creek and river crossings, but trades in the mountain views for long stretches through dense forest.

Most people take four days and three nights for this trip. This route gets you away from the crowds of Henrys Fork.

An even more leisurely option (read: longer) is the 46- to 49 mile round-trip route from Uinta trailhead. (See directions to the trailhead in the next chapter.) There is time to relax, soak up the adventure, and go fishing. There are loop options, or you could arrange a shuttle by friends or family to drop you off and meet you at a different trailhead a couple of weeks later.

Hikers should consider this as a multiple-day excursion with plenty to see and fish to catch along the way. Many make this a five-day, four-night outing, and some spend an entire week.

Start at the Uinta trailhead (sometimes labeled Wandin Campground) and follow the old road 0.8 mile to the Smokey Springs Day Use Area. Stay to the right. Then follow the trail along the Uinta River through the forest for 3 miles to the sheep bridge crossing the river. The trail splits at this point. The shorter trail 044 heads up the Uinta River drainage, turning west (left) at around 13 miles and continuing 11 miles to Kings Peak. (Uinta River Trail 044 meets Highline 025 in Painter Basin approximately 20 miles into the hike.)

The other route from Uinta trailhead adds about 1.5 miles one way and logs 7,250 feet in elevation gain thanks to two additional passes—but by extension is incredibly scenic. It crosses the sheep bridge at 3.8 miles to Trail 043 as described in Chain Lakes and Lake Atwood in the next chapter. Once on 043 you will start hitting a series of switchbacks, climbing more than 1,000 feet over 5 miles to Lower Chain Lake.

The trail passes the four lakes of Chain Lakes—possible camping areas—and then heads over Roberts Pass to the Lake Atwood Basin. Continue past Lake Atwood—surrounded by Allred Lake, Allen Lake, Carrot Lake, B–29 Lake, and Lake George Beard, all possible camp spots. The main trail then climbs over Trail Rider Pass and drops into the Painter Basin below Kings Peak. Once at the three-way junction of Trails 043, 044, and 025, turn west on 025. Another option from 025 after another mile is to take Trail 068 at the junction to Gunsight Pass and then the Dome Peak Cutoff from Henrys Fork trail to the top.

UINTA TRAILHEAD

The first time I drove across the bridge over the Uinta River, I had to stop the car and get out. I had not seen so much water coming out of the Uintas before, being accustomed to hiking and fishing as a kid around the smaller Upper Prove River off Highway 150. Up the canyon, there are a couple dozen basic tent sites along the river, spread between a campground and a group area—sometimes accessible earlier in the season given the mostly paved access and relatively low 7,700 feet in elevation.

Hikes begin at the picnic area and signed "Uinta Trailhead." It's sometimes labeled Wandin Campground on maps, but signage at the trailhead indicates camping is not permitted. The road is typically closed beyond, adding around 0.8 mile of dirt road travel to the hikes. Though fishing and horseback expeditions no longer depart from the defunct U Bar Wilderness Ranch, expect plenty of equestrian traffic on these trails. As always, carry bug spray, watch your step, and take your time—this is an extremely rocky drainage. Even if you don't summit Kings Peak as described above, there are plenty of reasons to extend your stay. The following trails can easily combine into a scenic loop of 40 or more miles.

See trails 56 through 58 for Uinta Trailhead.
Maps: USGS Bollie Lake, USGS Fox Lake, USGS Mount Emmons, and USGS Kings Peak; *USDA Forest Service High Uintas Wilderness*; *Trails Illustrated High Uintas Wilderness*

Trail contacts: Ashley National Forest, Forest Supervisor, 355 North Vernal Ave., Vernal, UT 84078, (435) 781-1181; Duchesne Ranger District, 85 West Main, Duchesne, UT 84021, (435) 738-2482

FINDING THE TRAILHEAD

From Heber City, take US 40 east 99 miles to Roosevelt. Then take SR 121 north for 11 miles to Neola. Head north 17 miles on the mostly paved Road 118, 0.8 mile past the Uinta Canyon Campground to the marked trailhead.

The Uinta trailhead has room for forty vehicles; amenities include toilets and a stock ramp. There is no water at the trailhead. Camping is available at Uinta Canyon Carnpground.

Popular with hikers and horse packs, Uinta Canyon trails are long, rocky, often steep, and always beautiful.

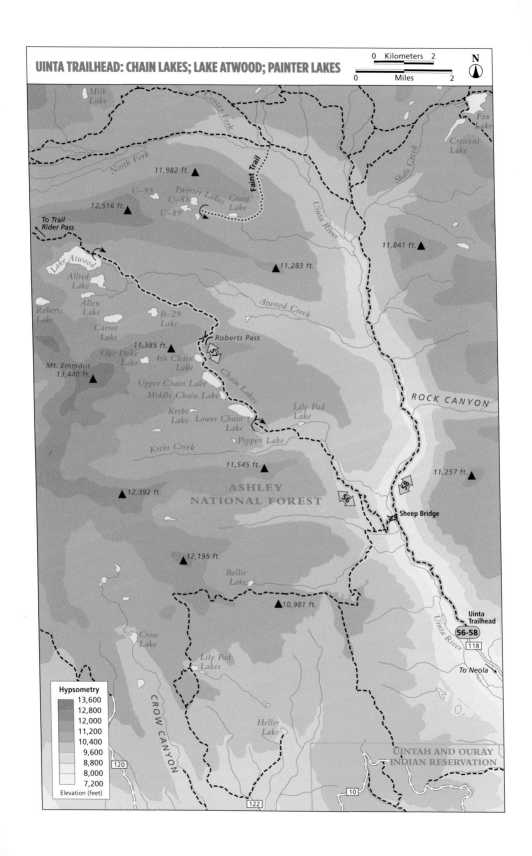

0 Kilometers 2

0 Miles 2

N

Milk Lake

Center Fork

Fox Lake

North Fork

Crescent Lake

11,982 ft. ▲

Faint Trail

Shale Creek

U-93

12,516 ft. ▲

Painter Lakes
U-88
U-89

Graig Lake

Uinta River

11,841 ft. ▲

To Trail Rider Pass

Lake Atwood

11,283 ft. ▲

Allred Lake

Atwood Creek

Allen Lake

Roberts Lake

B-29 Lake

Carrot Lake

Roberts Pass

ROCK CANYON

11,385 ft. ▲

57

Oke Doke Lake

4th Chain Lake

Mt. Emmons
13,440 ft. ▲

Chain Lakes

Upper Chain Lake

Middle Chain Lake

Krebs Lake

Lower Chain Lake

Lily Pad Lake

Pippen Lake

Krebs Creek

11,545 ft. ▲

11,257 ft. ▲

ASHLEY
NATIONAL FOREST

58

12,392 ft. ▲

56

Sheep Bridge

12,195 ft. ▲

Bollie Lake

10,981 ft. ▲

Uinta River

Uinta Trailhead

56-58

118

Crow Lake

To Neola

Lily Pad Lakes

CROW CANYON

Hypsometry

13,600
12,800
12,000
11,200
10,400
9,600
8,800
8,000
7,200

Elevation (feet)

Heller Lake

UINTAH AND OURAY
INDIAN RESERVATION

120

10

122

56 CHAIN LAKES

Chain Lakes are three connecting reservoirs and one natural lake. Campsites and horse pasture are somewhat limited at all four lakes, but they receive heavy camping and fishing anyway—and at times hikers report seeing more equestrians than hikers on this trail. During the late summer months, the reservoirs experience serious fluctuation, and angling pressure decreases rapidly. However, from July to mid-August pan-size brookies are abundant at all reservoirs and should produce fast fishing. Chain #4 is a natural lake located up a few steep switchbacks on a plateau. Anglers don't utilize this lake as much as the others, but this is often the best fishing hole during late summer.

See map and logistics on pages 151–152.
Start: Uinta trailhead
Distance: 19 to 20.2 miles out and back
Destination elevation: 10,893 feet

Approximate hiking time: 11 to 12 hours
Difficulty: Moderate—some steep sections
Usage: Heavy
Nearest town: Roosevelt, Utah
Drainage: Uinta River

THE HIKE

Access to Chain Lakes begins at the Uinta trailhead. After 0.8 mile along an old road, stay to the right and follow the rocky Uinta River Trail 3 miles north to a signed fork. Veer left (west) to the Sheep Bridge. Proceed east across the footbridge and up a thousand feet of rocky switchbacks before entering the High Uintas Wilderness area at around the 6-mile mark. Catch your breath, then follow the trail about 3 miles northwest to Krebs Basin and another mile to Lower Chain Lake. Campfires and wood stoves are prohibited within 0.25 mile of lakes in Chain Lakes Basin. Check with the Forest Service before pasturing, as overnight horse grazing may also be prohibited within 0.25 mile on either side of the trail from Lower Chain Lake to Upper Chain Lake.

A good place to set up base camp is Pippen Lake (sometimes called Island Lake). It sits in a meadow 0.5 mile southwest of Lower Chain's outlet. Pippen is distinguished by a small island near the south end of the shore and has excellent meadowland campsites. Plenty of horse pasture dominates the surrounding terrain. Pippen is one of the better

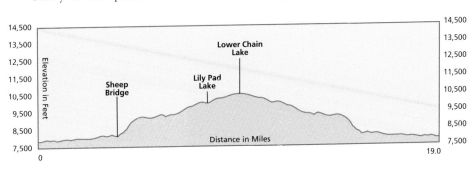

Morning at Lower Chain Lake, beneath a big sky and sporting an empty shoreline

fly-fishing lakes in the Uinta River drainage and sustains moderate angling use throughout the summer. You should have no problem filling your skillet with fresh mountain brook trout.

If you're looking to get off the beaten path, Oke Doke Lake is a good spot. This handsome lake is just 1 mile from Fourth Chain Lake. From Fourth Chain Lake or Roberts Pass, head west along the south side of the ridge that extends from Mount Emmons. Oke Doke Lake is on the eastern base of Mount Emmons in a high cirque. No campsites or horse pasture exists. Light angling pressure often means exciting fishing for cunning cutthroat trout.

57 LAKE ATWOOD

Lake Atwood houses one of the largest brook trout populations in the High Uintas. With this in mind, you just may want to throw your line in here and forget about all the surrounding lakes. That said, Atwood receives most of the attention in this basin, and angling may be hampered by semi-crowded shorelines. Allred and Mount Emmons Lakes have the same problem. Although fast fishing usually occurs, so do crowds. This is partly because Atwood and Allred offer the best camping opportunities in Atwood Basin. Lake Atwood loses much of its appeal later in the summer, when it draws down about 15 feet.

See map and logistics on pages 151–152
Start: Uinta trailhead
Distance: 28.6 miles out and back
Destination elevation: 11,030 feet
Approximate hiking time: 16 hours

Difficulty: Difficult—some steep sections
Usage: Moderate
Nearest town: Roosevelt, Utah
Drainage: Uinta River

THE HIKE

From Uinta trailhead, take the rocky Uinta River Trail 3.8 miles north to a signed fork and veer left (west) to the Sheep Bridge. Cross the bridge and climb 1,000 feet of rocky switchbacks over 6 miles to Lower Chain Lake. Continue on the same trail 2 miles over Roberts Pass and into the Atwood Creek drainage. Lake Atwood is 3.6 miles northwest along the trail from the top of the pass. (One of the best ascents to the nearby 13,440-foot Mount Emmons climbs a steep ridge north and then west. The route departs the Atwood trail just before the Roberts Pass switchbacks north of Fourth Chain Lake.)

Other lakes in Atwood Basin include Roberts, George Beard, Carrot, and B–29. Roberts Lake is a typical alpine lake located in a cirque basin 1 mile southwest of Atwood. Follow a faint trail 1.5 miles west from Mount Emmons Lake. No campsites exist in this small windy basin, so angling pressure remains light for feisty cutthroat trout.

Two miles west on the trail from Atwood lies George Beard Lake (U–21). This lake sits in windswept terrain just below Trail Rider Pass. Most people ignore this water

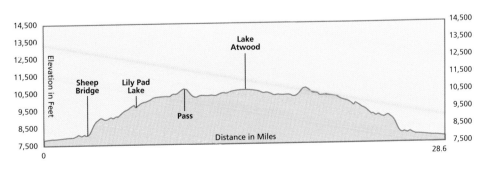

The Uinta trail forks at the 3.8-mile mark.

because there is no shelter, but this makes perfect conditions for the avid angler. That is, if there's fast fishing for wild trout—and there is. George Beard Lake contains a huge supply of wild brookies. Another lake that might be worth checking out, U–19, sits just 0.5 mile south of George Beard. Not many anglers make it this far.

58 PAINTER LAKES

Painter Lakes take after their name. They are scattered about like little dabs of acrylic on a painter's palette. This beautiful wilderness is characterized by gentle rolling hills and timbered terrain. Due to the remoteness and difficult travel to this basin, Painter Lakes remain blissfully free of people and debris.

See map and logistics on pages 151–152.
Start: Uinta trailhead
Distance: 32.5 miles out and back
Destination elevation: 11,030 feet

Approximate hiking time: 18 hours
Difficulty: High—cross-country travel
Usage: Light
Nearest town: Roosevelt, Utah
Drainage: Uinta River

THE HIKE

From Uinta trailhead, take the Uinta River Trail 3.8 miles north to the fork and continue straight on the trail up the Uinta River 9 miles to the junction with the trail coming down from Kidney Lakes. Stay left (northwest) 2 miles, following the Uinta River to North Fork Park. From North Fork Park, follow a vague trail 2 miles south up a steep and rugged 900-foot incline next to a small creek. The first lake you'll run into is Craig.

Craig is the only lake in this basin with a horse pasture; it also contains a good population of cutthroat trout. Although good campsites exist at Craig Lake, better accommodations exist at Painter Lakes U–88 and U–89. Following the inlet of Craig Lake 1 mile west, you'll find the first two Painter Lakes. These lakes sit only 100 yards apart. U–88 is the largest lake in the basin, so fishing may be better at this lake than at any of the others. Angling pressure is almost nil, and eager brook trout should be fighting one another to get to your lure first. But don't forget U–89. This lake fluctuates like a toilet bowl, but you never know; a big one may be lurking in its depths. Situated deep in the western part of Painter Lakes Basin is Lake U–93, located 0.75 mile west of U–88. U–93 is above timberline at an elevation of 11,400 feet, and there are no campsites or horse pasture. Angling is unpredictable. These cutthroat either bite or they don't, and if they do, they are small. Unless you're just out for a pleasure stroll, other lakes like U–88 and Craig will better fulfill your fishing desires.

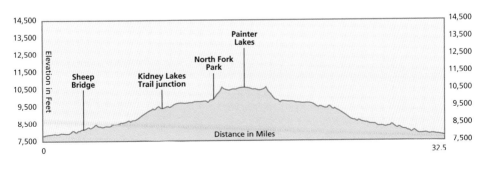

Follow the Uinta River north to Painter Lakes.

WEST FORK WHITEROCKS TRAILHEAD

There are a number of long, improved dirt roads that climb high onto the South Slope. West Fork Whiterocks presents the chance to explore multiple trailheads from one such road. A short 0.5-mile spur road about 7 miles before the Chepeta trailhead carries drivers to West Fork Whiterocks. The narrow FR 109 opens to a surprisingly spacious parking area suitable for multiple vehicles and trucks with stock trailers. From there, enjoy easy access to the West Fork and a set of outstanding, though often rocky, long-distance trails perfect for well-conditioned, surefooted backpackers and well-prepared equestrians—indeed, there's a lot of horse traffic here, so be sure to yield and watch your step. There are a couple of ATV-only trails (235 and 306) cutting northwest that offer access to additional trailheads and there are multiple loop options, including multi-day routes over high mountain passes.

See trails 59 through 62 for West Fork Whiterocks Trailhead.
Maps: USGS Fox Lake and USGS Chepeta Lake, *USDA Forest Service High Uintas Wilderness, Trails Illustrated High Uintas Wilderness*

Trail contacts: Ashley National Forest, Forest Supervisor, 355 North Vernal Ave., Vernal, UT 84078, (435) 781-1181

FINDING THE TRAILHEAD

From Heber City, take US 40 east 99 miles to Roosevelt. Then take SR 121 north for 11 miles to Neola. Follow SR 121 east about 5 miles to a junction. From the junction, follow a paved road north 3 miles to the town of Whiterocks. Keep on the road, heading north for 4 miles to another junction. At this point, follow Road 117, which winds east then north 18 miles to Pole Creek Junction. Then take Road 110 about 4 miles north to the West Fork junction. From here it's about 1 mile northwest to the West Fork trailhead; the road continues north another 7 miles to the Chepeta trailhead. There are numerous 4WD roads in the area, so stay on the road most traveled.

West Fork Whiterocks has parking for thirty vehicles as well as toilets, corrals, and a stock-unloading ramp.

Like Uinta Canyon, West Fork Whiterocks is a rocky drainage popular among equestrians and hikers with good ankles.

WEST FORK WHITEROCKS TRAILHEAD: QUEANT LAKE; FOX LAKE; KIDNEY LAKE; DAVIS LAKES

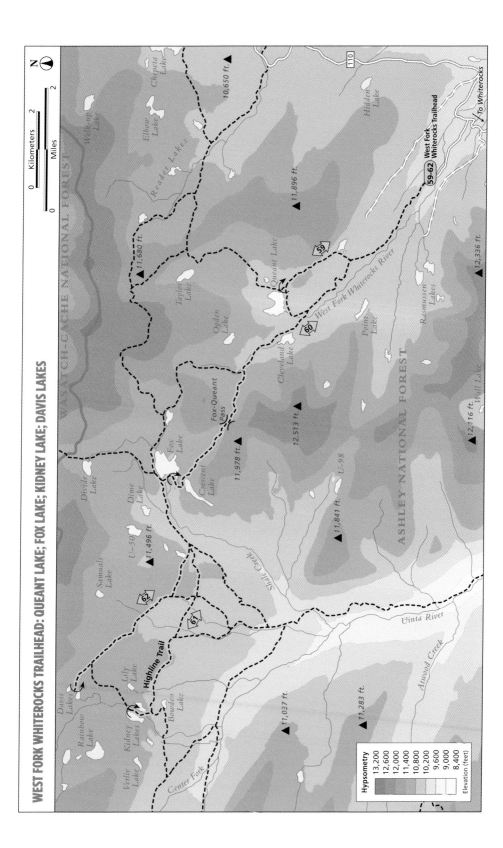

N

0   1   Kilometers   2

0   1   Miles   2

WASATCH-CACHE NATIONAL FOREST

ASHLEY NATIONAL FOREST

110

To Whiterocks

West Fork Whiterocks Trailhead
59-62

59

60

62

61

Highline Trail

West Fork Whiterocks River

Uinta River

Atwood Creek

Slate Creek

Center Fork

Chepeta Lake
Elbow Lake
Reader Lakes
Walk-up Lake
Taylor Lake
Ogden Lake
Queant Lake
Hidden Lake
Point Lake
Cleveland Lake
Rasmussen Lakes
Wall Lake
Fox-Queant Pass
Fox Lake
Crescent Lake
Divide Lake
Dime Lake
Samuals Lake
Davis Lakes
Rainbow Lake
Verlie Lake
Kidney Lakes
Lily Lake
Bowden Lake

10,650 ft.
11,896 ft.
11,680 ft.
12,336 ft.
12,116 ft.
12,513 ft.
11,978 ft.
11,841 ft.
1,496 ft.
11,037 ft.
11,283 ft.

U-98
U-50

Hypsometry

Elevation (feet)
13,200
12,600
12,000
11,400
10,800
10,200
9,600
9,000
8,400

59 QUEANT LAKE

A gentle hike, great camping, and a chance to get away from the campground masses—perhaps these are the reasons Queant Lake is so popular. While you're likely to have neighbors here, it's a whole lot better than spending the night with the RVs and roadside tenters. Besides, not all backpackers are loners. Many actually enjoy a little company, as long as backcountry etiquette is followed.

See map and logistics on pages 160–161.
Start: West Fork Whiterocks trailhead
Distance: 10 miles out and back
Destination elevation: 10,652 feet

Approximate hiking time: 7 hours
Difficulty: Easy, but long
Usage: Heavy
Nearest town: Roosevelt, Utah
Drainage: Whiterocks River

THE HIKE

From West Fork Whiterocks trailhead, the trail goes northwest 2 miles to a junction with the trail to Queant Lake. Turn right (northeast) in 0.5 mile to a small lake, then travel 2.5 miles northwest to the lake. Queant is also accessible by staying to the left on the West Fork Whiterocks Trail (048C) toward Fox and veering northeast at around 4.5 miles.

Queant Lake is big enough to handle several large groups. It's a long walk around its 57 acres, and there are plenty of campsites, horse pasture, and treatable spring water. Look for the latter along the northern shore. You will have little difficulty finding a ready-made camp. All you'll have to do is move in.

If Queant doesn't suit your tastes, head north another 0.75 mile to Ogden Lake. It sees far fewer hikers than Queant and offers just as many amenities. Campsites and horse pasture are abundant, and a large spring flows into the north end.

Angling at Queant, Ogden, and Cleveland Lakes may be only fair. This area entertains a lot of anglers. Plan on working a little harder here than you would on some of the more remote lakes, and stay with the basics. Small flies (#16) in the late evening and early morning should yield at least enough trout for a pleasant meal. There is also a good-looking stream below Queant that should produce some small trout.

Queant Lake is a great place to introduce someone to backpacking, particularly youngsters. The trip is not taxing, and there is a ton of room to run and explore without leaving the proximity of the lake. Everyone has to begin somewhere, and Queant Lake provides an ideal setting for beginners.

The West Fork of the Whiterocks River is an excellent fishing stream and the route to Queant Lake.

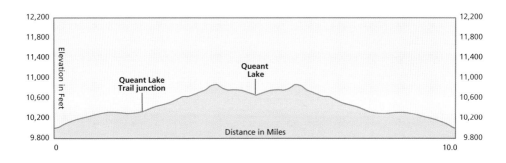

60 **FOX LAKE**

Although Fox is a primitive lake, it just doesn't always boast all the hallmarks of a designated Wilderness area. Large groups of campers bring horses loaded with all their "essentials" and settle in for a good time. Those who prefer a place that is a little less conspicuous may need to look elsewhere, depending on when you visit. Fox Lake gets more than its share of high-impact camping.

See map and logistics on pages 160–161.
Start: West Fork Whiterocks trailhead
Distance: 17 miles out and back
Destination elevation: 10,790 feet

Approximate hiking time: 11 hours
Difficulty: Difficult—due to Fox-Queant Pass
Usage: Heavy
Nearest town: Roosevelt, Utah
Drainage: Uinta River

THE HIKE

The best access to Fox begins at West Fork Whiterocks trailhead. From the trailhead, the trail goes northwest 2 miles to a junction with the trail to Queant Lake. Stay left (northwest) for 1.5 miles to Cleveland Lake. It's another 3.5 miles over the 11,388-foot Fox-Queant Pass to Crescent and Fox Lakes. Another route that is well traveled by horses starts in the Uinta River drainage. This trail runs next to the Uinta River for 10 miles to a three-way junction. At this point, take the northeast trail 3.5 miles up Shale Creek to Fox Lake.

Fox is a fluctuating reservoir that experiences a serious drawdown during the late summer months, and fishing success declines with the water level. Despite this, the lake frequently hosts large groups of backpackers or horse packs and had been a favorite of area Scouts. Campsites are found around the lake, while horse pastures are located north of Fox and west of Crescent Lake. Overall fishing pressure is considered moderate for brook and cutthroat trout.

Just southwest of Fox is Crescent Lake, a long narrow reservoir that fluctuates only moderately. Camping areas are all around the lake, but groups often have them occupied during the midsummer months. Angling usage is quite heavy at times. Best results may occur in the late evening while casting off the rocks. Cutthroat trout are the main species, but an occasional brookie may show up.

Other lakes in the Fox Lake area are Dollar, Brook, and Divide. Dollar Lake is sometimes called Dime Lake. This aesthetic lake is in a large meadow 1 mile northwest of Fox

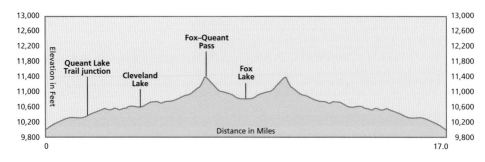

and features better-than-average campsites along with a generous supply of horse pasture. A good number of pan-size brookies inhabit the lake. As with the other lakes around here, Dollar sometimes receives heavy use from large groups that migrate from Fox Lake. Your best bet to escape the crowds is Brook Lake. It lies 1 mile east of Fox near the trail. Camping areas are available, and pressure is remarkably light. There is a 0.25 mile campfire restriction around Fox, Crescent, and Dime Lakes.

61 KIDNEY LAKES

Several lakes make up the Kidney Lakes Basin, and most receive substantial camping or fishing use. Kidney Lakes are no exception. Large recreational groups usually occupy both Kidney Lakes. Plenty of campsites can be found between the lakes and around West Kidney. Fishing is often good for brook trout and an occasional 1-pound rainbow. Moose are often seen feeding in the shallows of both Kidney Lakes. Be aware of these large animals and give them their space. Although usually docile, an upset moose is extremely dangerous.

See map and logistics on pages 160–161.
Start: West Fork Whiterocks trailhead
Distance: 25.1 miles out and back
Destination elevation: 10,850 feet

Approximate hiking time: 16 hours
Difficulty: Difficult—due to Fox-Queant Pass
Usage: Heavy
Nearest town: Roosevelt, Utah
Drainage: Uinta River

THE HIKE

Five different access points can be used for the Kidney Lakes area. The shortest route begins at the West Fork Whiterocks trailhead. The others start at Uinta River, Chepeta Lake, Hoop Lake, and Spirit Lake. But they are at least 3 miles longer. Excellent trails exist for each route, and stock-unloading ramps are present at every trailhead except Chepeta Lake.

From West Fork Whiterocks trailhead, the trail goes northwest 2 miles to a junction with the trail to Queant Lake. Stay left (northwest) for 1.5 miles to Cleveland Lake. It's another 4.5 miles over Fox-Queant Pass to Crescent and Fox Lakes. After you pass Fox Lake, there's a trail junction with the Highline Trail (025) just under 0.5 mile farther. Stay right (west) 0.5 mile to a junction with the trail to Davis Lakes. Stay on the Highline Trail (southwest) 3.2 miles to Kidney Lakes, turning north off the Highline Trail for the last 0.25 mile.

For secluded camping, try nearby Bowden or Lily Lake. Bowden has limited campsites but an endless supply of horse pasture. Lily is a quaint little lake surrounded by yellow water lilies. Campsites with horse pastures are just west of the lake. Lily receives only light pressure, even though it's only 0.5 mile from the Kidney Lakes.

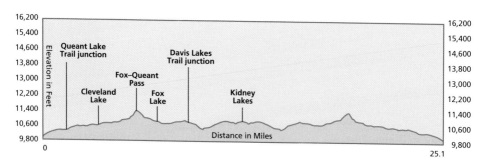

The first of many river and creek crossings on the long trail to Kidney Lakes

Along a well-marked trail, about a mile northwest of Kidney Lakes lies Rainbow Lake. The trail also leads to numerous lakes in the upper northwest portion of the basin (and completes a loop with the Davis Lakes Trail). These lakes are in high, windswept country. There are no decent camps up here. Rainbow Lake sees moderate to heavy fishing pressure but is mostly limited to day use. Don't forget about the lakes located above Rainbow Lake. These small bodies of water may bring a nice surprise, and the ones just below are certainly worth checking out. Expect to find a good mixture of brookies, rainbows, and cutthroat.

Nearby Davis Lakes present good angling opportunities too. They are a little over 1 mile north of Kidney Lakes and 250 yards north and south of each other. Both lakes get light use, and fly fishing can be fast for pan-size brookies.

There is a 0.25-mile campfire restriction in the Upper Uinta Basin, around Kidney Lakes and Verlie, Rainbow, Wilderness, Bowden, and Weeping Ledge Lakes, plus southwest of Kidney Lakes and north of Rainbow Lake .

62 DAVIS LAKES

Nestled in a high cirque, Davis Lakes offer a true alpine experience. The surrounding hills are composed of lush green grasses and scattered pines that may remind you of the Swiss Alps. Equestrians will appreciate all the space, pasture, and water for their animals, as well as the fact that horses cannot really roam any higher thanks to the steep divide rising behind them.

See map and logistics on pages 160–161.
Start: West Fork Whiterocks trailhead
Distance: 26 miles out and back
Destination elevation: 11,020 feet

Approximate hiking time: 16 hours
Difficulty: Difficult—due to Fox-Queant Pass
Usage: Light
Nearest town: Roosevelt, Utah
Drainage: Uinta River

THE HIKE

Davis Lakes are a little off the beaten path and don't see a lot of visitors. From West Fork Whiterocks trailhead, the trail goes northwest 2 miles to a junction with the trail to Queant Lake. Stay left (northwest) for 1.5 miles to Cleveland Lake. It's another 3.5 miles to Crescent and Fox Lakes. After you pass Fox Lake, there's a trail junction with the Highline Trail after around 0.5 mile. Follow Highline 0.7 mile to another trail junction with the trail to Davis Lakes. Turn right (north) and go 3.3 miles to Davis Lakes. The last 0.5 mile is cross-country travel to the northwest.

A loop trail passes just below Davis South. It can be accessed from either Kidney Lakes, or if you're coming from Fox Lake, by taking the Davis Lakes turnoff about 2 miles from Fox Lake. A sign marks the turnoff, and regardless of which trail you take, it is hard to follow in places. Keep your compass and map handy, and keep pointed toward the large cirque in the mountainside.

Best camping facilities are on the south side of Davis South Lake. A spacious existing campsite should accommodate groups of up to eight people. Treatable spring water flows into Davis South along the north shore. There is a 0.25-mile campfire restriction around Davis Lakes.

The north shore is also the deepest and is where most of the fish are. Plump, pan-size brookies can be easily harvested using a small fly or woolly worm. There is plenty of open shoreline where fly casters can have a ball. You won't catch big fish here, but you

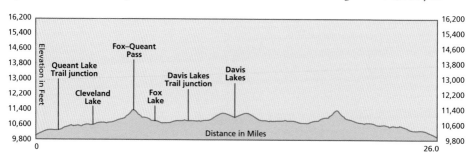

will probably catch as many as you want, for as long you want. Small brook trout also inhabit Davis North Lake but may be tougher to fool. For a change of pace, try fishing the small stream between the lakes or the outlet stream from Davis South.

Don't be surprised to see moose in the area. The large mammals are common between Davis Lakes and Kidney Lakes. Enjoy them at a distance, and you'll probably see them often. There are also deer and elk around, but they are much more wary.

CHEPETA TRAILHEAD

It's remarkable how far into the Uinta Mountains FR 110 reaches. Where it terminates at the rocky-shored Chepeta Lake, the road hits the Highline Trail, the range's famously high-elevation and remote point-to-point route. For that reason, Chepeta makes for an alternate starting point to Highline or a resupply stop. Friends or Trail Angels have been known to leave non-perishable, nutrient-dense foods sealed in plastic bags inside the vault restroom.

At 10,568 feet, Chepeta Lake is just south and east of the designated High Uintas Wilderness boundary, and only 3.5 miles as the crow flies from the North Slope's Spirit Lake—but it'd be a 14-mile hike over an 11,780-foot pass. There's no campground, but there are a few lakes to fish—Chepeta is stocked with brook trout that are ideally pursued from rubber rafts—and a variety of hiking distances, not to mention the chance to hike Highline, even if only for a few miles. Chances are you'll want to return for more.

See trails 63 through 65 for Chepeta Trailhead.
Maps: USGS Chepeta Lake and USGS Paradise Park, *USDA Forest Service High Uintas Wilderness*, *Trails Illustrated High Uintas Wilderness*

Trail contacts: Ashley National Forest, Forest Supervisor, 355 North Vernal Ave., Vernal, UT 84078, (435) 781-1181

FINDING THE TRAILHEAD

From Heber City, take US 40 east 99 miles to Roosevelt. Then take SR 121 north for 11 miles to Neola. Follow SR 121 east about 5 miles to a junction. From the junction, follow a paved road north 3 miles to the town of Whiterocks. Keep on the road, heading north for 4 miles to another junction. At this point, follow Road 117, which winds east then north 18 miles to Pole Creek Junction. Then take Road 110 about 11 miles north to the Chepeta Lake trailhead. There are ten parking spots, horse corrals, and vault restrooms.

A backpacker sets out on the 65-mile Highline Trail journey from Chepeta Trailhead to Hayden Peak.

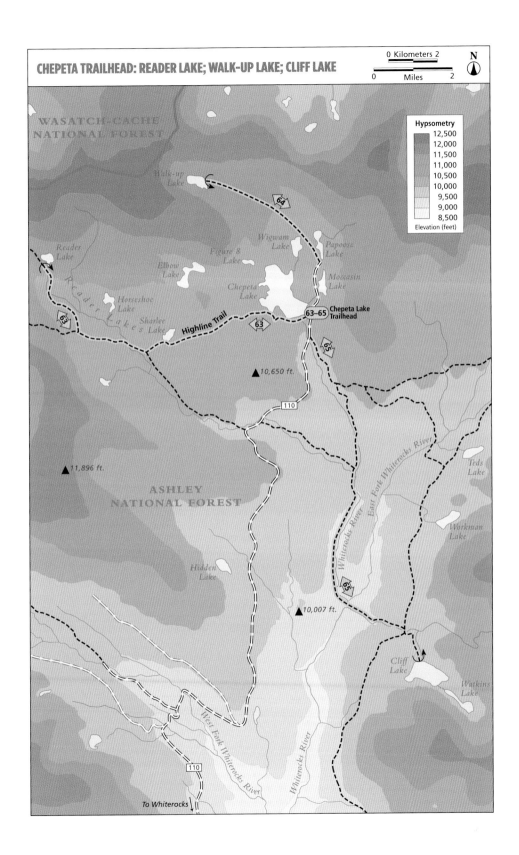

CHEPETA TRAILHEAD: READER LAKE; WALK-UP LAKE; CLIFF LAKE

0 Kilometers 2

0 Miles 2

N

Hypsometry

12,500
12,000
11,500
11,000
10,500
10,000
9,500
9,000
8,500
Elevation (feet)

WASATCH-CACHE
NATIONAL FOREST

Walk-up
Lake

64

Wigwam
Lake

Papoose
Lake

Reader
Lake

Figure 8
Lake

Elbow
Lake

Moccasin
Lake

R
e
a
d
e
r

Horseshoe
Lake

Chepeta
Lake

Chepeta Lake
Trailhead

Sharlee
Lake

L
a
k
e
s

63–65

63

Highline Trail

63

65

▲10,650 ft.

110

▲11,896 ft.

ASHLEY
NATIONAL FOREST

Teds
Lake

East Fork Whiterocks River

Workman
Lake

Hidden
Lake

Whiterocks River

65

▲10,007 ft.

Cliff
Lake

Watkins
Lake

West Fork Whiterocks River

Whiterocks River

110

To Whiterocks

63 **READER LAKE**

You might take a hint from this lake's name and bring a good book to read and binoculars to watch for wildlife. This is a good place to be alone and relax. Reader Lake is no longer managed as a fishery but does get some trout moving in from Reader Creek. Here is a respite for the non-fishing backpacker.

See map and logistics on pages 170–171.
Start: Chepeta Lake trailhead
Distance: 9 miles out and back
Destination elevation: 10,960 feet
Approximate hiking time: 6 hours

Difficulty: Moderate—some cross-country travel
Usage: Light
Nearest town: Roosevelt, Utah
Drainage: Whiterocks River

THE HIKE

Located at the head of Reader Lakes Basin, Reader Lake offers deluxe camping accommodations for the discriminating solitude seeker. Bubbling water, fresh from a mountain spring and easy to filter and treat, is served up cold with every meal. The lake borders timberline and provides a wonderful alpine ambience, complete with light afternoon thundershowers and warm, inviting sunsets. Okay, okay, so it's not always this inviting. Reader Lake is subject to the same unpredictable weather, mosquitoes, and hazards as

The serene setting of the 10-acre Reader Lake

the other 1,000 Uinta lakes. It is better than some and worse than others. However, it is seldom used and is a fine place to shack out for a while and ignore the rest of the world. There are even a couple of decent places to pitch a tent.

To reach Reader Lake, follow the Highline Trail west from the Chepeta Lake trailhead about 3 miles until you reach Reader Creek. Staying on the west side of the creek, follow it northwest another 1.5 miles to Reader Lake. Many opt to follow Highline for another 0.5 mile through the forest then depart the trail. Though marshy, stay close to the trees and watch for one or two large cairns in the meadow. The creek turns north up a slope at around 4.2 miles and the last 0.3 mile is steep and dense with trees and bushes. The lake is only 10 acres in size and shallow—you may see a moose run across the pond as if walking on water. It may first appear as a large pond, but there are no other large ponds in the area with which to confuse it.

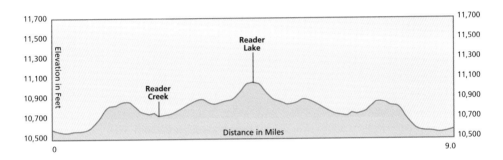

64 **WALK-UP LAKE**

Walk-Up Lake is not as easy as its name implies. You don't want to be in a hurry going through this country. It's both beautiful and treacherous. But cirque lovers will adore this bowl carved out eons ago when glaciers ruled the High Uintas, and solitude seekers should like this place, since it sees very few visitors.

See map and logistics on pages 170–171.
Start: Chepeta Lake trailhead
Distance: 7 miles out and back
Destination elevation: 11,114 feet
Approximate hiking time: 5 hours

Difficulty: Moderate—cross-country travel
Usage: Very light
Nearest town: Roosevelt, Utah
Drainage: Whiterocks River

THE HIKE

The easiest (but not easy) route to Walk-Up Lake is to first hike 1.3 miles north from the Chepeta Lake trailhead past Moccasin and Papoose Lakes. From there, hike northwest another 2.2 miles up steep, rocky slopes and meadows. It is a little tricky picking your way through the boulders, so plan on a little extra time.

Cirque lovers will adore this bowl, carved out eons ago when glaciers ruled the High Uintas. Steep slopes drop sharply into the clear water, which reaches a depth of 55 feet. That's pretty deep for a lake of only 18 acres.

Solitude seekers should also like this place. The lake sees very few visitors throughout the course of a year. You might expect it to receive considerably more pressure due to its proximity to popular Chepeta Lake, but its inaccessibility keeps it a quiet place. Despite its rugged access and appearance, there are some fair campsites located in grassy clearings just above the lake, though it's best to avoid these spots during a thunderstorm.

Brook trout are stocked occasionally. In a lake this deep, fish are usually more selective and have more defined feeding times. Early morning and late evening are when you are likely to have success at Walk-Up Lake. Just don't expect too much if you take a day hike into here to try some midday angling.

Make a stop at Papoose Lake on the trail to Walk-Up Lake.

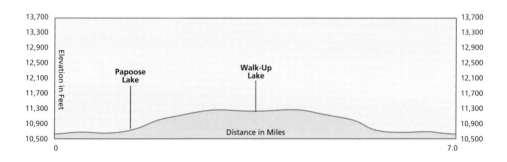

65 CLIFF LAKE

Simply put—this is quite a quiet, rugged place.

See map and logistics on pages 170–171.
Start: Chepeta Lake trailhead
Distance: 11.2 miles out and back
Destination elevation: 10,348 feet

Approximate hiking time: 7 hours
Difficulty: Moderate
Usage: Light
Nearest town: Roosevelt, Utah
Drainage: Whiterocks River

THE HIKE

Cliff Lake is about 5 miles from Chepeta Lake and offers a wilderness experience. From Chepeta Lake trailhead, follow the Highline Trail southeast 0.7 mile to a trail junction. Stay right (south) for 1.2 miles along the Whiterocks River and another trail junction. Cross the river and continue south along the river 2.2 miles to another river crossing. Cross the river again and climb 1.7 miles to the lake. The ladle-shaped Watkins Lake is 100 yards from the southern shore of Cliff Lake.

Additional lakes will be unveiled along this trail by returning on the Whiterocks Lake Trail northeast from Cliff then returning along Highline back to Chepeta. Sand, Teds, Workman, and Wooley Lakes are all known to maintain good fly fishing and many good campsites. Should you visit Cliff Lake? It's your call. There are no cozy camp spots, and spring water is nonexistent at the lake. However, Cliff Lake does get far less angling attention than any of the other lakes mentioned above and it's a memorable setting.

Cliff Lake may also be reachable by 4WD road. However, it is not advisable. Just beyond Johnson Creek, the road passes over several severe rough-rock ledges. Then it circles around Dead Horse Park, only to complete its deformity at the lake. To say the least, this road will torture the toughest truck. From Paradise Park Campground, the road to Cliff Lake is graded for about 6 miles. The last 3 miles are considered an ATV road. Good luck!

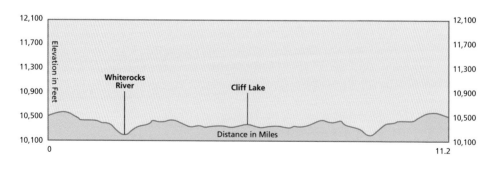

PARADISE PARK/ BLANCHETT TRAILHEAD

Among the more interesting features of the Paradise Park trailhead is the roughly 100-year-old Paradise Guard Station. Available to rent on Recreation.gov, the facility is described as RUSTIC (all caps)—but if you've been backpacking in the mountains it may feel like a resort. Up at Paradise Park Reservoir, access may be prohibited past the dam around the east side of the lake, but there is plenty of room to spread out across the western shores after carefully picking your way across the rocks, marsh, and cow pasture.

There are a lot of ATV tracks around the southwest side of the lake and nearby high-clearance roads offer plenty of miles of exploration and an advantage. The best trails near the lake require about 3 miles more to hike from Paradise Park than from Blanchett Park, but you'll need a high-clearance vehicle and possibly an ATV to reach it, depending on conditions. If you can reach it, Blanchett Park offers good camping options to set up base camp.

See trails 66 through 68 for Paradise Park/Blanchett Trailhead.
Maps: USGS Paradise Park and USGS Whiterocks Lake, *USDA Forest Service High Uintas Wilderness*, *Trails Illustrated High Uintas Wilderness*

Trail contacts: Ashley National Forest, Forest Supervisor, 355 North Vernal Ave., Vernal, UT 84078, (435) 781-1181

FINDING THE TRAILHEAD

From Vernal, drive west 15 miles to LaPoint. Turn north toward the Uinta Mountains, then drive another 30 miles to Paradise Park. You can start hiking from here, but if you have a sturdy high-clearance 4WD, keep heading north another 3 miles up FR 296 to an old logging road and continue 1.3 miles to Blanchett Park (this road may be impassable).

If you're coming from the Salt Lake City area, begin your journey to Paradise Park at Roosevelt. Take SR 121 north 10 miles to Neola. Keep following SR 121 another 14 miles east to the small community of LaPoint, then turn north and drive for 30 miles on the unpaved, though typically graded and improved dirt road.

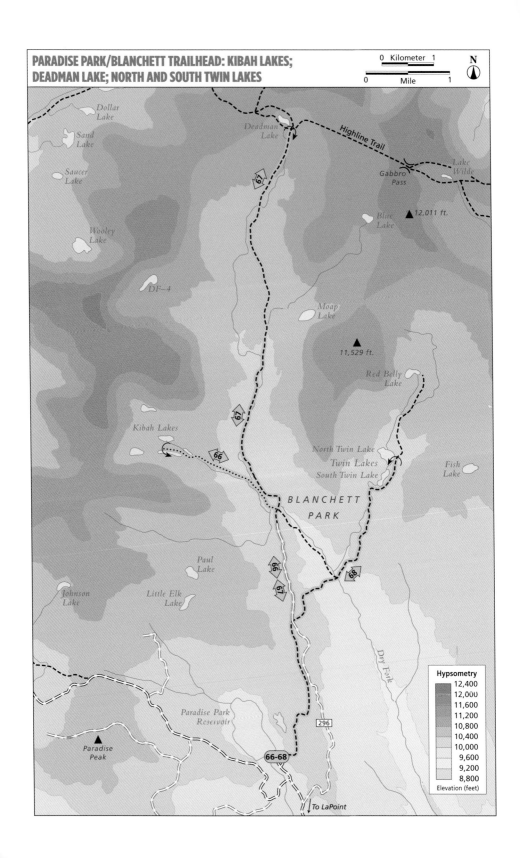

0   Kilometer   1

0   Mile   1

N

Dollar
Lake

Sand
Lake

Deadman
Lake

Highline Trail

Saucer
Lake

67

Gabbro
Pass

Lake
Wilde

Wooley
Lake

Blue
Lake

▲ 12,011 ft.

DF–4

Moap
Lake

▲
11,529 ft.

Red Belly
Lake

67

Kibah Lakes

66

North Twin Lake

Twin Lakes

South Twin Lake

Fish
Lake

BLANCHETT
PARK

Paul
Lake

Johnson
Lake

Little Elk
Lake

66

68

67

Dry Fork

Paradise Park
Reservoir

296

Paradise
Peak

66-68

↓ To LaPoint

Hypsometry

	12,400
	12,000
	11,600
	11,200
	10,800
	10,400
	10,000
	9,600
	9,200
	8,800

Elevation (feet)

According to legend, the Whiterocks District Ranger built the Paradise Guard Station in his spare time in the 1920s.

A pond covered in lily pads near the trail to Kibah Lakes

66 KIBAH LAKES

Since there are only poor campsites and horse access is nearly impossible, most people visiting Kibah Lakes are on day hikes from Paradise or Blanchett Park. To reach Blanchett Park, hike from a trailhead near the entrance to Paradise Campground or take the shorter route after driving about 3 to 4 miles to the end of jeep road FR 296, a northeast turn 0.5 mile south of Paradise Park Campground. Great camping areas and plenty of horse munchies are available at the park.

See map and logistics on pages 177–178.
Start: Blanchett or Paradise Park
Distance: 3 to 9.6 miles out and back
Destination elevation: 10,550 feet

Approximate hiking time: 4 to 7 hours
Difficulty: Moderate—cross-country
Usage: Moderate
Nearest town: Vernal, Utah
Drainage: Ashley Creek

THE HIKE

No real trail exists to Kibah Lakes beyond Blanchett Park. Hikers starting from the entrance to Paradise Campground will follow a generally well-marked trail for 1 mile. After the first mile past Paradise Park, the trail crosses several logging roads. During this 0.9-mile stretch, the trail and rock cairns are difficult to locate. The trail joins the jeep road and continues another 1.3 miles. Depending on conditions, ATVs may be able to continue to Blanchett Park. From Blanchett, travel cross-country 1 mile northwest over some nasty boulder fields to East Kibah (DF–11). This lake is identified by a rockslide along the north shore and a wet meadow to the northwest. Fishing is spotty at times, but occasionally a large trout can be netted.

Right next door to the southwest of East Kibah sits Finger Kibah. This lake takes after its name, as its shape portrays a finger. Angling should be a little faster here. Brook trout survive well in this lake, and a superb population is steadily maintained.

One-half mile west of Finger Kibah, you'll find West Kibah Lake. It rests at the base of a talus slope in the southwest corner of Kibah Basin. Fishing usage is light to moderate for brook trout, and it is possible to camp overnight here utilizing a primitive campsite.

Three hundred yards northwest of East Kibah is Island Kibah (DF–16). Surrounded by rocky, timbered ridges, a small island protrudes from its shallow water. Angler use is moderate for brookies.

North Kibah (DF–15) is located about 1 mile northwest of East Kibah. Because of low water levels during late summer, it tends to experience fish winterkill. However, this may be a good lake to catch some solitude.

67 DEADMAN LAKE

Although Deadman Lake lies in unsheltered, windy terrain, it gets a fair amount of visitation and used to be frequented by Scouts. A few fair campsites are found along the south shore, but horse pasture is a scarce commodity. Three other lakes reside near the head of Dry Fork Creek. From Deadman, these lakes are 1.5 to 5 miles away.

See map and logistics on pages 177–178.
Start: Blanchett or Paradise Park
Distance: 9.6 to 15.8 miles out and back
Destination elevation: 10,790 feet

Approximate hiking time: 7 to 10 hours
Difficulty: Moderate
Usage: Heavy
Nearest town: La Point, Utah
Drainage: Ashley Creek

THE HIKE

Deadman Lake can be reached from several access points, but the trail from Blanchett Park is the most feasible. From Paradise Park, go 3 miles up the 4WD road to Blanchett Park at the end of the road. Deadman Lake is just under 5 miles up a good trail following Dry Fork Creek. The trail splits in two directions upon reaching the lake. The east trail ventures over Gabbro Pass and into Lakeshore Basin; the west trail disperses into Whiterocks, Beaver Creek, and Carter Creek drainages. Hikers starting from the entrance to Paradise Campground will follow a generally well-marked trail for 1 mile. After the first mile past Paradise Park, the trail crosses several logging roads. During this 0.9-mile stretch, the trail and rock cairns are difficult to locate. Go another 1.3 miles to Blanchett Park then continue onto the Dry Fork Creek trail.

Reach Blue Lake by traveling 1.5 miles southeast from Deadman Lake over a bald mountain. This scenic lake sits at the top of a windswept basin on the northeast side of Dry Fork. No campsites exist. Blue Lake contains an excellent supply of hungry brook trout. Watch out for sheep dip here. In the midsummer months, rotational sheep grazing depreciates the aesthetic value of this beautiful basin.

From Blue, another scenic lake—Moap Lake—is easily reached. It is just a little over 1 mile south of Blue Lake at the base of a steep talus slope within a small cirque. No fish exist here, but it's a beautiful spot for solitude seekers and hermits.

If remote fishing is what you're after, then DF–4 is your kind of lake. Find it by following Reynolds Creek 1 mile to its spring source. Then head 1 mile over rough boulders

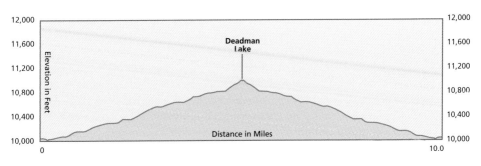

From Paradise Campground, it's just under 9 miles to Deadman Lake. Starting at Blanchett Park at the end of the high-clearance FR 296 shaves off a few miles.

into a cirque basin. Due to the rugged terrain, there are no camping areas. Angler utilization is very light, and fishing is often hot for feisty cutthroat trout. Allow yourself plenty of time to get back to base camp before dark!

68 NORTH AND SOUTH TWIN LAKES

Twin Lakes lie in marshy terrain characterized by open meadows interspersed with timber. Although these lakes receive heavy usage, many camping areas are available, especially around South Twin Lake. There is spring water at North Twin, but remember to filter it. Horse pasture is present at either lake, but South Twin has more. During summer, angling usage remains steady, and fishing is usually good.

See map and logistics on pages 177–178.
Start: Blanchett or Paradise Park trailhead
Distance: 5.4 to 9.2 miles out and back
Destination elevation: 10,300 feet

Approximate hiking time: 5 to 7 hours
Difficulty: Moderate
Usage: Heavy
Nearest town: Vernal, Utah
Drainage: Ashley Creek

THE HIKE

As with the other hikes in this area, two different starting points can be used for reaching Twin Lakes. Blanchett Park is closer, but adventurers without a 4WD vehicle will set out from Paradise Park trailhead and hike 1.9 miles to the confluence with the jeep trail. From there it's another 0.8 mile to Dry Fork Creek. Past Dry Fork Bridge, follow the Dry Fork/Twin Lakes Trail 1.9 miles north and east to the lakes. After the first mile past Paradise Park, the trail crosses several logging roads. During this stretch, the trail and rock cairns are difficult to locate.

If heavy pressure crimps your camping style, try Red Belly Lake. It receives a little less usage but gets some day use from hikers staying at Twin Lakes. Red Belly is located 1 mile north of Twin Lakes on the Dry Fork Trail. Campsites and horse pasture are on the southeast side of the lake. Angling pressure is considered moderate.

Another nice excursion from North Twin is Fish Lake. Begin near the east inlet of North Twin Lake. From the inlet, follow a hit-or-miss forest service trail 2.5 miles east to Fish. This pretty lake is at the foot of steep talus slopes on the west side of Marsh Peak. Meadows scattered with timber surround the outer portions of Fish Lake, along with good campsites and treatable spring water. Heavy usage is usually encountered throughout July and August. Litterbugs often plague all the lakes mentioned. Practice low-impact techniques, and leave this area better than you found it.

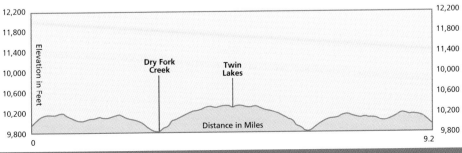

69 LEIDY PEAK (HIGHLINE) TO LAKESHORE LAKE

If sightseeing is on your agenda, then Lakeshore is a great place to visit. This picture-perfect lake rests in a meadow encased by partly timbered slopes and rolling tundra. The Alps from *The Sound of Music* come to mind. Oh and, unless you're traveling with small children, there is the matter of bagging Leidy Peak.

Start: Leidy Peak trailhead, near Hacking Lake and the Highline Trail
Distance: 10.4 miles out and back
Destination elevation: 10,792 feet
Approximate hiking time: 7 hours
Difficulty: Moderate
Usage: Moderate
Nearest town: Vernal, Utah
Drainage: Ashley Creek

Maps: USGS Leidy Peak, *USDA Forest Service High Uintas Wilderness, Trails Illustrated High Uintas Wilderness*
Trail contacts: Ashley National Forest, Forest Supervisor, 355 North Vernal Ave., Vernal, UT 84078, (435) 781-1181

FINDING THE TRAILHEAD

From Vernal, take the Taylor Mountain and Red Cloud Loop Scenic Backway toward East Park Reservoir; continue on toward Hacking Lake. You can camp at Hacking Lake or drive up the road another mile to the Leidy Peak trailhead at this eastern point on the Highline Trail. The total distance from Vernal is about 36 miles.

THE HIKE

The shortest route to Lakeshore Lake begins at Leidy Peak trailhead, on the east end of the Highline Trail above Hacking Lake; the other starts at Ashley Twin Lakes at the end of a high-clearance road. Both trails are well marked, though the trail from Hacking Lake can be difficult to follow as it goes around Leidy Peak. The Hacking Lake route is at least a mile shorter and can be reached by car. Ashley Twin Lakes can only be reached by jeep, after figuring out your way through a maze of brutally rocky roads.

From Leidy Peak trailhead, take the North Leidy Peak route of the Highline Trail west along the north side of Leidy Peak for 1.9 miles. Head west 1.3 miles to a fork and veer left 0.2 mile to a junction with the South Fork Ashley Trail. Alternatively, go 0.8 or 1.4 miles due south to one of two trail junctions heading west. There are a couple of Highline Trail paths on the south side of Leidy Peak but both routes travel around 2.5 miles to the fork. Stay left (west), go 0.2 mile to the second junction, and turn left (southeast). Lakeshore Lake is 0.9 mile from the second fork.

Lakeshore Lake is named for the basin. It is just off a good forest service trail in the upper end of Lakeshore Basin. Good campsites are present, along with an abundant supply of horse pasture and spring water. Sometimes, you can pinpoint a major source of potential waterborne illness. In this area, sheep grazing can foul the surrounding watershed. Be sure to treat all water before drinking.

LEIDY PEAK (HIGHLINE) TO LAKESHORE LAKE

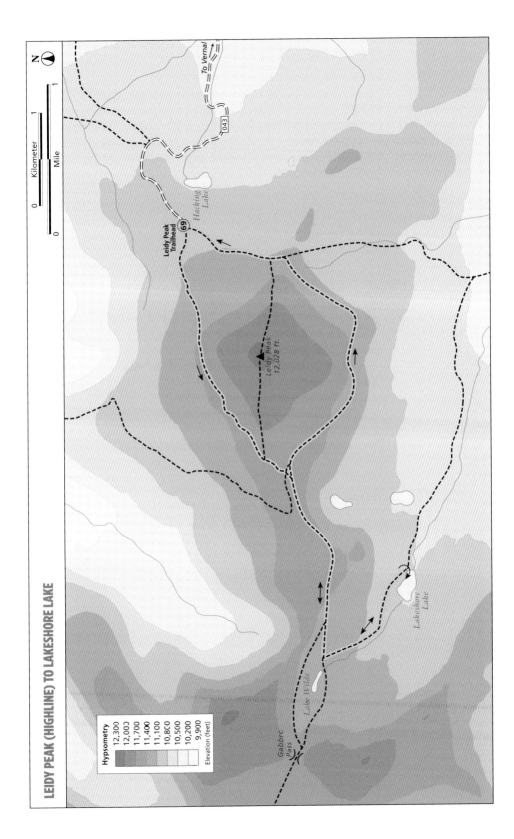

Hypsometry

Elevation (feet)
12,300
12,000
11,700
11,400
11,100
10,800
10,500
10,200
9,900

Leidy Peak Trailhead

69

Hacking Lake

To Vernal

043

Leidy Peak 12,028 ft

Gabbro Pass

Lake Wilde

Lakeshore Lake

Kilometer

Mile

N

Known as a decent fishing lake, Lakeshore holds a good population of fish. You should be able to catch enough for a tasty shore lunch.

Another lake in Lakeshore Basin is Lake Wilde, a cirque lake that sits on the trail 1 mile northwest of Lakeshore Lake at the base of Gabbro Pass. Do you like wind? You can have as much as you want here. During unsettled weather, the wind blows constantly and continues to blow even when you least expect it. No campsites or trout exist here, but several springs pop up around the lake.

Take your time as you explore this wonderful wilderness—and definitely take your camera.

If you have three or so extra hours, why not tackle the 12,028-foot Leidy Peak? Aside from snow lingering deep into summer on the northeast face, there are a lot of ways up. The shortest from the trailhead is a route up the east face, but the climb is not quite as steep from the west face.

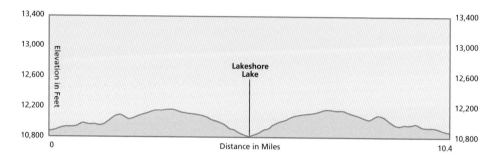

70 THE HIGHLINE TRAIL

You've heard of the Appalachian Trail and the Pacific Crest Trail. Maybe you've heard of the John Muir Trail in California. But have you heard of Utah's Highline Trail? With most of the trail above 10,000 feet, the 100-mile trek has a limited hiking season and its elevation commands respect. It takes a lot of stamina and willpower to take on a long hike lasting many days or even weeks—and may bring into immediate focus the reasons behind ultralight backpacking practices once you've gone just a few miles under the full weight of your pack. On that note, do not make Highline your first backpacking trip. Get in shape by taking on a trial trip or two—or three!—each time pushing your distance to know how many miles you are capable of covering in a day. But then, there is no "right way" to tackle Highline. If you are strong enough, conditioned enough, well prepared, and have enough time based on your chosen itinerary, then maybe you can join the elite long-haulers on the Highline Trail.

Start: Highline trailhead (west end) or McKee Draw (east end) or Leidy Peak trailhead (near east end)
Distance: 79 to 104 miles one way
Highest elevation: 12,600 feet
Approximate hiking time: Variable
Difficulty: Extremely difficult
Usage: Moderate
Nearest town: Kamas, Utah (west end), or Manila, Utah (east end)
Maps: USGS Hayden Peak, USGS Explorer Peak, USGS Red Knob, USGS Oweep Creek, USGS Garfield Basin, USGS Kings Peak, USGS Fox Lake, USGS Chepeta Lake, USGS Whiterocks Lake, USGS Leidy Peak, USGS Elk Park, USGS East Park Reservoir, and USGS Mount Lena; *USDA Forest Service High Uintas Wilderness, Trails Illustrated High Uintas Wilderness*
Trail contacts: Ashley National Forest, Forest Supervisor, 355 North Vernal Ave., Vernal, UT 84078, (435) 781-1181; Duchesne Ranger District, 85 West Main, Duchesne, UT 84021, (435) 738-2482; Uinta-Wasatch-Cache National Forest, Forest Supervisor, 857 West South Jordan Pkwy., South Jordan, UT 84095; Kamas Ranger District, 50 East Center St., Kamas, UT 84036, (435) 783-4338

FINDING THE TRAILHEAD

The Highline is the most popular trail of the High Uintas Wilderness. From Kamas, take the Mirror Lake Scenic Byway (Highway 150) 34 miles to a large sign on the east side of the road that says "Highline Trail." This trailhead has a listed capacity of twenty-four vehicles, but there are often considerably more parked here on busy weekends. This crowded trailhead is equipped with toilets, water, stock ramp, and nearby campsites. Highline is Trail 083 for 8 miles in the Uinta-Wasatch-Cache National Forest and Trail 025 for the 96 miles it winds through the Ashley National Forest.

The other end of the trail is at McKee Draw off U.S. 191. From Vernal, drive north on 191 (the Flaming Gorge–Uintas Scenic Byway) for 28.8 miles and turn left. About 0.5 mile up the road there is parking and a vault toilet. For the Leidy Peak trailhead, travel from Vernal by way of Taylor Mountain and Red Cloud Loop Scenic Backway toward East Park Reservoir and continue on toward Hacking Lake. You can camp at Hacking Lake or drive up the road another mile to the Leidy Peak trailhead at the eastern end of the Highline Trail. Total distance from Vernal is about 36 miles.

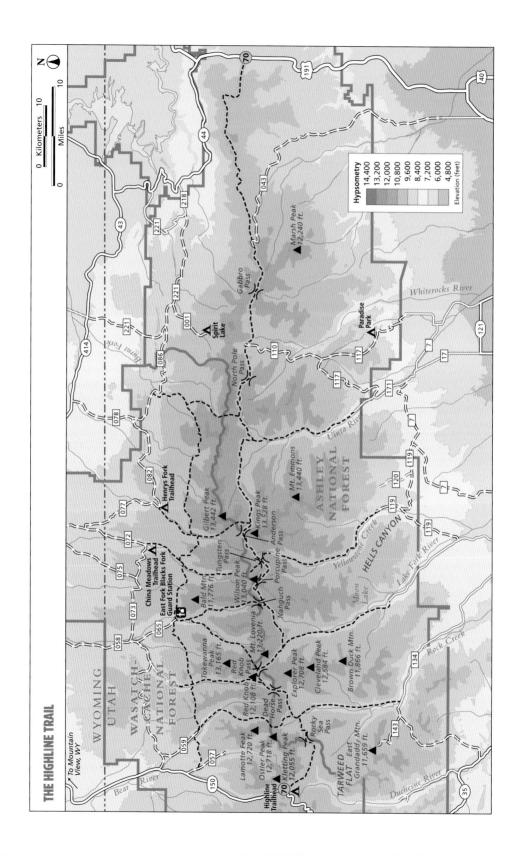

THE HIGHLINE TRAIL

N

Kilometers 10 0 10
Miles 0 10

Hypsometry
14,400
13,200
12,000
10,800
9,600
8,400
7,200
6,000
4,800
Elevation (feet)

WYOMING
UTAH

WASATCH-CACHE NATIONAL FOREST

ASHLEY NATIONAL FOREST

To Mountain View, WY

Bear River

Henrys Fork Trailhead

China Meadows Trailhead

East Fork Blacks Fork Guard Station

Spirit Lake

Marsh Peak 12,240 ft.

Gabbro Pass

North Pole Pass

Whiterocks River

Paradise Park

Gilbert Peak 13,442 ft.

Kings Peak 13,528 ft.

Anderson Pass

Mt. Emmons 13,440 ft.

Tungsten Pass

Bald Mtn. 11,776 ft.

Wilson Peak 13,040 ft.

Porcupine Pass

Nanguch Pass

Uinta River

Yellowstone Creek

HELLS CANYON

Tokewanna Peak 13,165 ft.

Red Knob Pass

Mt. Lovenia 13,220 ft.

Explorer Peak 12,708 ft.

Cleveland Peak 12,584 ft.

Brown Duck Mtn. 11,866 ft.

Moon Lake

Lake Fork River

Rock Creek

Lamotte Peak 12,720 ft.

Ostler Peak 12,718 ft.

Red Knob Pass 12,108 ft.

Dead Horse Pass

Kletting Peak 12,055 ft.

Rocky Sea Pass

Highline Trailhead

TARWEED FLAT

East Grandaddy Mtn. 11,659 ft.

Duchesne River

The view below Nahguch Pass looking east over Porcupine Lake along the Highline Trail's path through Porcupine Pass, the 12,236-foot route between Wilson Peak and Porcupine Peak.
PHOTO BY MATT MCKELL/UTAH DIVISION OF WILDLIFE RESOURCES

THE HIKE

The trail begins at either the Highline trailhead west end (at Hayden Peak off Highway 150), Highline trailhead east end (at McKee Draw off U.S. 191), or at the Leidy Peak trailhead near the eastern end of the High Uinta Mountains. An underappreciated fourth option starts at Chepeta trailhead and logs *only* 65 miles of hiking. You will surely still receive impressed and possibly envious looks when you tell people you backpacked 65 miles mostly above 10,000 feet. But thanks to the visual impact of the west end—and the more gradual start of McKee Draw for the full point-to-point trail—many choose to start from the east and head west.

Indeed, if you need a little time to acclimate to elevation, a strong case can be made for starting from the eastern side. At around 8,200 feet, it may come as less of a shock to your system than the approximately 10,800 feet at Leidy or 10,150 at Hayden. But if you're tackling Highline, the truth is you've come prepared, and you're conditioned for long distance and high elevation. For some, starting at a lower elevation may have little overall effect on the total wear and tear of this lengthy trek.

A high-elevation lake alongside the Highline Trail between Chepeta Lake and Reader Lake

The Highline Trail takes you up and down eight mountain passes. They are (east to west) Gabbro, North Pole, Anderson, Tungsten, Porcupine, Red Knob, Dead Horse, and Rocky Sea. These passes are what make this journey something special. From atop the backbone of the High Uintas, you'll witness one spectacular vista after another.

Almost all the Highline experience happens on the south slope of the Uintas. The main exception is where the trail takes a brief detour over Dead Horse Pass into the West Fork Blacks Fork drainage. After less than 4 miles, the trail winds its way back to the south slope over Red Knob Pass. There are also a couple of short 1.5- to 2-mile stretches on the east side that cross onto the North Slope. Those are about 10 miles into the trek and where the trail first begins flirting with 10,000 feet above sea level.

Because much of the Highline Trail is above timberline, plan carefully where to spend your nights. Choose camps with pines for shelter from wind and rain. Low stands of pines are also the safest place to be when lightning is flashing. Speaking of bad weather, allow yourself at least a couple of extra days to complete this hike. You might get holed up for a while waiting for the skies to settle down.

Camps near water can also help with planning when and where you filter and refill hydration bladders and bottles. If starting from the east, East Park Reservoir and Little Brush Creek beckon a mere 4 miles in because trailside water is comparatively scarce for the 20-mile stretch between East Park and Hacking Lake, which is near the Leidy Peak trailhead to Highline. Inspect and carry larger-scale topographical maps (those with smaller ratios and greater detail) for possible springs and creeks along the way. Fortunately, this stretch of the trail all occurs ahead of the first major mountain pass. After Leidy Peak, water is abundant and there are camp options at Deadman, Whiterocks, Chepeta, Reader,

Highline Trail carves a high-elevation path along the South Slope near the divide, with options to bag a few peaks along the way, including Wilson (center) and Kings (far right). PHOTO BY MATT MCKELL/UTAH DIVISION OF WILDLIFE RESOURCES

Fox, Kidney, North Star, Dead Horse, Ledge, and Carolyn Lakes, as well as near multiple other basin lakes or creeks.

As for mileage, that can vary wildly due to hiker skill and fitness, terrain, and trail conditions. Average pace may range from 1 to 3 miles per hour, meaning 20-minute miles at the fast end and hour-long miles at the slower end. A 20-mile day at an average of 2 miles per hour means 10 hours of hiking, with a pack, and potentially with one or more mountain passes adding thousands of punishing feet of elevation both up and down. Plan for shorter, stretch hiking goals, and always have a Plan B and C on your map if conditions change or your speed varies, taking into account the needs and pace of others in your group.

It should go without saying that excellent physical conditioning is a prerequisite for this alpine adventure. The steep, rocky miles will tear at your muscles, and the high mountain passes will take your breath away. But then, so will the scenery.

Red Castle Peak and Red Castle Lakes are jewels of the North Slope. PHOTO BY MATT MCKELL/
UTAH DIVISION OF WILDLIFE RESOURCES

PART 3: I-80 TO THE NORTH SLOPE

There are a series of unpaved, though typically well-maintained, roads running west to east along much of the North Slope that are often collectively known as the North Slope Road. Yet for adventurers heading to the Uintas from Utah and Wyoming, a large portion of the North Slope can be reached via I-80 and the Fort Bridger exit to Mountain View. The North Slope is heavily wooded and wetter than the South Slope. While some hikes are shorter and not as steep as the South Slope, there's plenty of elevation, distance, and some of the range's most scenic destinations to keep people entertained for hours or days.

With the exception of a couple of key trailheads, crowds are sometimes lighter on the North Slope. That said, the line between the North Slope and South Slope passes many drivers by without notice on Highway 150—though it draws a sharp line between drainages. (Hikes 1 through 20 in Part 1 fall on the South Slope and 21 through 32 are on the North Slope.) The divide is easily identified on the trail, of course, as it takes the form of named mountain passes that may be the most difficult part of your journey. The westernmost hikes in this section are also accessible from Highway 150. Road access can be problematic on some drainages, and 4WD is recommended for some trailheads.

EAST FORK BEAR RIVER AREA

It's worth pausing to consider how far some of the water up here travels. While the main stem of the Bear River forms at the confluence of Stillwater Fork and Hayden Fork near the Stillwater Campground, the East Fork tributary to the Bear River joins just 3 miles north. As the crow flies, the Great Salt Lake is roughly 75 miles west of the East Fork Bear River trailhead, but the Bear River winds some 350 miles to the northernmost point of the Wasatch Mountains in southeastern Idaho before bending back south on its journey to Great Salt Lake. Though your journeys from the trailheads in this area will be much shorter, they can be no less epic. Stunning high-elevation lakes and designated Wilderness experiences await.

See trails 71 and 72 for East Fork Bear River Area.
Maps: USGS Christmas Meadows and USGS Red Knob, *USDA Forest Service High Uintas Wilderness, Trails Illustrated High Uintas Wilderness*

Trail contacts: Uinta-Wasatch-Cache National Forest, Forest Supervisor, 857 West South Jordan Pkwy., South Jordan, UT 84095; Bear River Ranger Station, 32 miles south of Evanston, Wyoming, on the Mirror Lake Scenic Byway, (435) 642-6662

FINDING THE TRAILHEAD

From Evanston, take the Mirror Lake Scenic Byway (Highway 150) south about 30 miles to the East Fork of the Bear River turnoff. This road is often referred to as the North Slope Road. Follow this road east 1.5 miles to a junction. Take Road 059 south about 4 miles to East Fork Bear River trailhead. There's a vault toilet and a few places to park around the loop. You may need a 4WD vehicle for the last mile when wet. At the time of printing, the Hinckley Scout Ranch, whose turnoff is about 0.25 mile before the East Fork Bear River trailhead, remained "temporarily closed," with no recreation permitted. That closure blocks the best access to the Boundary Creek Trail to Scow Lake. (In a 4WD vehicle or ATV, hikers can access Boundary Creek from FR 120 or from Wolverine ATV trail 301.)

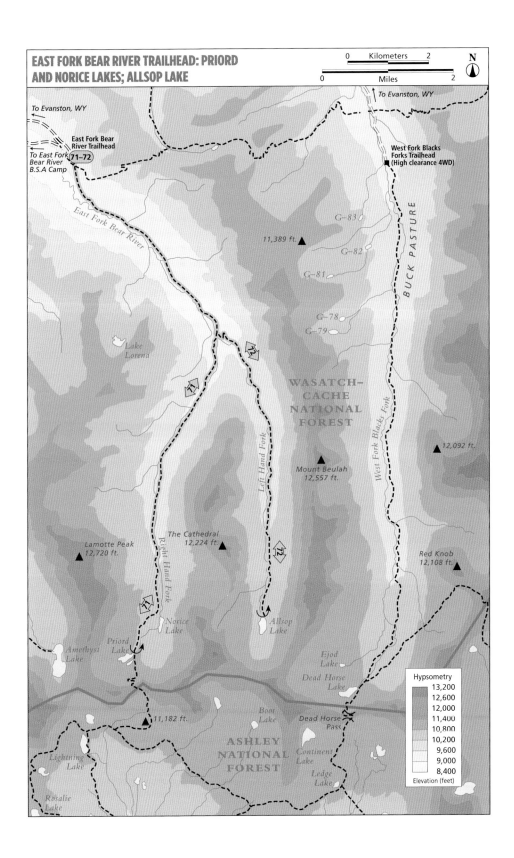

0   Kilometers   2

0   Miles   2

N

To Evanston, WY

To Evanston, WY

East Fork Bear
River Trailhead

71–72

To East Fork
Bear River
B.S.A Camp

West Fork Blacks
Forks Trailhead
(High clearance 4WD)

East Fork Bear River

G–83

11,389 ft.

G–82

G–81

BUCK PASTURE

G–78

G–79

*Lake
Lorena*

72

71

WASATCH–
CACHE
NATIONAL
FOREST

Left Hand Fork

West Fork Blacks Fork

12,092 ft.

Mount Beulah
12,557 ft.

*The Cathedral
12,224 ft.*

72

Lamotte Peak
12,720 ft.

Right Hand Fork

Red Knob
12,108 ft.

71

*Norice
Lake*

*Allsop
Lake*

*Priord
Lake*

*Amethyst
Lake*

*Ejod
Lake*

*Dead Horse
Lake*

Hypsometry

13,200
12,600
12,000
11,400
10,800
10,200
9,600
9,000
8,400
Elevation (feet)

11,182 ft.

*Boot
Lake*

*Dead Horse
Pass*

ASHLEY
NATIONAL
FOREST

*Continent
Lake*

*Lightning
Lake*

*Ledge
Lake*

*Rosalie
Lake*

The trailhead to the East Fork Bear River area with some of the 2002 burn scar visible on the range

71 PRIORD AND NORICE LAKES

The hikes of the North Slope can feel increasingly remote the farther east you go. Here on the western side, proximity to Highway 150 can lead to considerable traffic at this trailhead. Despite sometimes muddy conditions, the East Fork Bear River drainage receives moderate to heavy usage from equestrians, backpackers, ambitious day hikers, and grazing cows on the open range—so keep chase-prone dogs on a leash and, you know, watch your step.

See map and logistics on pages 194–195.
Start: East Fork Bear River trailhead
Distance: 16.5 miles out and back
Destination elevation: 10,470 feet

Approximate hiking time: 11 hours
Difficulty: Moderate
Usage: Moderate
Nearest town: Evanston, Wyoming
Drainage: Bear River

THE HIKE

Start your journey on the East Fork Bear River Trail, 0.5 mile southeast of the former Hinckley Scout Ranch turnoff. Follow the East Fork Trail 4 miles southeast to the Right Hand–Left Hand Fork Trail junction. Then go south on the Right Hand Fork Trail by crossing the river. There is no bridge here or at additional water crossings. Though not especially deep, spring runoff can make for fast water. The trail deteriorates when traveling through bogs and deadfall. When this occurs, following the stream will take you to Norice Lake. From Norice, the trail becomes difficult to locate. Just head south for 0.5 mile, then west 0.25 mile, and you'll find Priord Lake.

Priord sits at the head of the Right Hand Fork drainage. A rugged cirque basin encircles this timberline lake, and the lake itself is a pretty emerald green. Camping areas exist east of the lake, and spring water is present. However, horse pasture and firewood are limited. Windy conditions may hinder fly casting, but the fish should be cooperative, since Priord Lake only receives light fishing use for cutthroat trout.

Norice is shallow, but despite the depth, this lake contains an excellent population of cutthroat trout. Norice is a meadow lake that is quite boggy in spots. This means one thing: It is a perfect breeding ground for bugs and mosquitoes. Don't forget your repellent!

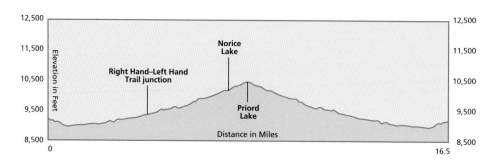

The trail to Priord and Norice

Experienced, well-prepared hikers with good wayfinding ability can turn this trail into a loop with Allsop via Yard Pass to the North of Yard Peak (or other low points along the ridge), but be prepared for cross-country travel, a scramble up, and a steep descent.

72 ALLSOP LAKE

What a pretty hike. The East Fork Bear River Trail caresses a wide, flowing river while steering leisurely by ruins of old log cabins, lush green meadows, and sky-reaching pines. Possible camping areas exist all along the river and all the way to the Allsop-Priord junction. After the junction, the Left Hand Fork Trail ascends high along the side of a steep ravine. Here you'll find a stunning overlook of consecutive waterfalls gushing down a sheer rock canyon.

See map and logistics on pages 194–195.
Start: East Fork Bear River trailhead
Distance: 17 miles out and back
Destination elevation: 10,580 feet
Approximate hiking time: 11 hours

Difficulty: Moderate—one steep section
Usage: Moderate
Nearest town: Evanston, Wyoming
Drainage: Bear River

THE HIKE

Start your journey on the East Fork Bear River Trail, 0.5 mile south of the B.S.A. turn-off. Follow the East Fork Trail 4 miles southeast to the Right Hand–Left Hand Fork Trail junction. Turn left (east) up Left Hand Fork. Allsop Lake is 4.5 miles up Left Hand Fork. The Allsop Lake Trail slowly gains altitude as exotic mountain peaks appear through the tops of gangling conifers. Once out of these tall strands of trees, a tantalizing view of The Cathedral and Allsop Basin is sighted just beyond a long stretch of meadows.

Allsop is a beautiful bluish-green lake nestled within a spectacular talus and timbered, sloped basin. Excellent campsites with superb spring water sources are plentiful at the lake, while horse pasture can be found nearby or downstream. Fishing for cutthroat is often consistent from Allsop's open shorelines. However, sudden stiff winds may ravage a long-distance cast. Pack some spinners or bait for those unexpected gusts. Other angling prospects can be found in the Left Hand or East Fork of the Bear River.

The Cathedral will tantalize peak baggers with its chiseled peak rising to the northwest of Allsop Lake. It stretches high over the tree line to 12,224 feet. As with most peaks in the Uintas, you'll not find a designated trail, just the usual assemblage of rock slabs, scree, and talus. For experienced hikers, non-technical ascents may be possible from the northeast shoulder or the south from the ridge between Allsop and Priord. Likewise, the nearby 12,706-foot Yard Peak will present fields of potentially unstable boulders to hop, but is also a non-technical climb.

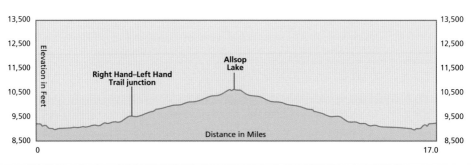

EAST FORK BLACKS FORK AREA

Just as the previous chapters marveled at the path of the Bear River, this chapter pauses to appreciate the awesome source waters of the Blacks Fork. These waters travel the other way, east along the North Slope to its ultimate drainage into the Green River and Flaming Gorge Reservoir.

There are two area trailheads, one on the West Fork and one on the East Fork. Thanks to 5+ miles of tricky high-clearance road and a river crossing, the West Fork trailhead is not included in this book. (Though there's great, easily accessible fishing at the confluence of the West Fork and East Fork found on this route.) At the East Fork Blacks Fork trailhead, you're just a couple of miles from the High Uintas Wilderness, whether you set out to the south or to the east. Either way, this is truly a trailhead to the vastness of the range: The out-and-backs are substantial hikes and they're connected to lengthy loops over high-mountain passes that can keep you deep in wilderness for days.

See trails 73 through 75 for East Fork Blacks Fork Area.
Maps: USGS Mount Lovenia, USGS Bridger Lake, and USGS Mount Powell; *USDA Forest Service High Uintas Wilderness*; *Trails Illustrated High Uintas Wilderness*

Trail contacts: Uinta-Wasatch-Cache National Forest, Forest Supervisor, 857 West South Jordan Pkwy., South Jordan, UT 84095; Bear River Ranger Station, 32 miles south of Evanston, Wyoming, on the Mirror Lake Scenic Byway, (435) 642-6662

FINDING THE TRAILHEAD

From Evanston, take the Mirror Lake Scenic Byway (Highway 150) south about 30 miles to the East Fork of the Bear River turnoff. This road is often referred to as the North Slope Road. Follow this road east about 20 miles to a junction just past Lyman Lakes. Then take the south road (Road 065) just a little over 5 miles to East Fork Blacks Fork trailhead.

This trailhead has ten parking places at the upper trailhead and twenty at the lower trailhead. Good campsites and toilets are located at the upper trailhead. There is a bridge to cross the river to the east of the campground.

Scenic mountain landscape surrounds the East Fork of the Blacks Fork River.

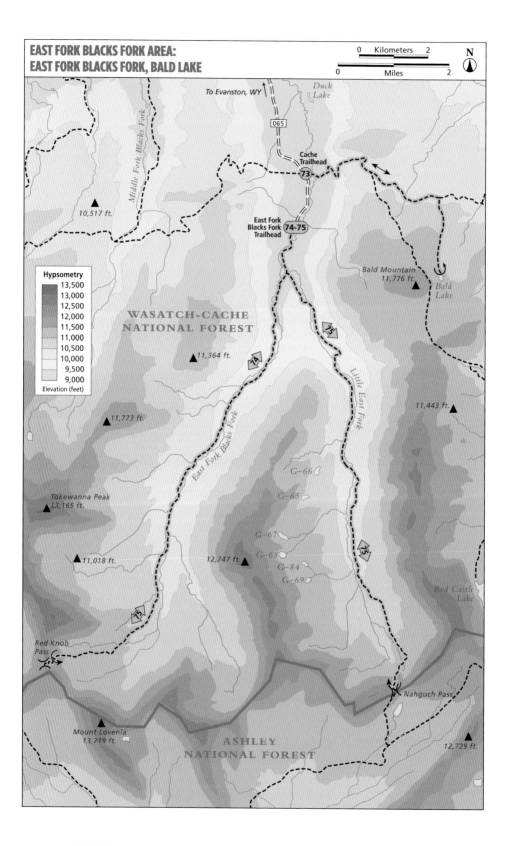

EAST FORK BLACKS FORK AREA:
EAST FORK BLACKS FORK, BALD LAKE

0 Kilometers 2

0 Miles 2

N

To Evanston, WY

Duck Lake

065

Cache Trailhead

73

East Fork Blacks Fork Trailhead 74-75

Bald Mountain 11,776 ft. ▲

Bald Lake

▲ 10,517 ft.

Middle Fork Blacks Fork

Hypsometry

	13,500
	13,000
	12,500
	12,000
	11,500
	11,000
	10,500
	10,000
	9,500
	9,000

Elevation (feet)

WASATCH-CACHE NATIONAL FOREST

▲ 11,364 ft.

74

75

Little East Fork

▲ 11,443 ft.

▲ 11,773 ft.

East Fork Blacks Fork

G-66

G-65

Tokewanna Peak ▲ 13,165 ft.

G-67

G-68

75

▲ 11,018 ft.

12,747 ft. ▲

G-84

G-69

Red Castle Lake

75

Red Knob Pass

Nahguch Pass

Mount Lovenia 13,219 ft. ▲

ASHLEY NATIONAL FOREST

▲ 12,729 ft.

73 BALD LAKE

Bald Lake is probably the only lake in the Smiths Fork drainage containing campsites that still only receive light fishing and camping use. This natural cirque lake harbors a large population of brook trout. Stocking has been discontinued, since natural reproduction has consistently met its quota. You should have no problem filling your skillet here.

Bald Lake sits near a glacial talus slope with a snowy ice pack that is the main source of water for this alpine lake. Small, stunted pines dot the north and east shorelines where a few sheltered campsites are found. Just south of the lake, a spectacular panorama of the upper Smiths Fork drainage awaits your viewing.

See map and logistics on pages 201 and 204.
Start: East Fork Blacks Fork trailhead
Distance: 10 miles out and back
Destination elevation: 11,030 feet
Approximate hiking time: 7 hours

Difficulty: Difficult—some steep, cross-country travel
Usage: Light
Nearest town: Mountain View, Wyoming
Drainage: Smiths Fork

THE HIKE

This hike begins from East Fork Blacks Fork and takes a 0.5-mile connector trail to the Bear River, or 0.5 mile might be shaved by starting on the Bear River Smiths Fork trail (Cache trailhead) where it crosses Road 065—but there's no bridge across the river. Over the course of 1.4 miles, Bear River Smiths Fork takes a few large switchbacks right up the slope gaining around 1,000 feet in elevation before leveling at the boundary to the High Uintas Wilderness. Here, the trail becomes the North Slope Highline Trail. At 2.5 miles, a right fork follows the lightly trafficked Bald Mountain Trail (the long route to Red Castle Lake), but you should continue straight for 2.3 miles to the junction with the West Fork Smiths Fork Trail. At this point, you may be able to roughly follow a stream cross-country, southwest 1.5 miles to Bald Lake. Keep your map, GPS, and insect repellent handy, and be prepared to cross marshy areas.

No other lakes exist in the vicinity; Bald Lake is alone. Chances are you will be too if you choose this hike. Here's a great place to spend the weekend and beat the crowds (aside from the crowds of mosquitos earlier in the season). Relax, breathe deep, and enjoy it.

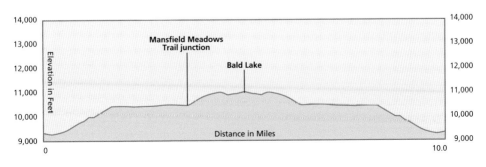

Some high mountain passes are inaccessible much of the summer. Red Knob is no exception. After a long, hard winter, the northeast side of Red Knob Pass is plagued with snowdrifts until the middle of August. You may try your luck during late July, but it could be a rugged trip. Snowdrifts are difficult to cross when hoisting a heavy pack; so is the East Fork River when the snowfields melt and fill its banks to capacity. Even when these mountains experience a light winter, Red Knob should not be attempted from the East Fork Trail until mid-July.

See map and logistics on pages 201 and 204.
Start: East Fork Blacks Fork trailhead
Distance: 20 to 28 miles out and back (with longer loop options)
Destination elevation: 12,200 feet

Approximate hiking time: 14 hours
Difficulty: Moderate to difficult— several river crossings
Usage: Light
Nearest town: Evanston, Wyoming
Drainage: East Fork Blacks Fork

THE HIKE

East Fork has no lakes. The main purpose of this drainage is as a route for hikers making the 50-mile trek from the Highline trailhead or the 26-mile loop trail that ventures around Mount Lovenia, the Upper Lake Fork drainage, and then back through Little East Fork. The trail begins at the footbridge northeast of the East Fork Campground. From the bridge, follow a well-used trail 1 mile south to another footbridge that crosses over the Little East Fork River. Just beyond the bridge, the trail forks to the right and to the left. Both trails take off to the south, then connect again in the upper portion of the Lake Fork drainage. From the fork, it is 10 miles to Red Knob Pass.

Scenery in the East Fork Blacks Fork is spectacular. Mount Lovenia and other high peaks surround the narrow, ridged canyons, which sometimes stay snowcapped year-round. Beautiful lodgepole pines cover the valley floor, while prolonged rivers ease through the misty meadows. Scenic campsites can be found along the trail, and firewood is plentiful for the overnight camper.

Occasionally, moose can be spotted grazing in the open meadows. It is a good idea to keep your distance from these animals. Moose are sometimes intrepid and may attack.

If a destination is a must for your journey (and you're late enough in the season to find Red Knob Pass free of snow), you do have some options. The east-to-west Highline

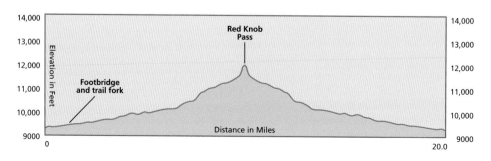

Fishing the East Fork of the Blacks Fork with a view of Quandary Peak. PHOTO BY MATT MCKELL/ UTAH DIVISION OF WILDLIFE RESOURCES

A cabin left behind from the turn-of-the-century "tie-hack" era—laborers for the railroad producing ties from timber by hand. PHOTO BY MATT MCKELL/UTAH DIVISION OF WILDLIFE RESOURCES

Trail joins up at Red Knob Pass. At a saddle below Red Knob Pass around 11.5 miles from the trailhead, the 12,108-foot Red Knob Peak is just under 0.5 mile. It's also 3.5 miles to Dead Horse Lake (a stunning lake typically accessed on the 16-mile, round-trip trail West Fork Blacks Fork), which means—you guessed it—another loop is possible if you have around 38 miles in you.

75 LITTLE EAST FORK

Open, windswept tundra dotted with alpine lakes characterizes this remote hike. The Little East Fork Blacks Forks drainage has several tiny, high lakes that almost nobody visits. Camping opportunities are few, firewood is scarce, spring water is hard to find, horse pasture is scant, and there are no trails to the lakes. If you're looking for solitude and a chance to discover some unknown waters, here it is. You've got to have a sense of adventure, but you'll know you've been to some of the least-traveled country these mountains have to offer.

See map and logistics on pages 201 and 204.
Start: East Fork Blacks Fork trailhead
Distance: 12 to 20 miles out and back
Highest elevation: 11,527 feet

Approximate hiking time: 8 to 14 hours
Difficulty: Moderate
Usage: Light
Nearest town: Evanston, Wyoming
Drainage: East Fork Blacks Fork

THE HIKE

The trail forks about 1.3 mile from the East Fork Blacks Fork trailhead, where the East Fork and the Little East Fork come together. Follow the trail to the left (southeast). From this point it's 4 miles to where you might turn to G–66 and G–65. Go another 1.5 miles to the creek coming from G–67 and G–68. Go another 1.5 miles to the creek from G–84 and G–69. It is about 2.3 miles to Nahguch Pass from there.

G–66 is the most logical choice to establish a base camp. There are several campsites, and spring water can be found. It is also the first lake you will encounter. You will need GPS and a topographical map and compass to find G–66, or any of these lakes.

The lakes still carry numbers as names to most hikers, but they have also taken on names over the years according to forest service officials. They are G-65 (Jarrod Lake), G-66 (Lake Nikki), G-67 (Lake Kelli), G-68 (Lake Kimberly), and G-69 (Chad Lake).

Fishing opportunities may be great, or they may be lousy. Stocking schedules are irregular, and winterkill could take its toll, but the fishing may still be excellent at times. There are several of these small lakes within a few miles of one another. A good horse can make its way around up here, but there isn't much pasture—camp by the lower meadows.

The Little East Fork Trail serves as the main sheep thoroughfare for the upper portions of the Lake Fork drainage. If you take either route after mid-July, be prepared to encounter flocks of sheep. Take precautions where drinking water is concerned.

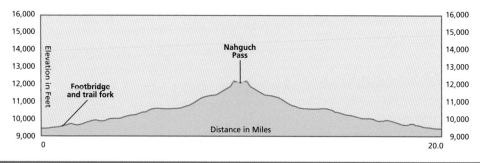

CHINA MEADOWS TRAILHEAD

Though Highway 150 hikes described in Part I of this guide are some of the most accessible, China Meadows is a popular trailhead that is well worth the extra drive time and unpaved road travel to reach. There's a small campground with a few reservable sites (plus dispersed sites near the trailhead) and nearby China Lake offers up arctic grayling, brook, and cutthroat trout. Carry cash for a trailhead fee.

Of course, those arriving from the north via Mountain View, Wyoming, will have noticed the multiple reservoirs, lakes, and campgrounds along the route pointing to the recreational appeal of this area. But for those who have come for the hiking, in addition to the excellent Hessie Lake and long-distance trek to the Highline Trail, the crown jewel of the Smiths Fork drainage is Red Castle Lake. At sunset, you'll quickly understand how it got its name.

See trails 76 and 77 for China Meadows Trailhead.
Maps: USGS Bridger Lake and USGS Mount Powell, *USDA Forest Service High Uintas Wilderness*, *Trails Illustrated High Uintas Wilderness*

Trail contacts: Uinta-Wasatch-Cache National Forest, Forest Supervisor, 857 West South Jordan Pkwy., South Jordan, UT 84095; Mountain View Ranger District, 321 Highway 414, PO Box 129, Mountain View, WY 82939, (307) 782-6555

FINDING THE TRAILHEAD

From Mountain View, take Highway 410 south about 6 miles to a junction. Then take Road 017 (CR 283), a well-maintained gravel road, south about 8.5 miles to a fork and continue onto Road 072, which meanders about 11 miles past Stateline Reservoir and multiple campgrounds to China Meadows.

The China Meadows trailhead has fifty parking places and offers campsites, toilets, corrals, and a stock ramp.

The East Fork Smith's Fork winds through China Meadows on its path down the North Slope.

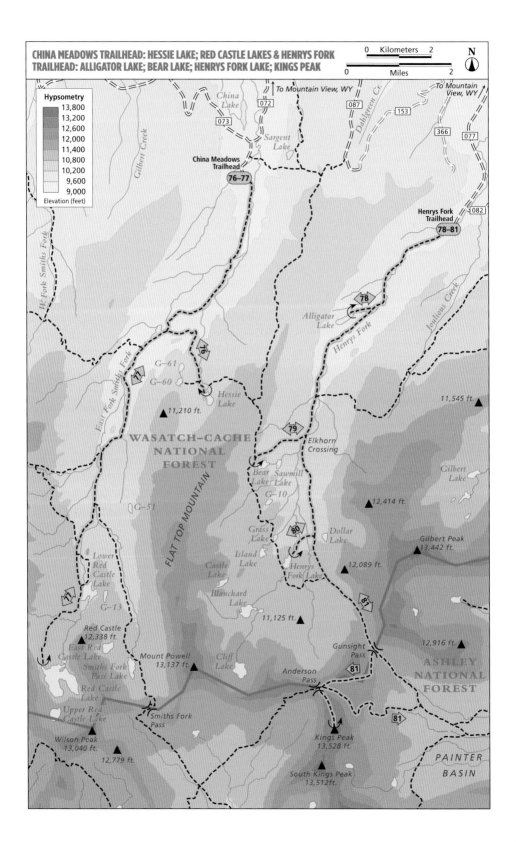

CHINA MEADOWS TRAILHEAD: HESSIE LAKE; RED CASTLE LAKES & HENRYS FORK
TRAILHEAD: ALLIGATOR LAKE; BEAR LAKE; HENRYS FORK LAKE; KINGS PEAK

0   Kilometers   2
0   Miles   2

N

Hypsometry
13,800
13,200
12,600
12,000
11,400
10,800
10,200
9,600
9,000
Elevation (feet)

China Lake
072
073
Sargent Lake
To Mountain View, WY
087
153
366
077
Dahlgreen Cr.

China Meadows Trailhead
76–77

Henrys Fork Trailhead
78–81
082

Gilbert Creek

W. Fork Smiths Fork

78
Alligator Lake
Henrys Fork
Jmllons Creek

76

G–61
77
G–60

East Fork Smiths Fork

Hessie Lake

▲ 11,210 ft.

11,545 ft. ▲

WASATCH–CACHE
NATIONAL
FOREST

79
Elkhorn Crossing

Bear Lake Sawmill Lake
G–10

G–51

Gilbert Lake

▲ 12,414 ft.

FLAT TOP MOUNTAIN

Grass Lake
Island Lake
80
Dollar Lake

Gilbert Peak
13,442 ft. ▲

Henrys Fork Lake
▲ 12,089 ft.

Lower Red Castle Lake

G–13

77

Castle Lake

Blanchard Lake

11,125 ft. ▲

81

12,916 ft. ▲

Red Castle
12,338 ft. ▲
East Red Castle Lake
Smiths Fork Pass Lake
Red Castle Lake

Mount Powell
13,137 ft. ▲

Cliff Lake

Anderson Pass

Gunsight Pass

81

ASHLEY
NATIONAL
FOREST

Upper Red Castle Lake

Smiths Fork Pass

81

Wilson Peak
13,040 ft. ▲

▲ 12,779 ft.

Kings Peak
13,528 ft. ▲

PAINTER
BASIN

South Kings Peak
13,512 ft.

76 HESSIE LAKE

Expect heavy weekend pressure at this popular lake. Several well-used camping areas are found along the east and south sides of the lake. However, firewood is limited. Heavily timbered shorelines make fly casting difficult, and for some reason cutthroat trout are quite skeptical. But by late evening, the fish become a little hungry and not so particular.

See map and logistics on pages 209–210.
Start: China Meadows trailhead
Distance: 11.5 miles out and back
Destination elevation: 10,620 feet
Approximate hiking time: 7.5 hours

Difficulty: Moderate
Usage: Heavy
Nearest town: Mountain View, Wyoming
Drainage: Smiths Fork

THE HIKE

This heavily timbered lake lies at the base of a rocky point in the East Fork of Smiths Fork drainage. Access starts at the south side of China Meadows Campground. Take the East Fork trail 3.5 miles south to the Henrys Fork Trail junction. Then head east toward

Hessie Lake is accessed via the China Meadows trailhead. PHOTO BY MATT MCKELL/UTAH DIVISION OF WILDLIFE RESOURCES

Henrys Fork 2 miles to the Hessie Lake turnoff. Travel another 0.25 mile west and you'll be at Hessie Lake. Though there are some boardwalks, be prepared for marsh and river crossings—and 800 feet of elevation gain over the last 2 miles after leaving behind the popular Red Castle trail.

A couple of other lakes in the proximity of Hessie are G–60 and G–61. These lakes are easily located by following their outlet stream that crosses the trail just east of the Hessie Lake turnoff. G–60 is the first lake you'll run into. This small meadow lake is situated at the base of a timbered ridge. Excellent campsites can be found near the lake, and plenty of horse pasture and spring water are available. Light to moderate fishing pressure is sustained by stocked brook trout.

Find G–61 by following the inlet of G–60 up a steep, timbered ridge 0.125 mile to the south. This shallow lake sits in partially timbered terrain at the base of Flat Top Mountain. Camping areas are present, and lots of horse pasture can be found in the large park to the west and north. Spring water is limited, especially in the late summer months. G–61 is subject to winterkill, but it has been experimentally stocked with brook trout anyway. You might want to give it a try. This lake receives little angling use, which means it could produce a big thrill.

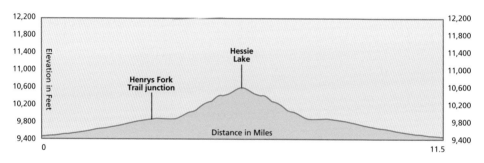

77 RED CASTLE LAKES

Red Castle Lake is one of the largest and deepest lakes in the High Uintas. Red Castle is set in a beautiful steep-walled basin. The reddish-colored mountain is shaped like a medieval castle.

See map and logistics on pages 209–210.
Start: China Meadows trailhead
Distance: 24 miles out and back
Destination elevation: 11,295 feet
Approximate hiking time: 14 hours

Difficulty: Moderate—one steep section
Usage: Moderate
Nearest town: Mountain View, Wyoming
Drainage: Smiths Fork

THE HIKE

From China Meadows trailhead, the trail follows the East Fork Smiths Fork River south 3.5 miles to the Henrys Fork Trail junction. Continue southwest 0.7 mile to another junction. Stay left, following the river. In about 1.8 miles the trail crosses a tributary of the creek and encounters another junction 0.5 mile farther on. Stay left and go 0.8 mile to another trail junction. Go right for 0.6 mile to a short set of switchbacks, then continue another 0.6 mile. At the next trail junction stay left and go 0.6 mile to Lower Red Castle Lake.

Lower Red Castle is a popular scenic lake resting in a large alpine meadow. Camping and fishing pressure are extremely heavy here too, but good campsites are available. Fires are prohibited at Lower Red Castle Lake.

Red Castle Lake is another 2.9 miles from Lower Red Castle Lake with a sharp gain in elevation on the last mile.

Campsites are nonexistent near the lake but can be found, along with running water, at the timbered area to the north. Other areas are exposed and can be hammered by wind. Angling and camping usage is excessively heavy on weekends, and fishing is considered only fair for pan-size cutthroat. Because of the size, depth, and popularity of this lake, an inflatable raft may increase the number and size of fish in your creel. If inflatables are used, use extreme caution. Red Castle is subject to sudden high winds and rapid weather changes. Life jackets are essential!

Upper Red Castle is in a rugged cirque basin, just 0.125 mile south of Red Castle. This lake is known as a poor fishery, but occasionally a large cutthroat trout is netted. No camping areas exist in this windy basin, but spring water is abundant.

East Red Castle is in a steep-walled basin at the east base of Red Castle Peak. Ice-cold spring water for filtering can be acquired from several different sources, but campsites, firewood, and horse pasture are not readily available. However, there are several good camping areas in the timbered areas to the northeast, along with a generous supply of horse pasture. You can easily reach East Red Castle from the inlet of Lower Red Castle Lake by picking your way up a steep hill to the east, then around the mountain.

This lake receives moderate fishing pressure for large but wary cutthroat trout. Try a #16 red or black ant at sundown. If the weather is foul, which happens a lot up here, tie on a small silver spinner. It's okay to fish in the rain if you can stay dry, but if lightning starts, head for shelter.

East Red Castle Lake sits at the base of Red Castle Peak. PHOTO BY MATT MCKELL/UTAH DIVISION OF WILDLIFE RESOURCES

Smiths Fork Pass Lake is said to have better angling. This lake is noted for its open terrain and irregular shorelines that make fly casting a pleasure. Due to the nature of this country, prospects for campsites and firewood are poor. Good camping areas and shelter are located in the wooded areas to the north, and spring water is present around the lake. This lake is next to the trail in a large cirque basin, 11 miles from either China Meadows or the East Fork Blacks Fork Campground.

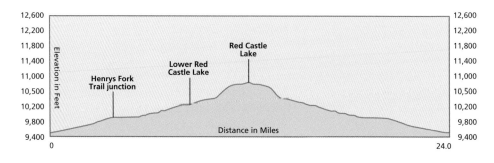

Red Castle is one of the most distinct landmarks in the Uinta Mountain range and certainly one of the most photogenic. PHOTO BY MATT MCKELL/UTAH DIVISION OF WILDLIFE RESOURCES

Compared with most trails in the High Uintas, the East Fork Smiths Fork Trail is like a freeway. It is well tread, and aging bridges are built over every major river crossing. But don't let these statements fool you. After a hard rain, horses and cows riddle the trail with tracks of slippery, slimy mud holes. And though the destination is among the prettiest in the Uintas, mountain pine bark beetles have taken a serious toll on the forest along the route.

HENRYS FORK TRAILHEAD

Another North Slope trailhead enters contention for winning the popularity contest in no small part thanks to Kings Peak. Though there are two other trails described in this book that access Utah's highest point, Henrys Fork is usually the most accessible—and clocks in at a reasonable 25 to 27.1 miles.

Unlike China Meadows, there are not a lot of campsites and no lakes to recreate on. Just a handful of established sites and a vault toilet plus some dispersed camping—great for setting up a base camp in the mountains from which to launch your backcountry adventures early the next morning. Otherwise, the primary destinations will be found several miles south of the trailhead, from a nearby lake with decent fishing to a view from the top of Utah.

See trails 78 through 81 for Henrys Fork Trailhead.
Maps: USGS Gilbert Peak NE, USGS Mount Powell, USGS Kings Peak; *USDA Forest Service High Uintas Wilderness*; *Trails Illustrated High Uintas Wilderness*

Trail contacts: Uinta-Wasatch-Cache National Forest, Forest Supervisor, 857 West South Jordan Pkwy., South Jordan, UT 84095; Mountain View Ranger District, 321 Highway 414, PO Box 129, Mountain View, WY 82939, (307) 782-6555

FINDING THE TRAILHEAD

From Mountain View, take Highway 410 south about 6 miles to a junction. Then take SR 017 (CR 283), a well-maintained gravel road, south about 12 miles to a fork. The east road (Road 077) heads south about 5 miles to Henrys Fork.

Henrys Fork trailhead has fifty parking places and is equipped with toilets, campsites, corrals, and a stock ramp.

The sun setting on the North Slope, looking up the valley to the south across Elkhorn Crossing from the trail to Henrys Fork Basin

78 ALLIGATOR LAKE

No, this lake is not a swamp where alligators feed. In fact, it's rather uncommon to encounter any reptile above 9,000 feet in the High Uintas. However, Alligator Lake can be enjoyed by human creatures, and its relatively shorter length and appealing name make it a good choice for families. Dominant pressure persists on weekends, but during the weekdays you should experience solitude.

See map on page 210 and logistics on page 216.
Start: Henrys Fork trailhead
Distance: 5.9 miles out and back
Destination elevation: 10,033 feet
Approximate hiking time: 4 hours

Difficulty: Easy
Usage: Heavy
Nearest town: Mountain View, Wyoming
Drainage: Henrys Fork

THE HIKE

To reach Alligator Lake, follow the Henrys Fork Trail 2.4 miles to a spur trail that parallels the lake's outlet. Good to excellent camping areas exist all around the lake, and angling is considered decent for pan-size brookies. The best fishing should take place along the north side. The south side is relatively shallow for some distance out.

There are also four or five campsites with tables, toilets, and fireplaces at the trailhead. Plenty of parking is available for hikers and equestrians, and a good road will ease you into the location. If you're able to grab a site (first come, first served), Alligator Lake would make a nice day excursion for kids while the old folks just lie back and enjoy a nap.

79 BEAR LAKE

Surrounded by mature pines, Bear Lake offers a quiet picture-book setting for the weary traveler. Its deep, placid waters seem to beckon, "Rest here, rest here." And a lot of hikers do. Bear Lake receives its share of backpackers that come to visit the popular Henrys Fork drainage. You might have some company here, but there are plenty of nice campsites, and the pine trees will serve as privacy barriers.

See map on page 210 and logistics on page 216.
Start: Henrys Fork trailhead
Distance: 13.5 miles out and back
Destination elevation: 10,767 feet
Approximate hiking time: 8 hours

Difficulty: Moderate
Usage: Moderate
Nearest town: Mountain View, Wyoming
Drainage: Henrys Fork

THE HIKE

To reach Bear Lake, simply follow the Henrys Fork Trail about 5.4 miles to Elkhorn Crossing. There a sign will direct you west along the North Side/Slope Highline Trail into Henrys Fork Basin. Just stick with the trail, which passes right next to Bear Lake.

As always, bring some means of water purification, even when drinking spring water, which can be found to the east 0.25 mile at Sawmill Lake. Horses won't find a lot to eat around these parts, so if you have pack animals, keep going up the trail.

There are numerous existing campsites at Bear Lake. Please don't build any more. As with any heavily used area, use low-impact camping techniques, and lend a hand gathering any leftover litter.

Bear and Sawmill Lakes have good populations of brook trout that provide fast fishing at times. These deep lakes can be fished successfully with either fly or spinner. Just keep your offerings small and work them slowly. You'll catch fish. For a change of pace, try the little creek connecting the two lakes. But practice your stealth. If these wild trout see or hear you, you won't see them.

An evening at Bear Lake can produce some beautiful sunsets.

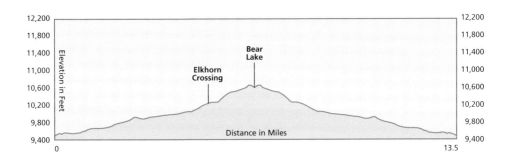

80 HENRYS FORK LAKE

Henrys Fork is a beautiful alpine mountain basin. Winding streams flow through misty meadows, and tall pines hiss in the wind while caressing big boulder formations. Campsites are plentiful below timberline, and fishing for brook and cutthroat trout is exciting at most lakes and rivers. It's a great place to visit. Though not as pressured as Dollar Lake, you may nevertheless have company here.

See map on page 210 and logistics on page 216.
Start: Henrys Fork trailhead
Distance: 15.5 to 18 miles out and back or partial loop
Destination elevation: 10,830 feet

Approximate hiking time: 10 to 11 hours
Difficulty: Moderate
Usage: Heavy
Nearest town: Mountain View, Wyoming
Drainage: Henrys Fork

THE HIKE

Henrys Fork features an excellent forest service trail that has a gradual climb. However, this trail is not too scenic and seems long until you arrive at Elkhorn Crossing, 5.4 miles from the trailhead. From here, many hikers opt for the loop trail into Henrys Fork Basin, passing by Bear Lake, Grass Lake, and Island Lake before running into the western shore of Henrys Fork after 4 miles of hiking. (It's only slightly longer to loop around to Dollar Lake for the return hike.) Or from Elkhorn Crossing, the trail heads south across the river and through the basin. Watch for cairns to mark the way. These rock piles are spaced along the trail to Gunsight Pass and beyond. Kings Peak is located on the other side of the pass and is the highest point in Utah (elevation 13,528 feet). After about 2 miles, at Dollar Lake turn southwest and go 0.5 mile cross-country to Henrys Fork Lake.

Henrys Fork Lake offers the best accommodations for a base camp. It has several excellent campsites along the east shore and ample running water flowing into and out of the lake. With the exception of Cliff, Castle, and Blanchard, all other lakes in this basin afford good camping areas and shelter.

Fishing can be unpredictable at most lakes and streams in the area. If there is no action at one lake, move to another. There are many to choose from that are increasingly distant and experience little visitation. The best angling might happen at Cliff Lake. For access, follow the inlet of Henrys Fork 1 mile south to Blanchard Lake, then follow the inlet of Blanchard another mile south to Cliff. After you pass Blanchard, the terrain is composed of rocky shelves and small waterfalls.

Diverging trails at Elkhorn Crossing. Take the trail to Bear Lake to reach Henrys Fork.

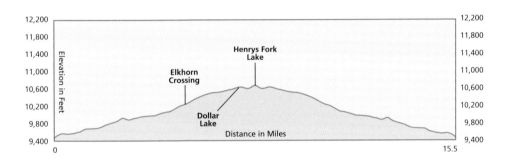

81 **KINGS PEAK**

There's a long way and then there are longer ways to reach Kings Peak. This is a long way. Utah's tallest mountain reaches to 13,528 feet in elevation. While that means Utah can claim no 14ers in its lineup of summits, there is something about the remoteness of Kings Peak and the effort it takes to reach it that adds to the sense of accomplishment. Of course, dedicated hikers never tire of the thrill of reaching virtually any mountaintop, but this one will make you work. While the main trail will tally just over 27 miles round-trip, if you can manage some non-technical scrambling up some rocks, you can shave off a couple of miles.

See map on page 210 and logistics on page 216.
Start: Henrys Fork trailhead
Distance: 25 to 27.1 miles out and back
Destination elevation: 13,528 feet
Approximate hiking time: Variable

Difficulty: Difficult—steep sections, rocky
Usage: Heavy
Nearest town: Mountain View, Wyoming
Drainage: Henrys Fork

THE HIKE

Admit it. You've had your eye on this one ever since you heard about it. Maybe that was when *National Geographic* named it one of the best hikes in the world a few years ago. If you're an inexperienced hiker, though, it's probably best to look elsewhere first and work your way up to this one. Its 4,100 feet in elevation gain, unpredictable weather in the form of afternoon thunderstorms, mosquitos, and rocky scrambles to the summit are not to be taken lightly. But if you have some miles behind you, have checked current conditions, and are prepared for the journey, let's get it done.

Depending on your timing and hiking speed, you could get an early start and make a long day of it: Plan on around 12 to 14 hours. Many opt to backpack in and include an overnight or two with a base camp at Dollar Lake (the most popular choice, aka potentially the least serene), Henrys Lake, or below Gunsight Pass. Thankfully, there are plenty of water sources you can filter and treat along the route, and, because of its popularity, the trail is mostly easy to follow until the unmarked rocky scramble up loose rocks to the top.

It all starts at Henrys Fork trailhead at around 9,420 feet. There's a gentle incline through some trees before reaching a low bridge at 2.4 miles. The right fork follows the creek up to Alligator Lake. Continue straight. At 5.4 miles there's a major intersection called Elkhorn Crossing. The first fork west heads into Henrys Fork Basin while the next fork east heads to Beaver Creek. You have the option to turn into Henrys Fork Basin to establish a base camp in a lower traffic area or proceed south along the well-tread trail through a beautiful meadow toward Dollar Lake, at the 7.4 mile-marker. Utah's third-highest mountain, Gilbert Peak, is due east of Dollar, and peak baggers can find a route there starting just south of the lake. It's one more mile to the junction with the return loop from Henrys Fork Basin.

The Henrys Fork trail ascends Gunsight Pass to reach Kings Peak, and the top of Utah, at center.
PHOTO BY MATT MCKELL/UTAH DIVISION OF WILDLIFE RESOURCES

Continuing southeast, the trail begins to ascend more noticeably for about a mile before a quick set of switchbacks up to Gunsight Pass at 11,852 feet and 10.2 miles in. At the pass, the primary trail drops down approximately 400 feet in elevation into Painter Basin where it meets up with the Highline Trail, then turns west and begins the steep ascent toward Kings Peak. Some hikers opt to take one of a couple feasible Gunsight/ Dome Peak Cutoff routes from Gunsight Pass, following a path up the right side of the ridge requiring some rocky scrambling before meeting up with Highline after 1.1 to 1.4 miles. From there, all hikers share the last mile or so to the top of Kings Peak, in all its rocky glory. Unless you're racing a storm, plan some time to sit and take in the views. Note that some years snow can linger at higher elevations deep into July, possibly necessitating the use of traction devices on your hiking boots and other gear.

Many years, snow will linger on mountain peaks of the High Uintas deep into July. Check conditions and hike prepared.

82 WEST FORK BEAVER CREEK TO GILBERT LAKE

If fly fishing is your thing, then Gilbert Lake might be your idea of heaven. Plenty of open shoreline and lots of eager trout make this a good fly-fishing lake. This lake is a must for fly fishers seeking fast action for brookies and cutthroat trout. Make sure your casting arm is in good shape. It will give out long before the fish do.

Start: West Fork Beaver Creek
Distance: 17.4 miles out and back
Destination elevation: 10,905 feet
Approximate hiking time: 10.5 hours
Difficulty: Moderate
Usage: Moderate
Nearest town: Mountain View, Wyoming
Drainage: Beaver Creek
Maps: USGS Kings Peak, *USDA Forest Service High Uintas*

Wilderness, Trails Illustrated High Uintas Wilderness
Trail contacts: Uinta-Wasatch-Cache National Forest, Forest Supervisor, 857 West South Jordan Pkwy., South Jordan, UT 84095; Mountain View Ranger District, 321 Highway 414, PO Box 129, Mountain View, WY 82939, (307) 782-6555

FINDING THE TRAILHEAD

From Mountain View, take Wyoming State Highway 414 southeast of Mountain View for 21.5 miles. At Lonetree, turn right onto CR 290, then left onto CR 291. After 5 miles, turn right on FR 078 and travel for 3 miles. Turn right on FR 082 and drive 1.7 miles. Turn right to stay on FR 082 and continue for 3.4 miles to a turn, signed for West Fork Beaver Creek, and continue approximately 0.5 mile to the trailhead. High clearance may be necessary near the end of the route, especially if it has been raining. There are eight parking spaces. GPS or the USDA Forest Service map is helpful for finding this one.

THE HIKE

From the trailhead, the trail heads southwest. You'll enter designated Wilderness at around 4.5 miles. At 5.7 miles, there is signage for the North Slope Highline and Middle Beaver. Turn left, cross the river, then head south following the signs toward Gilbert Lake, down the West Fork Beaver Trail. Gilbert Lake is 3 miles up the valley over fairly gentle terrain.

Equestrians are attracted to this area too. Horse pasture is plentiful around the lush meadows, and flowing water is everywhere. Campsites are well suited to horse travelers

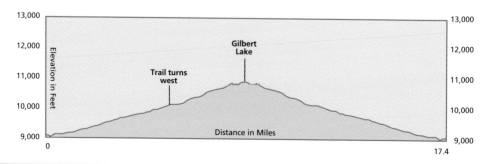

WEST FORK BEAVER CREEK TO GILBERT LAKE AND MIDDLE BEAVER CREEK TO BEAVER LAKE

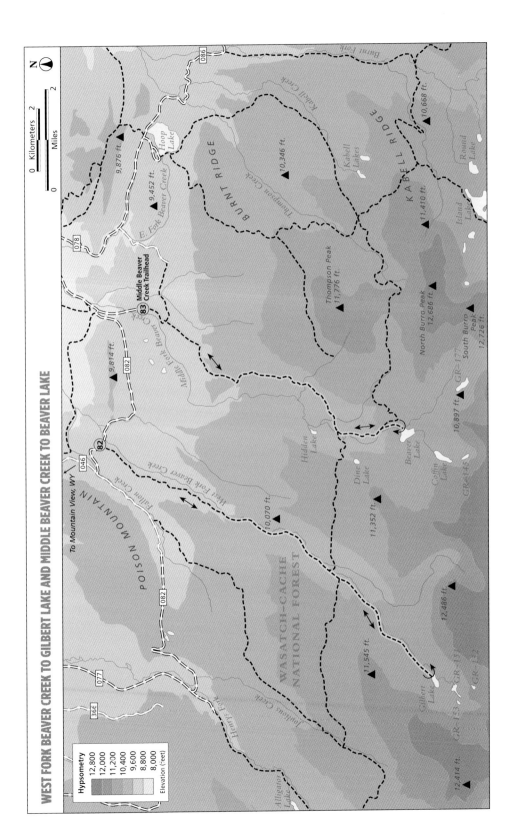

Hypsometry

Elevation (feet)

12,800
12,000
11,200
10,400
9,600
8,800
8,000

N

0 Kilometers 2

0 Miles 2

To Mountain View, WY

POISON MOUNTAIN

WASATCH-CACHE
NATIONAL FOREST

BURNT RIDGE

KABELL RIDGE

Burnt Fork

Hoop Lake

Middle Beaver Creek Trailhead

E. Fork Beaver Creek

Middle Fork Beaver Creek

Kabell Creek

Thompson Creek

Kabell Lakes

Round Lake

Island Lake

Coffin Lake

Branch Lake

Dine Lake

Hidden Lake

West Fork Beaver Creek

Fallon Creek

Henrys Fork

Jonthaus Creek

Gilbert Lake

Alligator Lake

9,876 ft.

9,452 ft.

9,814 ft.

10,346 ft.

10,668 ft.

11,410 ft.

Thompson Peak
11,776 ft.

North Burro Peak
12,626 ft.

South Burro Peak
12,726 ft.

10,897 ft.

12,486 ft.

11,352 ft.

10,070 ft.

11,545 ft.

12,414 ft.

GR-151

GR-451

GR-132

GR-145

GR-177

366

077

046

082

082

078

086

82

83

It's a short, but considerably rough, road to the West Fork Beaver Creek trailhead.

who want to set up a large base camp. The best camping is found on the south side of Gilbert Lake or in the trees just north of GR–151. Because of the moist nature of the area, mosquitoes are often a problem. Plan your trip late in the summer, and always bring along lots of repellent and cover up.

Although Gilbert Lake can offer fine fishing, check out some of the other lakes nearby. They are probably just as good, and maybe even better. South of Gilbert Lake lie GR–151, GR–152, and GR–153. These lakes and their connecting streams are stuffed with fish that seldom see an artificial lure. As with most other lakes in the High Uintas, great fishing is never guaranteed. If the lakes are not producing, then check out the streams. They can be hot when the lakes are not.

The trail to Gilbert Lake is sometimes hit-or-miss and there might be a lot of deadfall obscuring the route, so check your map and compass often. There are several wet areas along the route, and a good riding horse or waterproof boots can serve you well to keep your feet dry. There is also a moderately difficult (steep, time-consuming, and rocky!) 3-mile route up Gilbert Peak from Gilbert Lake.

A brook trout from the Beaver Creek drainage. PHOTO BY MATT MCKELL/UTAH DIVISION OF WILDLIFE RESOURCES

83 MIDDLE BEAVER CREEK TO BEAVER LAKE

Beaver Lake is characterized by timbered shorelines, with shallow water prevailing on the east side of the lake. Excellent campsites are in a large park to the west, and several sources of treatable spring water and horse pasture are available in nearby meadows. Brook trout and a few cutthroat inhabit this lake.

See map on page 227.
Start: Middle Beaver Creek trailhead
Distance: 13.6 miles out and back
Destination elevation: 10,505 feet
Approximate hiking time: 9 hours
Difficulty: Moderate
Usage: Heavy
Nearest town: Mountain View, Wyoming
Drainage: Beaver Creek

Maps: USGS Fox Lake, *USDA Forest Service High Uintas Wilderness*, *Trails Illustrated High Uintas Wilderness*
Trail contacts: Uinta-Wasatch-Cache National Forest, Forest Supervisor, 857 West South Jordan Pkwy., South Jordan, UT 84095; Mountain View Ranger District, 321 Highway 414, PO Box 129, Mountain View, WY 82939, (307) 782-6555

FINDING THE TRAILHEAD

Take Wyoming State Highway 414 southeast of Mountain View for 21.5 miles. At Lonetree, turn right onto CR 290, then left onto CR 291. After 5 miles, turn right on FR 078 and travel 3 miles. Turn right on FR 082 and drive 1.7 miles. Turn right on FR 164 and follow for approximately 1.5 miles past Georges Park picnic area to the Middle Beaver Creek trailhead. High clearance may be necessary near the end of the route, especially if it has been raining. There are ten parking spots.

THE HIKE

Beaver Lake is located in the Middle Fork of Beaver Creek drainage. From Middle Beaver Creek trailhead, the trail heads southwest. There's a sharp gain in elevation and a switchback around 0.8 mile and then some rolling terrain as the trail winds south and west across rocky creek crossings and an open meadow (whose trail might be muddled and horse-trampled) for 4 miles. At the next junction, stay to left and go another 1.5 miles to the lake.

Just southwest of Beaver lies Coffin Lake. Coffin gets its name from its oblong shape and small shelves surrounding the water. No trail exists to the lake, but you can find it by

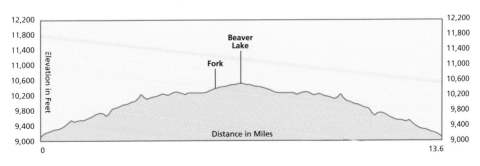

Stunning views of the Middle Fork of the Beaver Creek Drainage are a reward for hiking off trail to Coffin Lake. PHOTO BY MATT MCKELL/UTAH DIVISION OF WILDLIFE RESOURCES

following the inlet of Beaver 0.75 mile south then west to the base of some steep talus slopes. Rough and rocky describes the wilderness around this lake. Horse travel is quite difficult, and camping areas are a poor prospect. On the bright side, angling usage is light for unsophisticated cutthroat trout.

Other lakes you might happen upon in the Beaver Lake Basin are Hidden and Dine. Hidden Lake lies 0.5 mile north of Long Meadow. There is no trail, but access is not difficult. Anglers and backpackers alike often pass up this lake. There is no spring water here, but there are several good camping areas near the inlet.

Discover Dine Lake by following the inlet of Hidden Lake 1 mile southwest, or 0.5 mile west of Long Meadow. This lake is surrounded by rocky, timbered terrain and has a talus slope bordering the water on the southwest. Due to the rugged nature of this country, only mediocre campsites are available. There is no horse pasture in the vicinity, but there's plenty of spring water. Although Dine Lake has been stocked throughout the years, it will sometimes experience winterkill during harsh winters.

HOOP LAKE TRAILHEAD

A quintessential High Uintas destination, Hoop Lake offers a few dozen reservable developed campsites with drinking water plus a handful of smaller sites and group sites. It all caters to campers, anglers, boaters, equestrians, hikers, and backpackers seeking easy access to the High Uintas Wilderness. Beyond Island Lake described in this chapter, the trail climbs over the divide from the North Slope to the South Slope, meeting up with the Highline Trail and all that remarkable route accesses.

See trails 84 through 85 for Hoop Lake Trailhead.
Maps: USGS Fox Lake, *USDA Forest Service High Uintas Wilderness, Trails Illustrated High Uintas Wilderness*
Trail contacts: Uinta-Wasatch-Cache National Forest, Forest Supervisor, 857 West South Jordan Pkwy., South Jordan, UT 84095; Mountain View Ranger District, 321 Highway 414, PO Box 129, Mountain View, WY 82939, (307) 782-6555

FINDING THE TRAILHEAD

Take Wyoming State Highway 414 southeast of Mountain View for 21.5 miles. At Lonetree, turn right onto CR 290, then left onto CR 291. After 5 miles, turn right on FR 078 and travel for 3 miles. At the signed fork, stay left continuing south and then east for 3.8 miles. There's a Hoop Lake trailhead for horses on the east side of the lake as well as past the dam on the southwest side. There's a horse ramp and at least thirty parking spaces.

A faint trail along the south side of Hoop Lake sets out toward Kabell Lakes.

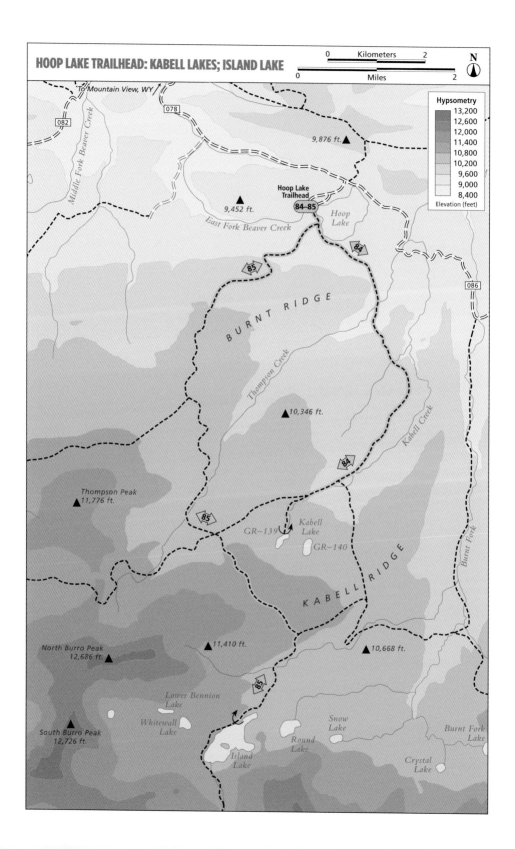

HOOP LAKE TRAILHEAD: KABELL LAKES; ISLAND LAKE

Kilometers
0   2

Miles
0   2

N

Hypsometry

13,200
12,600
12,000
11,400
10,800
10,200
9,600
9,000
8,400
Elevation (feet)

To Mountain View, WY

082

078

9,876 ft. ▲

Middle Fork Beaver Creek

Hoop Lake Trailhead

9,452 ft. ▲

84–85

East Fork Beaver Creek

Hoop Lake

84

086

85

BURNT RIDGE

Thompson Creek

10,346 ft. ▲

84

Thompson Peak
11,776 ft. ▲

Kabell Creek

85

GR–139

Kabell Lake

GR–140

KABELL RIDGE

Burnt Fork

North Burro Peak
12,686 ft. ▲

11,410 ft. ▲

10,668 ft. ▲

85

South Burro Peak
12,726 ft. ▲

Lower Bennion Lake

Whitewall Lake

Snow Lake

Burnt Fork Lake

Round Lake

Island Lake

Crystal Lake

84 KABELL LAKES

Even though the Kabell Lakes area is popular, campsites are scarce and heavy timber surrounds the shoreline. You may ask, "Why then is this place so popular?" Probably because Kabell is the only lake destination within a day's hiking distance (round-trip) that can be reached from the ever-popular Hoop Lake.

See map and logistics on pages 231–232.
Start: Hoop Lake trailhead
Distance: 10.4 miles out and back
Destination elevation: 10,348 feet
Approximate hiking time: 7 hours

Difficulty: Easy to moderate
Usage: Moderate
Nearest town: Mountain View, Wyoming
Drainage: Burnt Fork

THE HIKE

To get to Kabell Lakes, follow the trail from Hoop Lake to the south of Hoop Lake approximately 4 miles through Kabell Meadows, near where you'll officially enter the High Uintas Wilderness. At the upper portion of the meadows, the trail forks to the south and southwest. From here, take the trail south a couple hundred yards up Kabell Ridge. A side trail then takes off to the southwest, ending at Kabell Lakes in about 0.8 mile.

Angler usage is moderate for pan-size cutthroat trout. No decent camping areas are located in the lake vicinity, but a few wannabes with horse pasture exist along the outlet in the meadows to the north. There is spring water on the south side of the lake. You could see a lot of great country, eat lunch at the lake, fish a little, and be back at the campground before dark.

Signage at the trailhead to Kabell and Island Lake trails

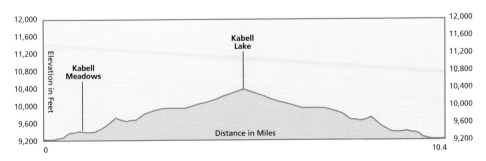

85 ISLAND LAKE

Many lakes in the High Uintas claim the name of Island. However, this lake is the king of all the Island Lakes—mainly because it's the biggest. Island Lake is reached from either Hoop or Spirit Lake. The Spirit Lake Trail is about a mile longer, but the elevation gain is 1,000 feet less.

See map and logistics on pages 231–232.
Start: Hoop Lake trailhead
Distance: 15.5 miles out and back
Destination elevation: 10,777 feet
Approximate hiking time: 10 hours

Difficulty: Moderate
Usage: Heavy
Nearest town: Mountain View, Wyoming
Drainage: Burnt Fork

THE HIKE

From Hoop Lake, the trail climbs southwest up a steep incline then over the more gradual slope of Burnt Ridge 3.5 miles to a trail junction. The trail to the right goes to Beaver Lake. Stay left, descending to Thompson Creek. The trail follows the stream briefly, then crosses it and comes to a trail crossing about 1.8 miles from the last junction. Continue straight across the other trail and climb up and over Kabell Ridge 1.5 miles to another junction with the trail descending into Burnt Creek. Turn right (south) and go 1 mile to the lake. (Another route continues past the turnoff to Kabell Lakes in chapter 84. Hike 1.3 miles to Highline North Slope and head west 2.2 miles.)

Island is a large alpine lake located in the southwest corner of the Burnt Fork drainage. It receives fairly heavy usage. Excellent campsites exist around the lake; treatable spring water is located along the south shore. Angling is often good for brook and cutthroat trout using small flies or spinners. Throughout the summer, Island Lake experiences a gradual drawdown, as irrigation water is needed downstream.

The farther you get from Island Lake, the better the solitude. Round Lake receives moderate pressure yet features excellent campsites, horse pasture, and spring water.

Snow Lake is impossible for horse travel, which makes fishing pressure for cutthroat trout all the lighter, but camping areas are nonexistent.

Whitewall and the Bennion Lakes can be worth a visit. They receive light angling use for brook and cutthroat trout. Several springs and campsites with plenty of horse pasture can be found on the west side of Whitewall Lake. Access from Island Lake is west through a large meadow, then up a timbered slope. Get your map and compass out. The best fishing should be at Lower Bennion.

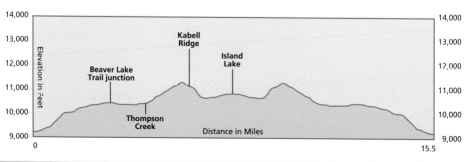

SPIRIT LAKE TRAILHEAD

Utahns may recognize Summit County as home to high-end hotel, ski, mountain bike, spa, and shopping experiences thanks to the world-renowned outdoor adventure base camp known as Park City. Spirit Lake, by comparison, feels like a frontier outpost in the easternmost extreme of the county, which may explain the cabin names at the nearby lodge: Sacagawea, Lewis & Clark, Nessmuk, among others.

Spirit Lake sits at 10,180 feet above sea level in Utah's Ashley National Forest. In fact, the lake and its trailheads are a 3-hour drive from Park City and accessed through Wyoming via I-80 and a series of unpaved county and forest roads. That remoteness can translate to some serious solitude. This chapter illustrates just four of the destination lakes accessed from two trailheads near Spirit Lake.

See trails 86 through 89 for Spirit Lake Trailhead.
Maps: USGS Chepeta Lake and USGS Whiterocks Lake, *USDA Forest Service High Uintas Wilderness*, *Trails Illustrated High Uintas Wilderness*

Trail contacts: Ashley National Forest, Supervisor's Office, 355 North Vernal Ave., Vernal UT 84078, (435) 781-1181; Flaming Gorge Ranger District, 25 West Highway 43, Manila, UT 84046, (435) 784-3445

FINDING THE TRAILHEAD

From Mountain View, take Wyoming Highway 414 east then south about 20 miles to Lonetree. After about 10 miles east on Highway 414 is a three-way junction that provides access to Spirit and Browne Lakes. At this junction, take the south dirt road (Road 221) 13 miles to a junction with a posted sign. Road 001 winds west then south 7 miles to Spirit Lake.

The Spirit Lake trailhead to Tamarak and Fish Lakes has about five parking places and can accommodate you with excellent campsites, toilets, water, a café with limited hours, rustic lodging, horse rentals, and a stock ramp. The trailhead to Daggett and Anson Lakes is located next to the road on the east side of Spirit Lake. There are limited pull-off parking options so the nearby campground might be the best option.

Dock and amenities near Spirit Lake Lodge, rustic accommodations near the Spirit Lake trailhead

SPIRIT LAKE TRAILHEAD: TAMARACK LAKE; FISH LAKE; DAGGETT LAKE; ANSON LAKES

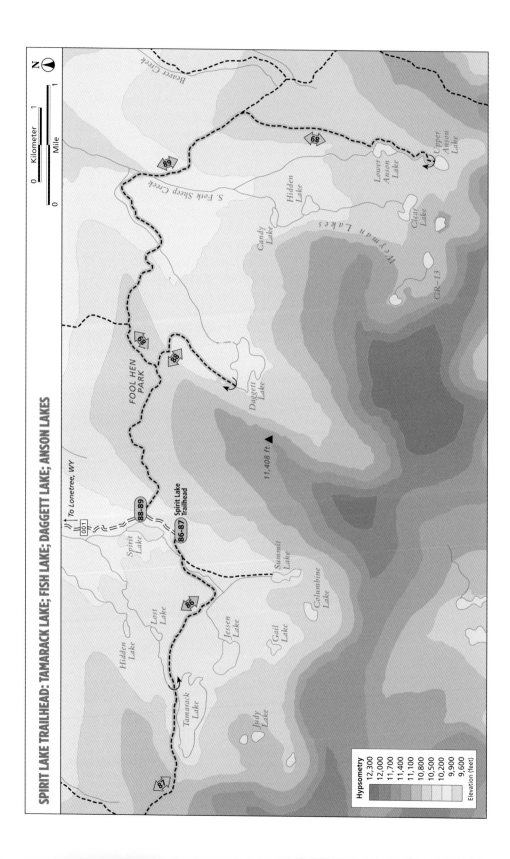

86 TAMARACK LAKE

If you're looking for a nice excursion for the entire family, then Tamarack Lake is a good choice. A well-maintained (but sometimes very rocky!) forest service trail takes off from the southwest side of Spirit Lake Campground. From here, it is only 1.4 miles south then west on the Middle Fork Trail. The trail splits about 1 mile from the trailhead, but both trails reunite near the east side of Tamarack Lake. The left-hand trail is a little bit longer but passes Jessen Lake; the right-hand trail heads straight to Tamarack Lake.

See map and logistics on pages 235–236.
Start: Spirit Lake trailhead
Distance: 2.8 miles out and back
Destination elevation: 10,429 feet
Approximate hiking time: 2 hours

Difficulty: Easy
Usage: Heavy
Nearest town: Mountain View, Wyoming
Drainage: Sheep Creek

THE HIKE

From Spirit Lake, the trail heads southwest for 0.6 mile to the creek then turns northwest for 0.8 mile to the lake. Sections of the trail are very rocky and require extra care to avoid twisted ankles or bruises, but the relatively short distance and multiple lake options will keep all hikers engaged. Just remember: Even though it's only 200 feet of elevation gain, this hike starts above 10,000 feet. Take it slow and drink plenty of water.

Tamarack is the biggest body of water in the Sheep Creek drainage. Although it receives heavy usage, brook and a few cutthroat trout are maintained by stocking and natural reproduction. The best campsites are on the east side. Perhaps the best campsite is located just a hundred yards south down the trail where it splits off and heads south toward the lake. This site can accommodate a large group. Spring water seeps up along the south shoreline, and horse pasture is present to the east.

Just southeast of Tamarack lies Jessen Lake. Both are about the same type of lake, except Jessen is half the size and has no real campsites. It sits right next to the trail in rocky, timbered country.

If these lakes contain too many people for your taste, try Lost Lake. Get there by following the outlet of Tamarack Lake 0.5 mile northeast. Lost Lake has several campsites to choose from, and angling usage remains relatively light. Lost Lake is more or less a shallow pond, but good water exchange enables cutthroat trout to survive the winter.

There are no campsites or springs 0.25 mile north at Hidden Lake, but hikers and anglers will likely find solitude there.

Judy Lake, perched upon a rocky and timbered bench within a scenic alpine basin, can provide fantastic brook trout angling. Follow a steep ridge up the southeast side of Tamarack, then head southwest. Fish a spinner down deep and get ready for some hard-hitting action. Gail Lake may also produce good opportunities. It receives little attention and is deep enough to support a fair supply of cutthroat trout.

Signage announces your arrival at Tamarack Lake, a short, but rocky hike from Spirit Lake.

87 **FISH LAKE**

For strong hikers looking for some real wilderness, circle *this* Fish Lake on your map. Seriously, Fish Lake sits within the boundaries of the designated High Uintas Wilderness area, which means dedicated hikers and folks on horseback will uncover the protected solitude and primitive recreation that make America's Wilderness so special.

See map and logistics on pages 235–236.
Start: Spirit Lake trailhead
Distance: 11.2 miles out and back
Destination elevation: 10,880 feet
Approximate hiking time: 6.5 hours

Difficulty: Moderate—one steep section, some cross-country
Usage: Light
Nearest town: Mountain View, Wyoming
Drainage: Sheep Creek

THE HIKE

Continuing along Tamarack Lake (see trail description above), the trail hits a set of steep, though reasonably short switchbacks that account for around 300 feet in elevation gain. While watching your step for jagged rocks in the trail, look for wildflowers along this forested section and take breaks as needed to acclimate to the elevation gain. The views back down over Tamarack are worth the pause.

The route (also known as the North Fork Sheep Creek Trail) eventually breaks clear of the conifers into a wide-open meadow at more than 10,800 feet above sea level. Here, the 12,722-foot South Burro and 12,676-foot North Burro peaks stand guard several miles to the north. Be careful as you cross the meadow taking in these surroundings: It is tempting to follow the odd screen of trees or continue along a path when you'll need to sweep the horizon for the next trail marker. Luckily, some of the cairns along Sheep Creek and the subsequent North Slope–Highline "B" Trail are monumental: human-sized stacks of stones built by hand. Oh, and around 3 miles in you'll hit the sign marked "High Uintas Wilderness." Don't be surprised if an elk or two cross your path.

The last leg of the journey is about 1 mile bearing south into a patch of forest where, after some winding through deadfall and broken trail segments, you'll arrive at the extreme west end of Fish Lake. Drop your pack and take a break: you've earned it.

It's difficult not to take time to throw a few casts into a lake called "Fish," but this remote lake in the Wilderness will be a welcome site to all.

88 DAGGETT LAKE

With shorter hikes to lakes on the other side of Spirit, Daggett gets a little less traffic. Afternoon thunderstorms also regularly turn the trail into a muddy, impassable mess. For those who make the trip, a beautifully nestled lake will reward the effort as well as offer one of the better rainbow fisheries in the High Uintas.

See map and logistics on pages 235–236.
Start: Spirit Lake trailhead
Distance: 5.6 to 6.9 miles out and back
Destination elevation: 10,462 feet
Approximate hiking time: 4.5 hours

Difficulty: Moderate—some steep sections
Usage: Heavy
Nearest town: Mountain View, Wyoming
Drainage: Sheep Creek

THE HIKE

The trail winds around swampy water holes, and a large meadow sits just south of the lake—prime habitat for a large assortment of mosquitoes and other bugs. To limit your exposure to these pesky critters, plan your trip after mid-August. By this time, hailstorms and other elements have diminished the insects' numbers.

Access to Daggett begins on the east side of Spirit Lake. Follow the well-groomed Browne–Spirit Lake Trail to the northeast to a switchback at around 0.6 mile. Continue south then east for about 1.7 miles to a junction. From here, the trail drops 400 feet down rocky switchbacks and to one of the outlets of Daggett Lake. Proceed along the outlet another 0.75 mile through a couple of boggy meadows and up a boulder ravine. Another, slightly shorter, route still shows on some maps departing from the trailhead and climbing 1 mile east up a steep slope and across Fool Hen Park before meeting up with the junction.

Daggett Lake plays host to a number of campsites along the northwest shore. Horse pasture is available in a meadow to the north, but spring water is hard to come by. This pretty lake receives moderate to heavy usage. Please help keep it clean.

Climbing the trail from Spirit to Daggett Lake

89 ANSON LAKES

People staying at the Spirit Lake Lodge might consider a long day trip to the Weyman Basin and Upper and Lower Anson Lakes. The lakes are popular with anglers, but the scenery alone is worth the walk.

See map and logistics on pages 235–236.
Start: Spirit Lake trailhead
Distance: 16 miles out and back
Destination elevation: 10,575 feet
Approximate hiking time: 9 hours

Difficulty: Moderate—some steep sections
Usage: Moderate
Nearest town: Mountain View, Wyoming
Drainage: Sheep Creek

THE HIKE

From the east side of Spirit Lake, follow the well-groomed Browne–Spirit Lake Trail to the northeast to a switchback at around 0.6 mile. Continue south then east for about 1.7 miles to a junction. Turn left and continue 0.3 mile to another junction. Stay right and descend a few hundred feet over 2 miles into South Fork Sheep Creek. After the second creek crossing, the trail climbs then levels off. About 2 miles from the creek crossing, turn right, heading south 1 mile to Anson Lakes.

The first lake you'll arrive at is Lower Anson. Upper Anson Lake is just a little farther. Follow a scant trail 0.25 mile south as it parallels the east side of the inlet to Lower Anson. Both lakes are in rugged and rocky terrain. There is one small camp on the south end of Lower Anson, but the best campsite is located a couple of hundred yards above Lower Anson Lake near the creek.

Fishing should be pretty good if the water is clear. Anson Lakes can get murky during rainy years. Natural reproduction keeps the brook trout population up. In fact, sometimes there are too many trout and they become stunted.

Leave your horses behind at Anson Lakes when traveling into the Weyman Lakes area. Treacherous terrain makes horses impractical. Expect the best fishing at either Clear or Hidden Lake, although Hidden will likely be murky if Anson Lakes are. Clear Lake is always clear and has some fat trout. Though angling can be slow, Candy Lake offers some big and tasty trout.

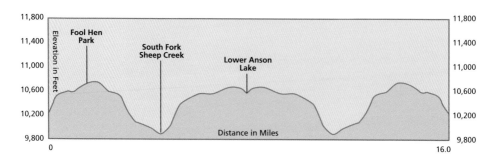

90 BROWNE LAKE AREA (LAMB LAKES OR POTTER)

The Browne Lake area is, in many respects, an outdoor recreation hub of the northeastern Uintas thanks to the campground; the cooling lake at 8,200 feet known for rainbow trout, brook trout, and kokanee salmon; and a network of ATV trails, including the historic Carter Military Trail. There are also three hiking and backpacking trailheads, though seasonal deadfall has made some navigation difficult—on a recent visit, the trail to Tepee was nowhere to be found.

Start: Browne Lake
Distance: 13 miles out and back
Destination elevation: 10,350 feet
Approximate hiking time: 8 hours
Difficulty: Difficult
Usage: Light
Nearest town: Mountain View, Wyoming
Drainage: Carter Creek

Maps: USGS Whiterocks Lake, *USDA Forest Service High Uintas Wilderness, Trails Illustrated High Uintas Wilderness*
Trail contacts: Ashley National Forest, Supervisor's Office, 355 North Vernal Ave., Vernal UT 84078, (435) 781-1181; Flaming Gorge Ranger District, 25 West Highway 43, Manila, UT 84046, (435) 784-3445

FINDING THE TRAILHEAD

From Mountain View, take Wyoming Highway 414 east then south about 20 miles to Lonetree. After about 10 miles east on Highway 414 is a three-way junction that provides access to Spirit and Browne Lakes. At this junction, take the south dirt Road 221 13 miles to a junction with a posted sign. Browne Lake is 8 miles east on Road 221.

Campsites, toilets, and water are located at Browne Lake, along with three different trailheads. Make sure to start on the correct trailhead (017).

THE HIKE

From the 017 trailhead, the trail traces a meadow and crosses fields where it's easy to lose site of the route. At a junction 2.5 miles in, turn left heading south toward Sheep Creek Canal through another grassy meadow. There's a bridge crossing the canal before continuing another 2 miles to a creek crossing on West Fork. (Another westbound trail branches to the right just ahead of the creek, so keep left.) After crossing the creek, it's

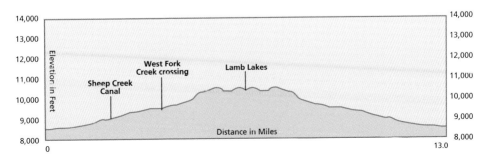

BROWNE LAKE AREA (LAMB LAKES OR POTTER)

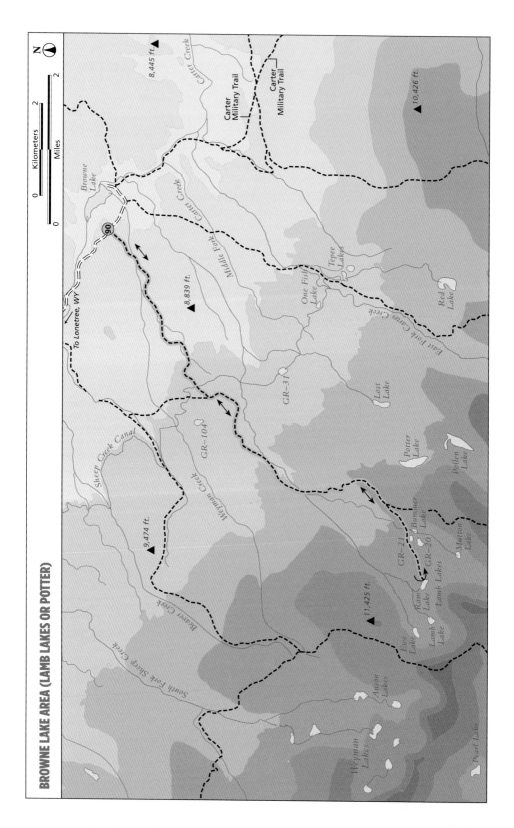

N

Kilometers
0   2

Miles
0   2

To Lonetree, WY

90

Browne Lake

8,445 ft.

Carter Creek

Carter Military Trail

Carter Military Trail

10,426 ft.

Carter Creek

Middle Fork

8,839 ft.

Sheep Creek Canal

9,474 ft.

GR-104

Weymus Creek

GR-31

One Fish Lake

Tepee Lakes

Red Lake

East Fork Carter Creek

Last Lake

Potter Lake

Pollen Lake

Mutton Lake

Bamaner Lake

GR-21

GR-20

Raw Lake

Lamb Lake

Lamb Lakes

Eve Lake

11,425 ft.

Beaver Creek

South Fork Sheep Creek

Anson Lakes

Weyman Lakes

Pearl Lake

The Browne Lake area features multiple trails for people on foot, horseback, or in ATVs.

around 2.5 miles to either Potter Lake or the Lamb Lakes area. The trail climbs the slopes toward the top of the ridge for about 1 mile. The route to Potter Lake branches left. Or, before reaching tree line, turn right off the trail and contour 1 mile to Lamb Lakes.

Though the landscape is rugged, backpackers will find suitable camping areas on the east side of Potter. The lake and East Fork Carter Creek areas (including Lower Tepee Lake) were treated by wildlife resources in recent years to remove non-native fish in an effort to establish native cutthroat trout.

Lamb Lakes can provide prime angling. However, fishing is unpredictable. Although these lakes receive little pressure, most have a history of winterkill during long, hard winters. In the summer months, there's an excellent elk population here. Signs of elk are everywhere, but actual sightings of these animals are rare. One sniff, sound, or sight of a human, and the only evidence of their existence will be the sound of hooves pounding through the trees.

Several lakes occupy Lamb Lakes Basin: Bummer, Mutton, Lamb, Ram, Ewe, GR–20, and GR–21. All these lakes are in rough and rocky, timbered country, and campsites are few and far between. Except for the Bummer Lake area, treatable spring water can be found at all the lakes.

To reach Mutton Lake, follow the inlet of Bummer Lake 0.5 mile south. This lake plays host to the best camping areas in Lamb Lakes Basin. Fishing pressure is considered light for stocked brook trout.

Lamb Lake is next to a steep rocky slope 1 mile west of Bummer. There is no trail, and the going gets rough when crossing over rocks and dead timber. This lake may also experience winterkill during harsh winters. For better angling possibilities, try Ram Lake. It is a little deeper and is fed by a fresh supply of spring water for filtering. Ram Lake is just 1 mile southwest of Bummer Lake.

Ewe Lake is a fishless pond sitting at the base of a talus slope 1 mile west of Bummer over very rough terrain. Get out and see this remote wilderness. Few people do.

Note: A 3.6-mile, round-trip trail near Browne Lake dam climbs Ute Mountain to the historic Ute Mountain Fire Tower National Historic Site (though the site is also accessible by car). Near the dam, the Old Carter Military Trail is a 35.6-mile route popular for off-highway vehicle (OHV) travel. It's worth hiking up 2 or 3 miles to get a sense of difficulty of travel through the rugged Uinta mountains from when the trail was built by the U.S. Army in the 1880s. Parts of it are challenging even for modern ATVs!

FALCONGUIDES'
THE ART OF HIKING

For many of us, a hike into the "wild" means loading up the SUV with expensive gear and driving to a toileted trailhead. Sure, you can mourn how civilized we've become—how GPS units have replaced natural instinct and Gore-Tex, true grit—but the silly gadgets of civilization aside, we have plenty of reason to take pride in how we've matured. With survival now on the back burner, we've begun to reason—and it's about time—that we have a responsibility to protect, no longer conquer, our wild places: that they, not we, are at risk. So please, do what you can. The following section will help you understand better what it means to "do what you can" while still making the most of your hiking experience. Anyone can take a hike, but hiking safely and well is an art requiring preparation and proper equipment.

TRAIL ETIQUETTE

Zero impact. Always leave an area just like you found it—if not better than you found it. Avoid camping in fragile, alpine meadows and along the banks of streams and lakes. Use a camp stove versus building a wood fire, required in some Uinta Mountain locations. Pack up all your trash and extra food. Bury human waste at least 100 feet from water sources under 6 to 8 inches of topsoil. Above tree line? It won't decompose. Pack it out. All of it. Don't bathe with soap in a lake or stream—use prepackaged moistened towels to wipe off sweat and dirt, or bathe in the water without soap.

Stay on the trail. It's true, a path anywhere leads nowhere new, but purists will just have to get over it. Paths serve an important purpose; they limit impact on natural areas. Straying from a designated trail may seem innocent but it can cause damage to sensitive areas—damage from which it may take years to recover, if the area can recover at all. Even simple shortcuts can be destructive. Furthermore, creating new trails leads to confusion and may lead to other hikers getting lost. So, please, stay on the trail. Some High Uintas trails are "cross-country," meaning there is no defined trail. In that case, tread lightly. With a group? Spread out to prevent creating a trail.

Leave no weeds. Noxious weeds tend to overtake other plants, which in turn affects animals and birds that depend on them for food. To minimize the spread of noxious weeds, hikers should regularly clean their boots, tents, packs, and hiking poles of mud and seeds. Also brush your dog to remove any weed seeds before heading into a new area.

Keep your dog under control. You can buy a flexi-lead that allows your dog to go exploring along the trail, while allowing you the ability to reel him in should another hiker approach or should he decide to chase a rabbit or deer—and worse for the dog, a porcupine. Always obey leash laws and be sure to bury your dog's waste or pack it out in sealed bags.

Respect other trail users. Often you're not the only one on the trail. With the rise in popularity of multiuse trails, you'll have to learn a new kind of respect, beyond the nod and "hello" approach you may be used to. First investigate whether you're on a multiuse trail, and assume the appropriate precautions. When you encounter motorized vehicles (ATVs, motorcycles, and 4WDs), be alert. Though they should always yield to the hiker, often they're going fast or are lost in the buzz of their engine to react to your presence. If you hear activity ahead, step off the trail just to be safe. Note that you're not likely to hear a mountain biker coming, so be prepared and know ahead of time whether you share the trail with them. Cyclists should always yield to hikers, but that's little comfort to the hiker. Be aware. When you approach horses or pack animals on the trail, always step quietly off the trail, preferably on the downhill side, and let them pass. If you're wearing a large backpack, it's often a good idea to sit down. To some animals, a hiker wearing a large backpack might appear threatening. Many national forests allow domesticated grazing, usually for sheep and cattle. This is noticeably true in many parts of the Uintas. The forest is part of the U.S. Department of Agriculture, after all. Make sure your dog doesn't harass these animals, and respect ranchers' rights while you're enjoying yours.

GETTING INTO SHAPE

Unless you want to be sore—and possibly have to shorten your trip or vacation—be sure to get in shape before a big hike. If you're terribly out of shape, start a walking program early, preferably 8 weeks in advance. Start with a 15-minute walk during your lunch hour or after work and gradually increase your walking time to an hour. You should also increase your elevation gain. Walking briskly up hills really strengthens your leg muscles and gets your heart rate up. If you work in a storied office building, take the stairs instead of the elevator. If you prefer going to a gym, walk on the treadmill or use a stair machine. You can further increase your strength and endurance by walking with a loaded backpack. Stationary exercises you might consider are squats, leg lifts, sit-ups, and push-ups. Other good ways to get in shape include biking, running, aerobics, and, of course, short hikes. Stretching before and after a hike keeps muscles flexible and helps avoid injuries.

PREPAREDNESS

It's been said that failing to plan means planning to fail. So take the necessary time to plan your trip. Whether going on a short day hike or an extended backpack trip, always prepare for the worst. Simply remembering to pack a copy of the *US Army Survival Manual* is not preparedness. Although it's not a bad idea if you plan on entering truly wild places, it's merely the tourniquet answer to a problem. You need to do your best to prevent the problem from arising in the first place. In order to survive—and to stay reasonably comfortable—you need to concern yourself with the basics: water, food, and shelter. Don't go on a hike without having these bases covered. And don't go on a hike expecting to find these items in the woods.

Water. Even in frigid conditions, you need at least two quarts of water a day to function efficiently. Add heat and taxing terrain and you can bump that figure up to one gallon. That's simply a base from which to work—your metabolism and your level of conditioning can raise or lower that amount. Unless you know your level, assume you need one gallon of water a day. Now, where do you plan on getting the water?

Preferably not from natural water sources, unless you are prepared to properly treat that water (see Treating water later in this section). These sources can be loaded with intestinal disturbers, such as bacteria, viruses, and fertilizers. *Giardia lamblia,* the most common of these disturbers, is a protozoan parasite that lives part of its life in water sources. The parasite spreads when mammals defecate in water sources. Once ingested, giardia can induce cramping, diarrhea, vomiting, and fatigue within two days to two weeks after ingestion. Giardiasis is treatable with prescription drugs. If you believe you've contracted giardiasis, see a doctor immediately.

Treating water. The best and easiest solution to avoid polluted water is to carry your water with you. Yet, depending on the nature of your hike and the duration, this may not be an option or may not be wise—one gallon of water weighs 8.5 pounds. In that case, you'll need to look into treating water. Regardless of which method you choose, you should always carry some water with you in case of an emergency. Save this reserve until you absolutely need it.

There are basically three methods of treating water: boiling, chemical treatment, and filtering. If you boil water, it's recommended you do so for 10 to 15 minutes. This is often impractical because you're forced to exhaust a great deal of your fuel supply. You can opt for chemical treatment, which will kill giardia but will not take care of other chemical pollutants and doesn't filter. Another drawback to chemical treatments is the unpleasant taste of the water after it's treated. You can remedy this by adding powdered drink mix to the water. Filters are the preferred method for treating water. Many filters remove giardia, organic and inorganic contaminants, and don't leave an aftertaste. Water filters are far from perfect, as they can easily become clogged or leak if a gasket wears out. It's always a good idea to carry a backup supply of chemical treatment tablets in case your filter decides to quit on you.

Food. If we're talking about survival, you can go days without food, as long as you have water. But we're also talking about comfort. Try to avoid foods that are high in sugar and fat like candy bars and potato chips. These food types are harder to digest and are low in nutritional value. Instead, bring along foods that are easy to pack, nutritious, and high in energy (e.g., bagels, nutrition bars, dehydrated fruit, gorp, and jerky). If you are on an overnight trip, easy-to-fix dinners include rice mixes with dehydrated potatoes, corn, pasta with cheese sauce, and soup mixes. For a tasty breakfast, you can fix hot oatmeal with brown sugar and reconstituted milk powder topped off with banana chips. If you like a hot drink in the morning, bring along herbal tea bags or hot chocolate. If you are a coffee junkie, you can purchase coffee that is packaged like tea bags. You can prepackage all of your meals in heavy-duty sealable plastic bags to keep food from spilling in your pack. These bags can be reused to pack out trash.

Shelter. The type of shelter you choose depends less on the conditions than on your tolerance for discomfort. Shelter comes in many forms—tent, tarp, lean-to, bivy sack, cabin, cave, etc. If you're camping in the desert, a bivy sack may suffice, but if you're above the tree line and a storm is approaching, a better choice is a three- or four-season tent. Tents are the logical and most popular choice for most backpackers, as they're lightweight and packable—and you can rest assured you always have shelter from the elements and bugs. Before you leave on your trip, anticipate what the weather and terrain will be like and plan for the type of shelter that will work best for your comfort level (see Equipment later in this section).

Finding a campsite. If there are established campsites, stick to those. If not, start looking for a campsite early—around 3:30 or 4:00 p.m. Stop at the first decent site you see. Depending on the area, it could be a long time before you find another suitable location. Pitch your camp in an area that's level. Make sure the area is at least 200 feet from fragile areas like lakeshores, meadows, and stream banks. And try to avoid areas thick in underbrush, as they can harbor insects and provide cover for approaching animals. There are 0.25-mile fire and firewood gathering restrictions around several lakes in the High Uintas Wilderness, meaning carry a backcountry stove or count your steps carefully if you absolutely must have a fire—which in some conditions, believe us, you truly don't want to risk.

If you are camping in stormy, rainy weather, look for a rock outcrop or a shelter in the trees to keep the wind from blowing your tent all night. Be sure you don't camp under trees with dead limbs that might break off and drop on top of you. Also, try to find an area that has an absorbent surface, such as sandy soil or forest duff. This, in addition to camping on a surface with a slight angle, will provide better drainage. By all means, don't dig trenches to provide drainage around your tent—remember you're practicing zero-impact camping.

If you're in bear country, steer clear of creek beds or animal paths. If you see any signs of a bear's presence (i.e., scat, footprints), relocate. You'll need to find a campsite near a tall tree where you can hang your food and other items that may attract bears, such as deodorant, toothpaste, or soap. Carry a lightweight nylon rope with which to hang your food. As a rule, you should hang your food at least 20 feet from the ground and 5 feet away from the tree trunk. You can put food and other items in a waterproof stuff sack and tie one end of the rope to the stuff sack. To get the other end of the rope over the tree branch, tie a good size rock to it, and gently toss the rock over the tree branch. Pull the stuff sack up until it reaches the top of the branch and tie it off securely. Don't hang your food near your tent! If possible, hang your food at least 100 feet away from your campsite. Alternatives to hanging your food are bear-proof plastic canisters and metal bear boxes. Also remember to cook 100 feet from camp and change out of clothes used to cook in.

Lastly, think of comfort. Lie down on the ground where you intend to sleep and see if it's a good fit. For morning warmth (and a nice view to wake up to), have your tent face east.

FIRST AID

I know you're tough, but get 10 miles into the woods and develop a blister and you'll wish you had carried that first-aid kit. Face it, it's just plain good sense. Many companies produce lightweight, compact first-aid kits. Just make sure yours contains at least the following:

- Band-Aids
- moleskin
- various sterile gauze and dressings
- white surgical tape
- an Ace bandage

- an antihistamine

- aspirin

- Betadine solution

- a first-aid book

- Tums

- tweezers

- scissors

- antibacterial wipes

- triple-antibiotic ointment

- plastic gloves

- sterile cotton tip applicators

- syrup of ipecac (to induce vomiting)

- thermometer

- wire splint

Here are a few tips for dealing with and hopefully preventing certain ailments:

Sunburn. Take along sunscreen or sunblock, protective clothing, and a wide-brimmed hat. If you do get a sunburn, treat the area with aloe vera gel, and protect the area from further sun exposure. At higher elevations, the sun's radiation can be particularly damaging to skin. Remember that your eyes are vulnerable to this radiation as well. Sunglasses can be a good way to prevent headaches and permanent eye damage from the sun, especially in places where light-colored rock or patches of snow reflect light up in your face.

Blisters. Be prepared to take care of these hike-spoilers by carrying moleskin (a lightly padded adhesive), gauze and tape, or adhesive bandages. An effective way to apply moleskin is to cut out a circle of moleskin and remove the center—like a doughnut—and place it over the blistered area. Cutting the center out will reduce the pressure applied to the sensitive skin. Other products can help you combat blisters. Some are applied to suspicious hot spots before a blister forms to help decrease friction to that area, while others are applied to the blister after it has popped to help prevent further irritation.

Insect bites and stings. You can treat most insect bites and stings by applying hydrocortisone 1 percent cream topically and taking a pain medication such as ibuprofen to reduce swelling. If you forgot to pack these items, a cold compress or a paste of mud and ashes can sometimes assuage the itching and discomfort. Remove any stingers by using tweezers or scraping the area with your fingernail or a knife blade. Don't pinch the area, as you'll only spread the venom. Some hikers are highly sensitive to bites and stings and may have a serious allergic reaction that can be life threatening. Symptoms of a serious allergic reaction can include wheezing, an asthmatic attack, and shock. The treatment for this severe type of reaction is epinephrine. If you know you are sensitive to bites and stings, carry a pre-packaged kit of epinephrine, which can be obtained only by prescription from your doctor.

Ticks. Ticks can carry diseases such as Rocky Mountain spotted fever and Lyme disease. The best defense is, of course, prevention. If you know you're going to be hiking through an area littered with ticks, wear long pants and a long-sleeved shirt. You can apply a permethrin repellent to your clothing and a DEET repellent to exposed skin. At the end of your hike, do a spot check for ticks (and insects in general). If you do find a tick embedded in your skin, coat the insect with petroleum jelly or tree sap to cut off its air supply. The tick should release its hold, but if it doesn't, grab the head of the tick firmly—with a pair of tweezers if you have them—and gently pull it away from the skin with steady, even pressure. Sometimes part of the tick lingers, but this should come out on its own. Clean the affected area with an antibacterial cleanser and then apply triple-antibiotic ointment. Monitor the area for a few days. If irritation persists or a white spot develops, see a doctor to rule out possible infection.

Poison ivy, oak, and sumac. These skin irritants can be found most anywhere in North America and come in the form of a bush or a vine, having leaflets in groups of three, five, seven, or nine. Learn how to spot the plants. The oil they secrete can cause an allergic reaction in the form of blisters, usually about 12 hours after exposure. The itchy rash can last from 10 days to several weeks. The best defense against these irritants is to wear clothing that covers the arms, legs, and torso. For summer, zip-off cargo pants come in handy. There are also nonprescription lotions you can apply to exposed skin that guard against the effects of poison ivy/oak/sumac and can be washed off with soap and water. If you think you were in contact with the plants, after hiking (or even on the trail during longer hikes) wash with soap and water. Taking a hot shower with soap after you return home from your hike will also help to remove any lingering oil from your skin. Should you contract a rash from any of these plants, use an antihistamine to reduce the itching. If the rash is localized, create a light bleach/water wash to dry up the area. If the rash has spread, either tough it out or see your doctor about getting a dose of cortisone (available both orally and by injection).

Snakebites. Snakebites are rare in North America. Unless startled or provoked, the majority of snakes will not bite. If you are wise to their habitats and keep a careful eye on the trail, you should be just fine. When stepping over logs, first step on the log, making sure you can see what's on the other side before stepping down. Though your chances of being struck are slim, it's wise to know what to do in the event you are.

If a nonvenomous snake bites you, allow the wound to bleed a small amount and then cleanse the wounded area with a Betadine solution (10 percent povidone iodine). Rinse the wound with clean water (preferably) or fresh urine (it might sound ugly, but it's sterile). Once the area is clean, cover it with triple-antibiotic ointment and a clean bandage. Remember, most residual damage from snakebites, venomous or otherwise, comes from infection, not the snake's venom. Keep the area as clean as possible and get medical attention immediately.

If you are bitten by a venomous snake, find a place to sit down several yards away from the snake, monitor your breathing, remove constrictive jewelry or clothing, and stay calm. An emergency evacuation may be necessary, and you'll need a clear head and a plan. If you have cell service or satellite messaging, call for help. If not, you may need to slowly walk in the direction of service, staying hydrated and calm. Don't run—you'll only increase the flow of blood throughout your system. Commercial snake bite kits are no longer used.

If it is your travel companion who's been bitten, treat them for shock if needed—make them comfortable, have them lie down, elevate their legs, and keep them warm. Avoid applying anything cold to the bite wound. Immobilize the affected area and remove any constricting items such as rings, watches, or restrictive clothing—swelling may occur.

Once they are stable and relatively calm, seek medical attention in the quickest feasible way. The victim should get treatment within 12 hours, ideally, which usually consists of a tetanus shot, antivenin, and antibiotics.

Dehydration. Have you ever hiked in hot weather and had a roaring headache and felt fatigued after only a few miles? More than likely you were dehydrated. Symptoms of dehydration include fatigue, headache, and decreased coordination and judgment. When you are hiking, your rate of fluid loss depends on the outside temperature, humidity, altitude, and your activity level. On average, a hiker walking in warm weather will lose four liters of fluid a day. That fluid loss is easily replaced by normal consumption of liquids and food. However, if a hiker is walking briskly in hot, dry weather and hauling a heavy pack, they can lose one to three liters of water an hour. It's important to always carry plenty of water and to stop often and drink fluids regularly, even if you aren't thirsty.

Heat exhaustion. Heat exhaustion is the result of a loss of large amounts of electrolytes and often occurs if a hiker is dehydrated and has been under heavy exertion. Common symptoms of heat exhaustion include cramping, exhaustion, fatigue, lightheadedness, and nausea. You can treat heat exhaustion by getting out of the sun and drinking an electrolyte solution made up of 1 teaspoon of salt and 1 tablespoon of sugar dissolved in a liter of water. Drink this solution slowly over a period of 1 hour. Drinking plenty of fluids (preferably an electrolyte solution/sports drink) can prevent heat exhaustion. Avoid hiking during the hottest parts of the day, and wear breathable clothing, a wide-brimmed hat, and sunglasses.

Hypothermia. Hypothermia is one of the biggest dangers in the backcountry, especially for day hikers in the summertime. That may sound strange, but imagine starting out on a hike in midsummer when it's sunny and 80 degrees out. You're clad in nylon shorts and a cotton T-shirt. About halfway through your hike, the sky begins to cloud up, and in the next hour a light drizzle begins to fall and the wind starts to pick up. Before you know it, you are soaking wet and shivering. More advanced signs include decreased coordination, slurred speech, and blurred vision. When a victim's temperature falls below 92 degrees, the blood pressure and pulse plummet, possibly leading to coma and death.

To avoid hypothermia, always bring a windproof/rainproof shell, a fleece jacket, tights made of a breathable, synthetic fiber, gloves, and hat when you are hiking in the mountains. Learn to adjust your clothing layers based on the temperature. If you are climbing uphill at a moderate pace you will stay warm, but when you stop for a break, you'll become cold quickly, unless you add more layers of clothing.

If a hiker is showing advanced signs of hypothermia, dress them in dry clothes and make sure they are wearing a hat and gloves. Place the person in a sleeping bag in a tent or shelter that will protect them from the wind and other elements. Give the person warm fluids to drink and keep them awake.

Frostbite. When the mercury dips below 32 degrees, your extremities begin to chill. If a persistent chill attacks a localized area, say, your hands or your toes, the circulatory system reacts by cutting off blood flow to the affected area—the idea being to protect and preserve the body's overall temperature. And so it's death by attrition for the affected area. Ice crystals start to form from the water in the cells of the neglected tissue. Deprived of heat, nourishment, and now water, the tissue literally starves. This is frostbite.

Prevention is your best defense against this situation. Most prone to frostbite are your face, hands, and feet, so protect these areas well. Wool is the material of choice because it provides ample air space for insulation and draws moisture away from the skin. Synthetic fabrics, however, have recently made great strides in the cold weather clothing market. Do your research. A pair of light silk liners under your regular gloves is a good trick for keeping warm. They afford some additional warmth, but more importantly they'll allow you to remove your mitts for tedious work without exposing the skin.

If your feet or hands start to feel cold or numb due to the elements, warm them as quickly as possible. Place cold hands under your armpits or bury them in your crotch. If your feet are cold, change your socks. If there's plenty of room in your boots, add another pair of socks. Remember, though, constricting your feet in tight boots can restrict blood flow and actually make your feet colder more quickly. Your socks need to have breathing room if they're going to be effective. Dead air provides insulation. If your face is cold, place your warm hands over your face, or simply wear a head stocking.

Should your skin go numb and start to appear white and waxy, chances are you have or are developing frostbite. Don't try to thaw the area unless you can maintain the warmth. In other words, don't stop to warm up your frostbitten feet only to head back on the trail. You'll do more damage than good. Tests have shown that hikers who walked on thawed feet did more harm, and endured more pain, than hikers who left the affected areas alone. Do your best to get out of the cold entirely and seek medical attention—which usually consists of performing a rapid rewarming in water for 20 to 30 minutes.

The overall objective in preventing both hypothermia and frostbite is to keep the body's core warm. Protect key areas where heat escapes, like the top of the head, and maintain the proper nutrition level. Foods that are high in calories aid the body in producing heat. Never smoke or drink alcohol when you're in situations where the cold is threatening. By affecting blood flow, these activities ultimately cool the body's core temperature.

Altitude sickness (AMS). High lofty peaks, clear alpine lakes, and vast mountain views beckon hikers to the high country. But those who like to venture high may become victims of altitude sickness (also known as acute mountain sickness—AMS). Altitude sickness is your body's reaction to insufficient oxygen in the blood due to decreased barometric pressure. While some hikers may feel lightheaded, nauseous, and experience shortness of breath at 7,000 feet, others may not experience these symptoms until they reach 10,000 feet or higher.

Slowing your ascent to high places and giving your body a chance to acclimatize to the higher elevations can prevent altitude sickness. For example, if you live at sea level and are planning a weeklong backpacking trip to elevations between 7,000 and 12,000 feet, start by staying below 7,000 feet for one night, then move to between 7,000 and 10,000 feet for another night or two. Avoid strenuous exertion and alcohol to give your body a chance to adjust to the new altitude. It's also important to eat light food and drink plenty of nonalcoholic fluids, preferably water. Loss of appetite at altitude is common, but you must eat!

Most hikers who experience mild to moderate AMS develop a headache and/or nausea, grow lethargic, and have problems sleeping. The treatment for AMS is simple: Stop heading uphill. Keep eating and drinking water, and take meds for the headache. You actually need to take more breaths at altitude than at sea level, so breathe a little faster without hyperventilating. If symptoms don't improve over 24 to 48 hours, descend. Once a victim descends 2,000 to 3,000 feet, the signs will usually begin to diminish.

Severe AMS comes in two forms: high altitude pulmonary edema (HAPE) and high altitude cerebral edema (HACE). HAPE, an accumulation of fluid in the lungs, can occur above 8,000 feet. Symptoms include rapid heart rate, shortness of breath at rest, AMS symptoms, dry cough developing into a wet cough, gurgling sounds, flu-like or bronchitis symptoms, and lack of muscle coordination. HAPE is life threatening, so descend immediately, at least 2,000 to 4,000 feet. HACE usually occurs above 12,000 feet but sometimes occurs above 10,000 feet. Symptoms are similar to HAPE but also include seizures, hallucinations, paralysis, and vision disturbances. Descend immediately—HACE is also life threatening.

Hantavirus pulmonary syndrome (HPS). Deer mice spread the virus that causes HPS, and humans contract it from breathing it in, usually when they've disturbed an area with dust and mice feces from nests or surfaces with mice droppings or urine. Exposure to large numbers of rodents and their feces or urine presents the greatest risk. As hikers, we sometimes enter old buildings, and often deer mice live in these places. We may not be around long enough to be exposed, but be aware of this disease. Symptoms are flu-like and appear about two to three weeks after exposure. After initial symptoms, a dry cough and shortness of breath follow. Breathing is difficult. If you even think you might have HPS, see a doctor immediately!

NATURAL HAZARDS

Besides tripping over a rock or tree root on the trail, there are some real hazards to be aware of while hiking. Even if where you're hiking doesn't have the plethora of venomous snakes, poisonous plants, insects, and grizzly bears found in other parts of the United States, there are a few weather conditions and predators you may need to take into account.

Lightning. Thunderstorms build over the Uinta Mountains almost every day during the summer. Lightning is generated by thunderheads and can strike without warning, even several miles away from the nearest overhead cloud. The best rule of thumb is to start leaving exposed peaks, ridges, and canyon rims by about noon. This time can vary a little depending on storm buildup. Keep an eye on cloud formation, and don't underestimate how fast a storm can build. The bigger they get, the more likely a thunderstorm will happen. Lightning takes the path of least resistance, so if you're the high point, it might choose you. Ducking under a rock overhang is dangerous, as you form the shortest path between the rock and ground. If you dash below tree line, avoid standing under the only or the tallest tree. If you are caught above tree line, stay away from anything metal you might be carrying, Move down off the ridge slightly to a low, treeless point and squat until the storm passes. If you have an insulating pad, squat on it. Avoid having both your hands and feet touching the ground at once and never lay flat. If you hear a buzzing sound or feel your hair standing on end, move quickly, as an electrical charge is building.

Flash floods. On July 31, 1976, a torrential downpour unleashed by a thunderstorm dumped tons of water into the Big Thompson watershed near Estes Park. Within hours, a wall of water moved down the narrow canyon, killing 139 people and causing more than $30 million in property damage. The spooky thing about flash floods, especially in Western canyons, is that they can appear out of nowhere from a storm many miles away. While hiking or driving in canyons, keep an eye on the weather. Always climb to safety if danger threatens. Flash floods usually subside quickly, so be patient and don't cross a swollen stream.

Bears. Most of the United States (outside of the Pacific Northwest and parts of the Northern Rockies) does not have a grizzly bear population, although some rumors exist about sightings where there should be none. Black bears are plentiful in the Uintas. Here are some tips in case you and a bear scare each other. Most of all, avoid scaring a bear. Watch for bear tracks (five toes) and droppings (sizable with leaves, partly digested berries, seeds, and/or animal fur). Talk or sing where visibility or hearing are limited. Keep a clean camp, hang food, and don't sleep in the clothes you wore while cooking. Be especially careful in spring to avoid getting between a mother and her cubs. In late summer and fall bears are busy eating berries and acorns to fatten up for winter, so be extra careful around berry bushes and oak brush. If you do encounter a bear, move away slowly while facing the bear, talk softly, and avoid direct eye contact. Give the bear room to escape. Since bears are very curious, it might stand upright to get a better whiff of you, and it may even charge you to try to intimidate you. Try to stay calm. If a black bear does attack you, fight back with anything you have handy. Do not play dead. Unleashed dogs have been known to come running back to their owners with a bear close behind. Keep your dog on a leash or leave it at home.

Mountain lions. Usually elusive and quiet, lions rarely attack people. If you meet a lion, give it a chance to escape. Stay calm and talk firmly to it. Back away slowly while facing the lion. If you run, you'll only encourage the curious cat to chase you. Make yourself look large by opening a jacket, if you have one, or waving your hiking poles. If the lion behaves aggressively, throw stones, sticks, or whatever you can while remaining tall. If a lion does attack, fight for your life with anything you can grab.

Moose. Because moose have very few natural predators, they don't fear humans like other animals. You might find moose in sagebrush and wetter areas of willow, aspen, and pine, or in beaver habitats. Mothers with calves, as well as bulls during mating season, can be particularly aggressive. If a moose threatens you, back away slowly and talk calmly to it. Keep your pets away from moose.

Other considerations. Hunting is a popular sport in the United States, especially during rifle season in October. Hiking is still enjoyable in many areas during that time, so just take a few precautions. First, learn when the different hunting seasons start and end in the area in which you'll be hiking. You can check by visiting wildlife.utah.gov. During this time frame, be sure to wear at least a blaze orange hat, and possibly put an orange vest over your pack. Don't be surprised to see hunters in camo outfits carrying bows or muzzleloader rifles. If you would feel more comfortable without hunters around, hike in national parks and monuments or state and local parks where hunting is not allowed.

NAVIGATION

Whether you are going on a short hike in a familiar area or planning a weeklong backpack trip, you should always be equipped with the proper navigational equipment—at the very least a detailed map and a compass.

Maps. There are many different types of maps available to help you find your way on the trail. Easiest to find are USDA Forest Service maps and BLM (Bureau of Land Management) maps. These maps tend to cover large areas, so be sure they are detailed enough for your particular trip. You can also obtain National Park Service maps as well as high-quality maps from private companies and trail groups. These maps can be obtained either from outdoor stores or ranger stations.

US Geological Survey topographic maps are particularly popular with hikers—especially serious backcountry hikers. These maps contain the standard map symbols such as roads, lakes, and rivers, as well as contour lines that show the details of the trail terrain like ridges, valleys, passes, and mountain peaks. The 7.5-minute series (1 inch on the map equals 2,000 feet, or about 0.38 mile on the ground) provides the closest inspection available. USGS maps are available by mail (US Geological Survey, Map Distribution Branch, PO Box 25286, Denver, CO 80225), or online at USGS.gov.

Map reading is a skill you can develop by first practicing in an area you are familiar with. To begin, orient the map so it is lined up in the correct direction (i.e., north on the map is lined up with true north). Next, familiarize yourself with the map symbols and try to match them with terrain features around you such as a high ridge, mountain peak, river, or lake. If you are practicing with a USGS map, notice the contour lines. On gentler terrain these contour lines are spaced farther apart, and on steeper terrain they are closer together. Pick a short loop trail and stop frequently to check your position on the map. As you practice map reading, you'll learn how to anticipate a steep section on the trail or a good place to take a rest break, and so on.

Compasses. First off, the sun is not a substitute for a compass. So, what kind of compass should you have? Here are some characteristics you should look for: a rectangular base with detailed scales, a liquid-filled housing, protective housing, a sighting line on the mirror, luminous alignment and back-bearing arrows, a luminous north-seeking arrow, and a well-defined bezel ring.

You can learn compass basics by reading the detailed instructions included with your compass. If you want to fine-tune your compass skills, sign up for an orienteering class or purchase a book on compass reading. Once you've learned the basic skills of using a compass, remember to practice these skills before you head into the backcountry.

GPS. If you are a klutz at using a compass, you may be interested in checking out the technical wizardry of the GPS (Global Positioning System) device. A GPS device is a handheld unit that calculates your latitude and longitude. The Department of Defense used to scramble the satellite signals a bit to prevent civilians (and spies!) from getting extremely accurate readings, but that practice was discontinued in May 2000, and GPS units now provide nearly pinpoint accuracy (within 30 to 60 feet).

There are many different types of GPS units available, and they range widely in cost. In general, all GPS units have a display screen and keypad where you input information. In addition to acting as a compass, the unit allows you to plot your route, easily retrace your path, track your traveling speed, find the mileage between waypoints, and calculate the total mileage of your route.

Before you purchase a GPS unit, keep in mind that these devices don't pick up signals indoors, in heavily wooded areas, or in ravines or deep valleys. They also rely on batteries. If you are counting on a GPS to protect your life, make sure you have extra batteries or map reading skills.

Pedometers. A pedometer is a small, clip-on unit with a digital display, phone app, or fitness watch that calculates your hiking distance in miles or kilometers based on your walking stride. Some units also calculate the calories you burn and your total hiking time. Pedometers are available at most large outdoor stores.

TRIP PLANNING

Planning your hiking adventure begins with letting a friend or relative know your trip itinerary so they can call for help if you don't return at your scheduled time. Always remember to let them know you have returned so Search and Rescue isn't sent into action looking for you. Your next task is to make sure you are outfitted to experience the risks and rewards of the trail. This section highlights gear and clothing you may want to take with you to get the most out of your hike.

EQUIPMENT

With the outdoor market currently flooded with products, many of which are pure gimmickry, it seems impossible to both differentiate and choose. The only defense against the maddening quantity of items thrust in your face is to think practically—and to do so before you go shopping. The worst buys are impulsive buys. Since most name brands will differ only slightly in quality, it's best to know what you're looking for in terms of function. Buy only what you need. You will, don't forget, be carrying what you've bought on your back. Here are some things to keep in mind before you go shopping.

Clothes. Clothing is your armor against Mother Nature's little surprises. Hikers should be prepared for any possibility, especially when hiking in mountainous areas. Adequate rain protection and extra layers of clothing are a good idea. In summer, a wide-brimmed hat can help keep the sun at bay. In the winter months the first layer you'll want to wear is a "wicking" layer of long underwear that keeps perspiration away from your skin. Wear long underwear made from synthetic fibers that wick moisture away from the skin and draw it toward the next layer of clothing, where it then evaporates. Avoid wearing long underwear made of cotton, as it is slow to dry and keeps moisture next to your skin.

The second layer you'll wear is the "insulating" layer. Aside from keeping you warm, this layer needs to "breathe" so you stay dry while hiking. A fabric that provides insulation and dries quickly is fleece. It's interesting to note that this one-of-a-kind fabric can be made out of recycled plastic. Purchasing a zip-up jacket made of this material is highly recommended.

The last line of layering defense is the "shell" layer. You'll need some type of waterproof, windproof, breathable jacket that will fit over all of your other layers. It should have a large hood that fits over a hat. You'll also need a good pair of rain pants made from a similar waterproof, breathable fabric. Some Gore-Tex jackets are pricey, but you should know that there are more affordable fabrics out there that work just as well.

Now that you've learned the basics of layering, you can't forget to protect your hands and face. In cold, windy, or rainy weather you'll need a hat made of wool or fleece and insulated, waterproof gloves that will keep your hands warm and toasty. As mentioned earlier, buying an additional pair of light silk liners to wear under your regular gloves is a good idea.

Footwear. If you have any extra money to spend on your trip, put that money into boots or trail shoes. Poor shoes will bring a hike to a halt faster than anything else. To avoid this annoyance, buy shoes that provide support and are lightweight and flexible. A lightweight hiking boot is better than a heavy, leather mountaineering boot for most day hikes and backpacking. Trail running shoes provide a little extra cushion and are made in a high-top style that many people wear for hiking. These running shoes are lighter, more flexible, and more breathable than hiking boots. If you know you'll be hiking in wet weather often, purchase boots or shoes with a Gore-Tex liner, which will help keep your feet dry.

When buying your boots, be sure to wear the same type of socks you'll be wearing on the trail. If the boots you're buying are for cold weather hiking, try the boots on while wearing two pairs of socks. Speaking of socks, a good cold weather sock combination is to wear a thinner sock made of wool or polypropylene covered by a heavier outer sock made of wool. The inner sock protects the foot from the rubbing effects of the outer sock and prevents blisters. Many outdoor stores have some type of ramp to simulate hiking uphill and downhill. Be sure to take advantage of this test, as toe-jamming boot fronts can be very painful and debilitating on the downhill trek.

Once you've purchased your footwear, be sure to break them in before you hit the trail. New footwear is often stiff and needs to be stretched and molded to your feet.

Hiking poles. Hiking poles help with balance and, more important, take pressure off your knees. The ones with shock absorbers are easier on your elbows and knees. Some poles even come with a camera attachment to be used as a monopod. And heaven forbid you meet a mountain lion, bear, or unfriendly dog, the poles can make you look a lot bigger.

Backpacks. No matter what type of hiking you do, you'll need a pack of some sort to carry the basic trail essentials. There are a variety of backpacks on the market, but let's first discuss what you intend to use it for. Day hikes or overnight trips?

If you plan on doing a day hike, a day pack should have some of the following characteristics: a padded hip belt that's at least 2 inches in diameter (avoid packs with only a small nylon piece of webbing for a hip belt); a chest strap (the chest strap helps stabilize the pack against your body); external pockets to carry water and other items that you want easy access to; an internal pocket to hold keys, a knife, a wallet, and other miscellaneous items; an external lashing system to hold a jacket; and a hydration pocket for carrying a hydration system (which consists of a water bladder with an attachable drinking hose).

For short hikes, some hikers like to use a fanny pack to store just a camera, food, a compass, a map, and other trail essentials. Most fanny packs have pockets for two water bottles and a padded hip belt.

If you intend to do an extended, overnight trip, there are multiple considerations. First off, you need to decide what kind of framed pack you want. There are two backpack types for backpacking: the internal frame and the external frame. An internal frame pack rests closer to your body, making it more stable and easier to balance when hiking over rough terrain. An external frame pack is just that, a frame attached to the exterior of the pack. An external frame pack is better for long backpack trips because it distributes the pack weight better and you can carry heavier loads. It's easier to pack, and your gear is more accessible. It also offers better back ventilation in hot weather.

The most critical measurement for fitting a pack is torso length. The pack needs to rest evenly on your hips without sagging. A good pack will come in two or three sizes and have straps and hip belts that are adjustable according to your body size and characteristics.

When you purchase a backpack, go to an outdoor store that has salespeople who are knowledgeable in how to properly fit a pack. Once the pack is fitted for you, load the pack with the amount of weight you plan on taking on the trail. The weight of the pack should be distributed evenly, and you should be able to swing your arms and walk briskly without feeling out of balance. Another good technique for evaluating a pack is to walk up and down stairs and make quick turns to the right and to the left to be sure the pack doesn't feel out of balance. Other features that are nice to have on a backpack include a removable day pack or fanny pack, external pockets for extra water, and extra lash points to attach a jacket or other items.

Sleeping bags and pads. Sleeping bags are rated by temperature. You can purchase a bag made of synthetic fiber, or you can buy a down bag. Down bags are more expensive, but they have a higher insulating capacity by weight and will keep their loft longer. You'll want to purchase a bag with a temperature rating that fits the time of year and conditions in which you are most likely to camp. One caveat: The techno-standard for temperature ratings is far from perfect. Ratings vary from manufacturer to manufacturer, so to protect yourself you should purchase a bag rated 10 to 15 degrees below the temperature you expect to be camping in. Synthetic bags are more resistant to water than down bags, but many down bags are now made with a Gore-Tex shell that helps to repel water. Down bags are also more compressible than synthetic bags and take up less room in your pack, which is an important consideration if you are planning a multiday backpack trip. Features to look for in a sleeping bag include a mummy-style bag, a hood you can cinch down around your head in cold weather, and draft tubes along the zippers that help keep heat in and drafts out.

You'll also want a sleeping pad to provide insulation and padding from the cold ground. There are different types of sleeping pads available, from the more expensive self-inflating air mattresses to the less expensive closed-cell foam pads. Self-inflating air mattresses are usually heavier than closed-cell foam mattresses and are prone to punctures.

Tents. The tent is your home away from home while on the trail. It provides protection from wind, snow, rain, and insects. A three-season tent is a good choice. These lightweight and versatile tents provide protection in all types of weather, except heavy snowstorms or high winds, and range in weight from 4 to 8 pounds. Look for a tent that's easy to set up and will easily fit two people with gear. Dome type tents usually offer more headroom and places to store gear. Other tent designs include a vestibule where you can store wet boots and backpacks. Some nice-to-have items in a tent include interior pockets to store small items and lashing points to hang a clothesline. Most three-season tents also come with stakes so you can secure the tent in high winds. Before you purchase a tent, set it up and take it down a few times to be sure it is easy to handle. Also, sit inside the tent and make sure it has enough room for you and your gear.

Cell phones and satellite communicators. Many hikers are carrying their cell phones or a satellite communicator into the backcountry these days in case of emergency and to take pictures. That's fine and good, but 1) know that cell phone coverage is often poor to nonexistent in valleys, canyons, and thick forest and 2) batteries and technology can fail. More important, people have started to call for help because they're tired or lost. Let's go back to being prepared. You are responsible for yourself in the backcountry. Use your brain to avoid problems, and if you do encounter one, first use your brain to try to correct the situation. Take a beat and don't panic. Only use your cell phone or SOS signal in true emergencies.

HIKING WITH CHILDREN

Hiking with children isn't a matter of how many miles you can cover or how much elevation gain you make in a day; it's about seeing and experiencing nature through their eyes.

Kids like to explore and have fun. They like to stop and point out bugs and plants, look under rocks, jump in puddles, and throw sticks. If you're taking a toddler or young child on a hike, start with a trail you're familiar with. Trails that have interesting things for kids, like piles of leaves to play in or a small stream to wade through during the summer, will make the hike much more enjoyable for them and will keep them from getting bored.

You can keep your child's attention if you have a strategy before starting on the trail. Using games is not only an effective way to keep a child's attention, it's also a great way to teach them about nature. Quiz children on the names of plants and animals. If your children are old enough, let them carry their own day pack filled with snacks and water. So that you are sure to go at their pace and not yours, let them lead the way. Playing follow the leader works particularly well when you have a group of children. Have each child take a turn at being the leader.

With children, a lot of clothing is key. The only thing predictable about weather is that it will change. Especially in mountainous areas, weather can change dramatically in a very short time. Always bring extra clothing for children, regardless of the season. In the winter, have your children wear wool socks and warm layers such as long underwear, a fleece jacket and hat, wool mittens, and good rain gear. It's not a bad idea to have these along in late fall and early spring as well. Good footwear is also important. A sturdy pair of high-top tennis shoes or lightweight hiking boots is the best bet for little ones. If you're hiking in the summer near a lake or stream, bring along a pair of old sneakers that your child can put on when they want to go exploring in the water. Remember when you're near any type of water, watch your child at all times. Also, keep a close eye on teething toddlers who may decide a rock or leaf of poison oak is an interesting item to put in their mouth.

From spring through fall, you'll want your kids to wear a wide-brimmed hat to keep their face, head, and ears protected from the hot sun. Also, make sure your children wear sunscreen at all times. Choose a brand without PABA—children have sensitive skin and may have an allergic reaction to sunscreen that contains PABA. If you are hiking with a child younger than 6 months, don't use sunscreen or insect repellent. Instead, be sure their head, face, neck, and ears are protected from the sun with a wide-brimmed hat, and that all other skin exposed to the sun is protected with the appropriate clothing.

Remember that food is fun. Kids like snacks, so it's important to bring a lot of munchies for the trail. Stopping often for snack breaks is a fun way to keep the trail interesting. Raisins, apples, granola bars, crackers and cheese, cereal, and trail mix all make great snacks. If your child is old enough to carry their own backpack, fill it with treats before you leave. If your kids don't like drinking water, you can bring boxes of fruit juice.

Avoid poorly designed child-carrying packs—you don't want to break your back carrying your child. Most child-carrying backpacks designed to hold a 40-pound child will contain a large carrying pocket to hold diapers and other items. Some have an optional rain/sun hood.

HIKING WITH YOUR DOG

Bringing your furry friend with you is always more fun than leaving him behind. Our canine pals make great trail buddies because they never complain and always make good company. Hiking with your dog can be a rewarding experience, especially if you plan ahead.

Getting your dog in shape. Before you plan outdoor adventures with your dog, make sure he's in shape for the trail. Getting your dog into shape takes the same discipline as getting yourself into shape, but luckily, your dog can get in shape with you. Take your dog with you on your daily runs or walks. If there is a park near your house, hit a tennis ball or play Frisbee with your dog.

Swimming is also an excellent way to get your dog into shape. If there is a lake or river near where you live and your dog likes the water, have him retrieve a tennis ball or stick. Gradually build your dog's stamina up over a 2- to 3-month period. A good rule of thumb is to assume your dog will travel twice as far as you will on the trail. If you plan on doing a 5-mile hike, be sure your dog is in shape for a 10-mile hike.

Training your dog for the trail. Before you go on your first hiking adventure with your dog, be sure he has a firm grasp on the basics of canine etiquette and behavior. Make sure he can sit, lie down, stay, and come. One of the most important commands you can teach your canine pal is to "come" under any situation. It's easy for your friend's nose to lead him astray or possibly get lost. Another helpful command is the "get behind" command. When you're on a hiking trail that's narrow, you can have your dog follow behind you when other trail users approach. Nothing is more bothersome than an enthusiastic dog that runs back and forth on the trail and disrupts the peace of the trail for others. When you see other trail users approaching you on the trail, give them the right of way by quietly stepping off the trail and making your dog lie down and stay until they pass.

Equipment. The most critical pieces of equipment you can invest in for your dog are proper identification and a sturdy leash. Flexi-leads work well for hiking because they give your dog more freedom to explore but still leave you in control. Make sure your dog has identification that includes your name and address and a number for your veterinarian. Other forms of identification for your dog include a tattoo or a microchip. You should consult your veterinarian for more information on these last two options.

The next piece of equipment you'll want to consider is a pack for your dog. By no means should you hold all of your dog's essentials in your pack—let him carry his own gear! Dogs that are in good shape can carry 30 to 40 percent of their own weight.

Most packs are fitted by a dog's weight and girth measurement. Companies that make dog packs generally include guidelines to help you pick out the size that's right for your dog. Some characteristics to look for when purchasing a pack for your dog include a harness that contains two padded girth straps, a padded chest strap, leash attachments, removable saddle bags, internal water bladders, and external gear cords.

You can introduce your dog to the pack by first placing the empty pack on his back and letting him wear it around the yard. Keep an eye on him during this first introduction. He may decide to chew through the straps if you aren't watching him closely. Once he learns to treat the pack as an object of fun and not a foreign enemy, fill the pack evenly on both sides with a few ounces of dog food in sealable plastic bags. Have your dog wear his pack on your daily walks for a period of 2 to 3 weeks. Each week add a little more weight to the pack until your dog will accept carrying the maximum amount of weight he can carry.

You can also purchase collapsible water and dog food bowls for your dog. These bowls are lightweight and can easily be stashed into your pack or your dog's. If you are hiking on rocky terrain or in the snow, you can purchase footwear for your dog that will protect his feet from cuts and bruises.

Always carry plastic bags to remove feces from the trail. It is a courtesy to other trail users and helps protect local wildlife.

The following is a list of items to bring when you take your dog hiking: collapsible water bowls, a comb, a collar and a leash, dog food, plastic bags for feces, a dog pack, flea/tick powder, paw protection, water, and a first-aid kit that contains eye ointment, tweezers, scissors, stretchy foot wrap, gauze, antibacterial wash, sterile cotton tip applicators, antibiotic ointment, and cotton wrap.

First aid for your dog. Your dog is just as prone—if not more so—to getting in trouble on the trail as you are, so be prepared. Here's a rundown of the more likely misfortunes that might befall your little friend.

Bees and wasps. If a bee or wasp stings your dog, remove the stinger with a pair of tweezers and place a mudpack or a cloth dipped in cold water over the affected area.

Porcupines. One good reason to keep your dog on a leash is to prevent him from getting a nose full of porcupine quills. You may be able to remove the quills with pliers, but a veterinarian is the best person to do this nasty job because most dogs need to be sedated.

Heat stroke. Avoid hiking with your dog in really hot weather. Dogs with heat stroke will pant excessively, lie down and refuse to get up, and become lethargic and disoriented. If your dog shows any of these signs on the trail, have him lie down in the shade. If you are near a stream, pour cool water over your dog's entire body to help bring his body temperature back to normal.

Heartworm. Dogs get heartworm from mosquitoes, which carry the disease in the prime mosquito months of July and August. Giving your dog a monthly pill prescribed by your veterinarian easily prevents this condition.

Plant pitfalls. Foxtails are pointed grass seed heads that bury themselves in your friend's fur, between his toes, and even get in their ear canal or nose. If left unattended, these nasty seeds can work their way under the skin and cause abscesses and other problems. If you have a long-haired dog, consider trimming the hair between his toes and giving him a summer haircut to help prevent foxtails from attaching to his fur. After every hike, always look over your dog for these seeds—especially between his toes and his ears.

Other plant hazards include burrs, thorns, thistles, and poison oak. If you find any burrs or thistles on your dog, remove them as soon as possible before they become an unmanageable mat. Thorns can pierce a dog's foot and cause a great deal of pain. If you see that your dog is lame, stop and check his feet for thorns. Dogs are immune to poison oak, but they can pick up the sticky, oily substance from the plant and transfer it to you.

Protect those paws. Be sure to keep your dog's nails trimmed so he avoids getting soft tissue or joint injuries. If your dog slows and refuses to go on, check to see that his paws aren't torn or worn. You can protect your dog's paws from trail hazards such as sharp gravel, foxtails, lava scree, and thorns by purchasing dog boots.

Sunburn. If your dog has light skin, he is an easy target for sunburn on his nose and other exposed skin areas. You can apply a nontoxic sunscreen to exposed skin areas that will help protect him from overexposure to the sun.

Ticks and fleas. Ticks can easily give your dog Lyme disease, as well as other diseases. Before you hit the trail, treat your dog with a flea and tick spray or powder. You can also ask your veterinarian about other options to repel fleas and ticks.

Mosquitoes and deerflies. These little flying machines can do a job on your dog's snout and ears. Best bet is to spray your dog with fly repellent for horses to discourage both pests.

Giardia. Dogs can get giardia, which results in diarrhea. It is usually not debilitating, but it's definitely messy. A vaccine against giardia is available.

Mushrooms. Make sure your dog doesn't sample mushrooms along the trail. They could be poisonous to him, but he doesn't know that.

When you are finally ready to hit the trail with your dog, keep in mind that national parks and many Wilderness areas do not allow dogs on trails. Your best bet is to hike in national forests, BLM lands, and state parks. Always call ahead to see what the restrictions are.

HIKE INDEX

ABOUT THE AUTHORS

Jeffrey Probst is an outdoors writer who divides his time between writing about backpacking and programming computers. A lifelong resident of the state of Utah, he has backpacked in the High Uintas for more than 30 years and has written articles for outdoors magazines. His favorite place to backpack is the High Uinta Mountains, where he enjoys fishing, finding solitude, and taking photographs.

A native of northern Utah, **Brad Probst** spends much of his time exploring the wilderness. For more than 25 years, he and his brother, Jeff, have dedicated at least one trip a year to visit a new lake in the High Uintas, although he also enjoys solo expeditions. When he's not hiking, fishing, sketching, or taking photographs, he draws maps, writes outdoor literature, and prepares gourmet meals while watching football or the Utah Jazz.

Brett Prettyman was the outdoors editor for the *Salt Lake Tribune* for twenty-five years. He is the author of *Fishing Utah* (FalconGuides) and a frequent writer and blogger on outdoor sports. He grew up learning to fish in central Utah and in the high-elevation lakes of the Uinta Mountains, which he still visits frequently.

Andrew Dash Gillman served in the state of Utah's office of tourism for nearly a decade. In that role, he contributed to and then led the remarkable content and creative team, including as writer and strategist for visitutah.com and as editorial director of *Utah Explorer's Guide* magazine. He continues to produce travel and outdoor adventure content for clients at his Place-Based Storytelling Company. He devotes his leisure time to writing a novel and running, as well as hiking, camping, and fishing throughout Utah and the American West—including some of the same spots he learned these activities in Utah's High Uintas. Get in touch at adngillman.com.

THE TEN ESSENTIALS OF HIKING

American Hiking Society

American Hiking Society recommends you pack the "Ten Essentials" every time you head out for a hike. Whether you plan to be gone for a couple of hours or several months, make sure to pack these items. Become familiar with these items and know how to use them.

1. Appropriate Footwear
Happy feet make for pleasant hiking. Think about traction, support, and protection when selecting well-fitting shoes or boots.

2. Navigation
While phones and GPS units are handy, they aren't always reliable in the backcountry; consider carrying a paper map and compass as a backup and know how to use them.

3. Water (and a way to purify it)
As a guideline, plan for half a liter of water per hour in moderate temperatures/terrain. Carry enough water for your trip and know where and how to treat water while you're out on the trail.

4. Food
Pack calorie-dense foods to help fuel your hike, and carry an extra portion in case you are out longer than expected.

5. Rain Gear & Dry-Fast Layers
The weatherman is not always right. Dress in layers to adjust to changing weather and activity levels. Wear moisture-wicking cloths and carry a warm hat.

6. Safety Items (light, fire, and a whistle)
Have means to start an emergency fire, signal for help, and see the trail and your map in the dark.

7. First Aid Kit

Supplies to treat illness or injury are only as helpful as your knowledge of how to use them. Take a class to gain the skills needed to administer first aid and CPR.

8. Knife or Multi-Tool

With countless uses, a multi-tool can help with gear repair and first aid.

9. Sun Protection

Sunscreen, sunglasses, and sun-protective clothing should be used in every season regardless of temperature or cloud cover.

10. Shelter

Protection from the elements in the event you are injured or stranded is necessary. A lightweight, inexpensive space blanket is a great option.

Find other helpful resources at AmericanHiking.org/hiking-resources